Songs of the Cowboys

Songs of the Cowboys

by

N. Howard ("Jack") Thorp

Variants, Commentary, Notes and Lexicon
BY AUSTIN E. AND ALTA S. FIFE

Music Editor: NAUNIE GARDNER

Clarkson N. Potter, Inc./Publisher NEW YORK

Table of Contents

*T*o the memory of

Kathy Dagel

and to

Gail I. Gardner

representing the many who have
created, preserved, or transmitted
the treasures of western song
for the enrichment of our national heritage

Acknowledgments

MANY INDIVIDUALS AND INSTITUTIONS have supplied materials, ideas, and technical and professional assistance in the preparation of this work. For contributing song texts and tunes used we are especially grateful to Ray and Olwyn Browne, Richard Dorson, Edith Fowke, Robert W. Gordon, Herbert Halpert, Stella M. Hendren, Frank A. Hoffmann, Joan O'Bryant, J. D. Robb, S. J. Sackett, and Ellen Stekert.

For placing institutional resources at our disposal we thank Frances Gillmor and the Arizona Folklore Archive; Nyle H. Miller and the Kansas State Historical Society; Rae Korson and the Music Division of the Library of Congress; Mary K. Dempsey and the Historical Society of Montana; the special collections sections of the State University of Iowa Library and of the library of the University of Oregon; the Texas Historical Society; and Mrs. Eleanor Westermeier and Pacific Northwest Farm Quad.

For financial support to facilitate travel and research, we are beholden to the John Simon Guggenheim Foundation and Utah State University's Division of Research.

Four colleagues have helped us with technical data for the lexicon: Arthur Holmgren and Allen Stokes have put us straight on western flora and fauna; Arthur Woodward and H. J. Swinney have checked our facts on frontier firearms, cowboy gear, and other aspects of pioneer technology.

J. Frank Dobie was generous with hospitality, anecdote, and unlimited access to his personal library. Neil M. Clark confirmed bio-

1

2 SONGS OF THE COWBOYS

graphical facts concerning Thorp. Wayland D. Hand has offered encouragement and wisdom all along the way.

Finally, we express appreciation to D. K. Wilgus for constant support, especially in those areas where our own resources are the most deficient.

AUSTIN AND ALTA FIFE

Logan, Utah
May, 1966

Introduction

THE COWBOY'S BRAND IS BURNED indelibly into the hide of every American. That the circumstances which gave rise to the cowboy image—the raising of cattle on the open ranges of the West —should no longer exist, is immaterial. Children play cowboys and Indians wearing costumes that are as evocative as they are unauthentic. A considerable percentage of our televised entertainment, movies, and popular songs seek an exotic locale, poetic images, and other dramatic effects on the ranges of the buffalo where you're not fenced in and where you love to roam but sure enough don't want to be buried. Lodges, motels, resorts, restaurants, and cocktail bars try to outdo each other in the selection of "five hundred percent" western images such as *El Rancho, Saddle Room, Wagon Wheel, Trailer Wranglers, Golden Spur, Stockman, Purple Sage, Pony Express, Cowpoke Corner,* or *Lariat*. External and internal decor conspire to reinforce the western image: wagon wheels, prairie schooners, horse gear, brands and branding irons, holsters, pistols, ox yokes, antlers, and mountings of cow horns skillfully extruded to outdo the proudest longhorn in all of Texas. Businessmen and suburbanites invest staggering sums to breed, buy, or train cow horses whose greatest feats will be to step high and fancy in the sheriff's posse at a Fourth of July parade, so bedizened as no genuine cow horse ever dreamed to be. The term "cowboy" has been absorbed, untranslated, in many of the languages of the world, and the popular image speakers of these languages make for themselves of the American is colored by what they have seen, read, or heard concerning this mass-

3

media cowboy who has really never existed save in the minds and hearts of men.

N. Howard ("Jack") Thorp is the first person who recognized in cowboy and western songs a creativity capable of serving as a nucleus around which a new culture might identify itself. The odyssey of 1889 to 1890, during which Thorp made the first systematic effort to track down a repertoire of cowboy and western songs, may well loom in our American culture somewhat as did Homer's early efforts to gather and preserve the heroic songs and poetry of ancient Greece. Thorp's effort approximately coincided with the interest of Owen Wister, Andy Adams, and others in exploiting the assets of cowboys and the West in fiction, and of Theodore Roosevelt in exploring the West, in illuminating its image in popular literature, and in using it for political gain.

The roots of the cowboy myth go back, of course, many years beyond Thorp. Our story would start with the descent upon American shores of small herds of cattle and of horses from the galleons of the explorers and *conquistadores* of Spain, France, Portugal, Britain. It would tell how these herds multiplied and extended their range over vast areas of the New World, either as wild bands or as the quasi-husbanded property of Indian tribes, the missions, or affluent *rancheros* and *haciendados;* how there came into being well-developed patterns of exploitation of these resources, including roundups or rodeos, roping, cutting, branding, skinning, herding, driving; how strife in what was to become Texas between *gringos* and *mexicanos* from the 1830's to the 1850's led to the mutual pillage of horses and cattle and the driving of herds over great distances, even into New Orleans; how the *gringos* won the area and how they established cattle empires in the wide-open spaces; and how they appropriated, adapted, and extended the *mexicanos'* exploitive techniques, including the transformation of the English language to accommodate the new enterprise, and the geographical and biological peculiarities of the new locale. We would tell how homesteaders and sod busters arrived with ploughs and with fences to pock the open ranges and deflect the cattle drives from their chosen routes. How steam-snorting iron horses pushed into the West. How they built railroad corrals and began moving herds to eastern markets in cattlecars. How barbed wire reduced the open ranges to private fenced domains or expanses of National Forest and Taylor grazing areas. How the Model T and its successors began to restrict the utility of cow horses, and how telephones came to circumscribe both privacy and loneliness. Thus, the cattle and the cowboys got fenced in indeed, but not their myth.

All this we would tell as a kind of backdrop in space and in time for the half-century between 1870 and 1920 that saw the cowboy myth emerge and blossom in its full glory prior to its devitalization through the phony commercializations to which it has been subjected since the 1920's. Ballads and songs of frontier life have abounded for every major episode in the settlement of the North American continent, and it may properly be said that "western" songs have always been with us. But to produce cowboy songs as Thorp knew and transmitted them, the juncture of several historical currents was required: a special brand of frontier horsemanship; a market for cowhides and, later, beef; frontier lawlessness; the projection of the railroads into the Great American West; the ascription of heroic qualities to western men who were formerly viewed with indifference, if not with scorn. A Thorp as collector, composer, singer, and publisher of cowboy songs was a necessary part of the process, as was a ballad critic like G. L. Kittredge, whose intellectual offspring—Lomax, Piper, Belden, Pound, Gordon, and others—made us realize that our heritage of homegrown Anglo-American song was also the stuff of which epics are made.

That during fifty years spent riding the range and raising cattle Jack Thorp rode cheek to jowl with the songs and stories he chose to preserve needs scarcely be said. But there are other insights to be gleaned from less known facts of his biography. We are reminded of the rancher born and reared in the Bryce Canyon (Utah) area who, on hearing the beauty of this never-never land expounded by a tourist, remarked laconically, "Well, it's a hell of a place to lose a cow!" Thorp was reared to maturity in a wholly different environment so that, unlike the native rancher, he brought perspectives that helped him see the cowboy locale and cowboy life with empathy as well as with objectivity.

He was born June 10, 1867, the third son of a wealthy New York lawyer. He attended Saint Paul's School in Concord, New Hampshire, and first came to know horseflesh on a polo team of which Theodore Roosevelt and other notables were members, and by visits during his early youth to a ranch in Nebraska operated by an older brother. Financial reverses wrecked his father's fortune, and Jack was forced to forego a higher education and to earn a living, which, until his mother's death in 1894, he did mostly by buying western ponies, shipping them east, and training them as polo horses. Having had practical experience as a civil engineer, he served for a time as superintendent of the Enterprise Mining Company at Kingston, Arizona. In 1897 he and a friend went to Seattle, intending to join gold seekers in Alaska. But the money between them was barely enough for one. They played freeze-out poker, and Jack, the loser, had to stay at home. Shortly thereafter he went to Peru on a railroading venture that failed. He worked his way back to San Francisco as a stoker, and returned to the cattle ranges of New Mexico, where he lived out a rich and adventurous life as a cowboy, and later as a rancher. We are told that he stood six feet two, that he was all muscle, and that his speech was "humorous and picturesque, with the imaginative exaggeration characteristic of men of the range." Further details concerning his life and work are to be gleaned from his autobiography.[1]

If Thorp's disembodied spirit should at this moment be riding circle on this author's effort to define his role in the evolution of the cowboy and western myth, he would no doubt be more perplexed than proud. Small indeed was the energy Thorp shed for the lore and literature of cowboys and the West compared to his nearly total submergence in cowboy and western life itself. Still, posterity will reap a rich reward from these gifts that were little more than incidental to him. His fifteen-hundred-mile horseback journey through New Mexico and Texas in 1889–90 was the first ballad-hunting adventure in the cowboy domain. His author-editor-publisher venture of 1908[2] produced the first collection of cowboy and western songs. In 1921 he expanded this frail collection (twenty-three songs) to a neat one hundred and one.[3] In 1926 he published an engaging but neglected collection of cowboy and western tales.[4] He authored sundry tales and articles in *New Mexico Magazine, The Cattleman,* and other journals,[5] including one of the best essays ever written on singing among cowboys and other westerners during the heyday of the cowboy era ("Banjo in the Cow Camps").[6] Finally, his autobiography, prepared during his mellow years, in collaboration with Neil

---

[1] Thorp and Clark.
[2] Thorp (1908).
[3] Thorp (1921).
[4] Thorp, *Tales.*
[5] Thorp and Clark, p. 14.
[6] Reprinted from *Atlantic Monthly,* CLXVI, 2 (August, 1940), pp. 195–203. Also appears as Chapter One of Thorp and Clark pp. 21–45.

McCullough Clark,[7] gives authentic and engaging images of cowboy and western life such as are to be found in few other books.

It is notable that Thorp made no distinction between folk songs and any other kind of songs. His ear and mind were attuned to melodies, lyrics, and singing styles that belonged to the cowboy locale. Quite properly he included traditional songs that had been reshaped to fit the cowboy's notion of reality, songs about cowboys and the West of his own composition, or songs by anyone else, provided they satisfied his idea of what a cowboy song ought to be. He was indeed quite indifferent to authorship; witness his own failure to claim songs for his own collection until after the "learned professor," to quote Thorp, had incorporated them in a less authentic but more widely publicized book of cowboy songs published in 1910.[8] Like most of the early editors of folk and popular songs, Thorp published lyrics without melodies. In his mature years he did give us tunes for "Sam Bass" and "On the Dodge,"[9] but that is all.

Readers of the present work should be forewarned about its scope and limitations. First of all, we wish to present the twenty-three songs of Thorp's 1908 work with sufficient cultural and historical perspective to illuminate the songs in all of their depth and, by thus illuminating them, to throw light upon significant aspects of the cowboy and western myth itself. To do this we have first given essential historical and critical facts, followed by Thorp's text as initially printed (quotations are exact, and include all of the original errors). From this point the treatment of each song depends upon the history and character of the song itself. If the form of the song has remained fairly stable and pretty much as Thorp gave it, we have jumped directly to our encounters with it in print and elsewhere. Where transformations of the song have been real but moderate we have added additional integral texts as necessary to illuminate significant transformations. A few of the songs have had a vegetative, a protean existence so complex that analysis is difficult. Here we have constructed a synthetic text in which all significant stanzas and all significant variants of these stanzas have been consolidated so that the total range of ideas treated by the song in its multiple appearances has been assembled. Never, of course, would the song have been sung, and never should

---

[7] Thorp and Clark.

[8] Lomax (1910).

[9] Thorp, *Banjo,* p. 198 (*infra* p. 17); Thorp and Clark, pp. 28 and 30.

it be sung, in these epic-poem-like dimensions. So, following this synthetic text, we have given significant but integral texts of the song in
sufficient number to illustrate some of the most revealing ways in which
the song has actually been sung in cowboy times and in cowboy country.

The music has presented unique problems, first because Thorp,
with the two exceptions previously noted, did not give melodies, and
second, because many of our other sources, especially the earliest ones,
typically come without music. Where significant texts do appear accompanied by the melodic line, we have given them. We have studied many
of the musical renditions of each song, from field recordings, from
78-rpm commercial records, and from printed texts. This done, we have
written a brief statement about the song's musical treatment and included
a sufficient number of musical transcriptions to illustrate its melodic
forms as we have encountered them.

A comprehensive index has been added, which includes all proper
names—persons, places, ranches, cattle brands, etc.—and other entries
that folklorists, historians, and other researchers in the humanities or the
social sciences might hope to find. We have also included a "cowboy
and western" lexicon for the particular purpose of directing attention to all those elements in the songs that illuminate the myth—vocabulary, images, plants, animals, events, and activities which converge to
form that cluster of ideas and images generally accepted as "cowboy and
western." There is also an index of titles and one of first lines.

Bibliography, for a study of this kind, is extremely complex. In a
normal critical work one would exclude popular and ephemeral sources
—the very sources which, in the realms of folk and popular tradition,
have the greatest meaning. These include field recordings of the songs
in oral tradition, sheet music, broadsides and song folios, commercial
recordings (especially during the heyday of the 78-rpm record), and
printings in newspapers and other ephemeral documents. All of these
sources we have combed. Yet we beg the reader's indulgence if occasional manifestations of the song have escaped us. We pretend to have
been conscientious without, however, presuming to have been exhaus-
tive. We have not presumed to follow popular manifestations of any of
the songs beyond the 1930's, nor have we pursued them in at least one
stream where they must surely occur from time to time, namely the
hymnals of the numerous western revivalist religious sects. Finally, we
have left the current era of the city-billy revival of the folk song—the

hooting of the hoots, the proliferation of the long-playing records, and the globe-encircling coils of magnetic tape—to younger and more ambitious scholars.

The perspective of another half-century will be necessary to see whether this resurgence will inflate the cowboy into a total image of America, or dissipate him until, like Beowulf or Roland, he shall ride slowly over the horizon and away into the dim but provocative forests of philology. Just seventy-five years ago Thorp rode back to the Bar W Ranch at Carrizozo, New Mexico, with his first thin packet of cowboy songs—his dust from that journey is still arriving.

Banjo in the Cow Camps[1]

by "Jack" Thorp

I

Now, boys, I'll tell you a story
Of a horse I owned long, long ago. . . .[2]

Words and banjo-strumming floated soft and clear on the night. I reined up in the brush to listen. It was pitch-dark where I was, Pecos River behind me, Roswell down that-a-way quite a piece, and somebody's chuck wagon just ahead, drawn up for the night in flat sand-dune country rich in grama grass and tabosa.[3] The campfire flickered and fell. I knew there would be maybe half a dozen men sprawled around it, their day's riding done, supper over, and a banjo-pickin' cowboy to tell a story under the stars: a story in verse, about their own country and

---

[1] Copyright © by The Atlantic Monthly Company, Boston, Massachusetts. CLXVII, 2 (August, 1940), pp. 195–203. Reprinted with permission. Annotation is by the Fifes.

[2] We have not been able to locate the source of this couplet.

[3] *grama grass . . . tabosa.* The "lingo" of cowboys and cowboy songs is enriched by Spanish vocabulary of the Southwest adopted and adapted to meet the needs of the new environment. *Webster's New Twentieth,* unabridged (2nd ed., 1960) defines grama grass as "any of various species of low grasses of the genus *Bouteloua,* as *Bouteloua olegostachya,* the mesquite grass or buffalo grass of Texas, New Mexico, and other western sections." *Tabosa,* not given by Webster, is probably *Hilaria Jamesiai,* a grass adapted to the arid climate of the Southwest and especially favored for grazing by the buffalo herds.

11

kind, in their lingo, home-grown and maybe as thorny as cactus. This one I was hearing now was about "a little steel dust the color of rust," the fastest cutting-horse in Texas—name of Dodgin' Joe.[4] It was a new song to me. As the final words died away, I rode into the light of the campfire. . . .

A young man's impulse sent me out on the road collecting cowboy songs almost fifty years ago. And it was more than thirty years ago, in the year 1908, that I made a dicker with a printer in Estancia, New Mexico, to print two thousand copies of the first little book of cowboy songs ever published. I paid the printer six cents per copy. The book was printed on rough stock and bound in red paper. There were fifty pages, twenty-four songs.[5]

I advertised in some Kansas papers that published patent sheets, and sold a good many of the books at fifty cents apiece. They were fragile, and most of the copies probably were torn to pieces or lost long ago. The few that are left fetch twenty-five dollars or so from collectors.[6]

Few people know of the difficulties encountered in gathering those first songs. Today you can find scores of cowboy ballads in songbooks accessible anywhere, and Tin-pan Alley manufactures new ones fresh every hour. In the '90's, with the exception of about a dozen, cowboy songs were not generally known. The only ones I could find I gathered piece-meal on horseback trips that lasted months and took me hundreds of miles through half a dozen cow-country states.[7]

On this evening I'm telling about, in March of '89, my first song

---

[4] Save for Thorp's reference here and in Thorp and Clark, p. 23, we have not yet encountered "Dodgin' Joe" either in our library research or in our field collecting. Too bad that the notebook into which Thorp transcribed two stanzas of "Dodgin' Joe," and other songs he did not print, has not survived!

[5] Though the table of contents of Thorp's book lists twenty-four items, the printer inadvertently put Mark Chisholm's name there as though it were a song title. The book actually contains twenty-three songs.

[6] Thorp was quite unaware that, as the first book of cowboy songs, his modest volume would become the "makin's of history." We doubt that more than twenty of the original two thousand copies have survived. Since 1940 the price has gone up to nearly $100 in the rare cases when a copy has appeared for sale.

[7] Most of the songs were gathered in Texas and New Mexico, although, on the trip in question, Thorp might possibly have touched the borders of Oklahoma and Arizona as well. He had previously encountered a few songs on his brother's ranch in Nebraska; by 1921 he had encountered them in several other western states.

hunt proper started. I had been looking for a couple of stray Bar W horses, and I was tired after a forty-five-mile ride. About to unpack and make a solitary camp, I spied fire in the distance. "What's the use of campin' by yourself?" I thought. So I rode to the camp which Nigger Add and his men had pitched at the tail of their chuck wagon.

Cowmen from Toyah, Texas, to Las Vegas, New Mexico, knew Add, and most of them at different times had worked on roundups with him. He was the L F D outfit's range boss, and worked South Texas colored hands almost entirely. Black though he was, Add was one of the best hands on the Pecos River, well liked, and in due time hero of a cowboy song himself.[8]

I hobbled out my horses and rustled a plate and cup from the chuck box; coffee and a pot of stew were kept hot all night at such camps. Having eaten my fill, I inquired who had been singing just before I came in. Heads nodded at a colored boy known as 'Lasses. I asked if he would mind singing the song again. He did it for me. But he knew only two verses—that's all. And none of the other hands in camp knew more. That was one of the difficulties encountered in the earliest effort to assemble the unprinted verse on the range. None of the cowboys who could sing ever remembered an entire song. I would pick up a verse or two here, another verse or two there.

After 'Lasses finished, I sang a song and so did several others. Somebody knew a couple of verses of "Sam Bass"—not the whole thing. The other songs they knew were about cotton patches, like one which celebrated a colored girl named Mamie—she picked her weight of cotton in the morning, 'twas said, then, with her feet under a bush and her head in the sun, went fast asleep. Cotton-picking songs were fine if you liked them, but they weren't what I was after. By the light of the fire I copied in my notebook the two verses of "Dodgin' Joe" which 'Lasses knew. Then I spread my tarp, wrapped my soogan[9] around me, and, with feet to the fire, fought off sleep for a while because a big idea was buzzing in my head. Here I was, I told myself, workin' for wages for the

---

[8] "Whose Old Cow": XXI of this book.

[9] *Tarp . . . soogan.* A bedroll was standard equipment for every cowhand. On trail herd or at roundup it was carried in the chuck wagon. When a puncher was "riding the chuck line," i.e., floating between jobs, it was tied behind the saddle. It was made up of a sheet of canvas, one or more soogans (i.e., blankets or homemade quilts), and sundry personal effects. See Adams, pp. 9 and 163.

Bar W. Nothing on my mind. Not much in my pocket: three dollars
or so, and no more comin'.

The cowboy's life is a dreary life, though his mind it is no load,
And he always spends his money like he found it in the road.[10]

Nigger Add had told me the two horses I was looking for were safe
in the L F D horse pasture; no need to worry more about them. I was
handy with horses, and in cow country somebody was always wantin'
horses broke; they paid wages for it. My saddle horse, Gray Dog, and my
pack horse, Ample, were my own property. Right here on my own range
I had ridden into Add's camp and heard part of a cowboy song brand-
new to me.

"If there's one here," I thought, "there must be plenty more off my
own range that I never heard."

So I made up my mind to keep driftin'.

Next morning when the mule star went to bed and the morning
star got up, I had breakfast and started. No trouble to say good-bye to
my job. When I got near the first post office a week or so later, I dropped
a letter in the box telling my boss where his two strays were, and adding
that one of his cowhands was a stray now too, and he should expect me
back when he saw my dust arrivin'.

"Add," I said, "how far is it to the next water?"

"Keep this draw ten or twelve miles, Jack," he told me. "You'll see
some cow trails comin' in. Head due east and you'll strike a dry lake."

I was on my way!

A couple of hours after leaving the chuck wagon I reached Comanche
Springs and there found two V T men watering a bunch of saddle
horses. The rest of the day I saw no one. Just me, a couple of horses, a
little rough country, a lot of rolling prairie; and at night, near the northeast end of Mescalero Valley, a lone camp and a dry one. I hobbled my
horses, laid out my bed in a chamise flat[11] where the brush was three to
four feet high, ate a snack, and made a fire to be sociable and show the
folks I was rich and had matches in my pocket.

---

[10] "The Cowboys Life." Several cowboy songs carry this title. Thorp gives it
as "The Pecos Stream," XVIII of this work.

[11] *Chamise* is probably the Spanish-American *Chamiso*, a small, close, densely
growing shrub *Adenostoma fascicolatum* of the rose family.

II

Maybe cowboy singing was an answer to loneliness. Maybe it was just another way of expressing good fellowship. Maybe it was several things. Something happened in the day's work, funny or sad, and somebody with a knack for words made a jingle of it; if it was liked, others learned it and passed it on. A ballad like "The Old Chisholm Trail,"[12] with its catching *come ti yi youpy* refrain, seems to have just grown. It was sung from the Canadian line to Mexico, and there were thousands of verses; nobody ever collected them all. Every cowboy knew some, and if he had a little whiskey in him, or was heading for town with wages in his pocket, he might make up a few. These weren't "cultured" songs. Sometimes the rhymes didn't match very well. Often the language was rough and for publication had to be heavily expurgated. But ballad-making and song-singing were living parts of cowboy life.

I have never attempted any highbrow explanations of cowboy balladry. Not long ago in a newspaper I read a piece about the "singin' families" of East Tennessee who by word of mouth kept alive scores of ballads they have never seen in a book. It was that way on the range. Singing songs, and making them too (homely, everyday songs, not highbrow stuff), seem as natural to human beings as washing herself is to a cat. And the faculty gets more practice when people are cut off in isolated groups.

Three or four days after crossing the Llano Estacado[13] (so flat, as Uncle Johnny Martin once said, that you could see the water in the bottom of a forty-foot well ten miles away), I was heading for the town of Tokio, up Red River way. I had started my travels toward Red River

---

[12] A favorite among cowboy songs so universal and so extended that its stanzas, written end to end in longhand, would span more territory than the commemorated trail itself along which cattle were driven from central Texas to rail heads in Kansas. It consists of a rhymed couplet plus a nonsense refrain—so easily accomplished that with a bit of practice one can *ad lib* his own stanzas:

There was a cowpuncher, his name was Thorp
He played a banjo, now he plays a harp.
Come a ti yi youpy . . . etc.

We have assembled nearly two hundred texts of this song.

[13] The *Llano Estacado* (Staked Plains) is an arid plateau in southeastern New Mexico and western Texas where large cattle empires had been established in the late 1800's. From 1540 to 1542 Coronado had explored the region, wintered there, and claimed it in the name of the King of Spain.

because an old cowman once told me that they did nothing much in that district but sing, cuss, and go to camp meetin'. Some miles short of Tokio I caught sight of a little ranch house and headed for it. The owner was busy slaughtering a beef. I turned to and helped him. We soon had the carcass cleaned and hung up. The rancher showed me the gate to his horse pasture; the grass looked fine and I decided to stay all night. Even if the owner had been away, I should have been welcome to go in and help myself to a meal and feed my horses. No doors were locked. All they asked was that you leave other things alone. If you wanted to, you might wash up the dishes you dirtied.

As we entered the house, I saw a banjo hanging on the wall.

"You play?"

The rancher said he did. So I went to my pack and got my mandolin-banjo.

We ate a hearty supper. I pushed back and started up a song. My host was soon singing too. Little square room with a light in it, lonely cabin miles from any neighbor. Fire in the stove, dishes dirty, bellies full. Banjos makin' melody. "Sassiety" enough for one night for a couple of horny cowhands. I don't know how many songs we sang that night. The coyotes must have gathered outside and laid off howlin' to listen.

Cowboy songs were always sung by one person, never by a group. I never did hear a cowboy with a real good voice; if he had one to start with, he always lost it bawling at cattle, or sleeping out in the open, or tellin' the judge he didn't steal that horse. Some of the cowboy actors and radio cowboys nowadays, of course, have very beautiful voices.

The cowboy hardly ever knew what tune he was singing his song to; just some old, old tune that he had heard and known as a boy. Very often the old familiar airs were used. Both "Little Joe the Wrangler" and "Little Adobe Casa" were sung to the air of "Little Old Log Cabin in the Lane."[14] "Sky High"[15] was sung to the tune of "Solomon Isaacs"; "Overland Stage"[16] to the air of "Son of a Gam-bo-leer." "The Little Cowgirl"[17] was sung to the tune of "Turkey in the Straw"; the people of

---

[14] I and VII of this work.

[15] We have not found this song elsewhere.

[16] A song with this title appears in Thorp's 1921 book (pp. 124–26) under his own signature. We have not encountered it elsewhere.

[17] Text is given by Thorp in his 1921 book, pp. 94–95. Not to be confused with "Our Little Cowgirl" (Lomax, Cattle, pp. 82–83).

Texas didn't know the National Anthem, but they all knew "Turkey in the Straw."

Two of the songs we sang that night, I know, were important for me. One was "Sam Bass." This famous song, if you don't remember, has to do with a cowboy turned train robber and outlaw, and betrayed by one of his pals. It is supposed to have been written by John Denton of Gainesville, Texas, about 1879. . . .[18] I first heard some of it sung at a dance hall in Sidney, Nebraska, and one of the boys in Nigger Add's camp had sung a couple of verses. My host this evening sang five verses, three of which I had not heard. Into the notebook they went. When I published my first little book, nearly twenty years later, I had found three more verses, making eight which appeared in the first printed version. But there were more. I printed eleven in my bigger book in 1921. This will indicate how songs grow. Versions were likely to vary from singer to singer. Verses were added, eliminated, altered, and otherwise "improved" as they went the rounds. In my first version of "Sam Bass" it was "Jonis" who was due to get a scorching "when Gabriel blows his horn"; in the later version it was "Jim Murphy." Take into account that many of the songs had to be dry-cleaned for unprintable words before they went to press, and you get some notion of the chore a song collector had who was only a cowboy himself.

The second song important for me that night was "The Death of Jesse James."[19] Two verses of it; just two. I got several additional verses some days later in the bunkhouse of the Craul and Jacobs cow spread west of Ringgold. And in Ringgold itself I got two more from an old cowpuncher, who I had been told was *dripping* with songs. I have noticed that the further you are from a gold strike, the richer it is. This old cowpuncher, and two other people in Ringgold who had been recommended to me as great singers, knew between them "My Bonnie Lies Over the Ocean,"[20] "Clementine,"[21] several revival songs, two French

---

[18] Three stanzas and melody given here which we omit. See X of this work.

[19] Jesse James comes near playing in our American culture the role Robin Hood has played in England. There are a half-dozen Jesse James ballads with intricate interlinking of texts and tunes.

[20] "My Bonnie" has become a favorite melody for "The Grand Roundup" (VI of this work), which is also sung to "In the Sweet By and By."

[21] Readers should recall that "Clementine" is a western mining ballad: "In a canyon, in a cavern/Excavating for a mine/Lived a miner, a forty-niner/And his daughter Clementine."

love songs—and the two final verses of "The Death of Jesse James." A song-hunter had to pick up his gold in small hunks where he found it.

III

A lot of singing on the range had nothing to do with cowboy songs as such. In different camps I encountered railroad, mountain, river, and granger songs, as well as sticky-sweet sentimental ballads like "Mollie Lou, Sweet Mollie Mine," and "My Little Georgie May." Cowboys weren't always singin' about "little dogies"[22] or "give me a home where the buffalo roam,"[23] and when they sang river songs it was generally something about running logs down a mountain stream. Railroad songs celebrated head-on collisions, or told how a brave conductor saved a train. Granger songs usually had something to do with a yoke of oxen, old Buck and Spot, and a boy who was tired of driving them to the plough and so quit home. These were part of the singing West too, but I was mainly interested in songs that had all the elements of the range—the cow range, and its special codes and points of view.

It is generally thought that cowboys did a lot of singing around the herd at night to quiet them on the bed ground. I have been asked about this, and I'll say that I have stood my share of night watches in fifty years and I seldom heard any singing of that kind. What you would hear as you passed your partner on guard would be a kind of low hum or whistle, and you wouldn't know what it was. Just some old hymn

[22] The reference here is to one of the most popular of trail songs, known usually under the title "Git Along Little Dogies." Genuinely cowboy in its origins, it has been used so much in the world of popular (i.e., commercial) music that it has lost most of its range flavor.

[23] "Home on the Range" became the object of a six-figure damage suit in the 1930's when, as Franklin D. Roosevelt's favorite song, it achieved world popularity. It was ironical that none of the claimants had any valid rights to authorship since the song had floated in the public domain for sixty years! Words were written by Brewster Higley VI, M.D., in 1873, and first printed (without music) in the *Kirwin* (Kansas) *Chief*, February 26, 1876. Music was added by one of the pioneer doctor's acquaintances, Daniel E. Kelley, who, typically, did not set his melody in musical notation. For a full account see "The Story of 'Home on the Range'" by Kirke Mechem in *The Kansas Historical Quarterly*, XVII, 4 (November, 1949), pp. 313–39. Thorp rightly excluded it from his 1908 work, if he had encountered it by then, because it is not a cowboy song. The noun "range" as used in modern commercialized forms of the song does not appear in the Higley-Kelley version.

tune, like as not—something to kill time and not bad enough to make the herd want to get up and run.[24]

Cowboy songs, as I said, were often sung to old familiar airs. Failing these, there was a kind of standard monotonous tune used over and over that even uneducated fingers could pick out on the banjo. A young friend who has listened to me hum it says the tune looks like this in printed notes:—

Things that cowboys liked, things they hated, incidents of the here and reflections on the hereafter—these were the chief themes of their songs. Their ways were rough, but they knew gold from glitter when they saw it. They judged a man not by his boasts, but by what he could and did do when the time came for action. They played hard practical jokes, but the best of them could "take it" when their jokes back-fired. No theme of cowboy balladry illustrates these characteristics better than the one incorporated in "The Educated Feller," "Cowboys Victimized," "The Zebra Dun," and others built around the same essential situation.[25]

Who wrote the cowboy songs? The authorship of many of them is doubtful or unknown. Often the authors, if they hailed from the range direct, didn't bother or care to acknowledge authorship. Thus "The Campfire Has Gone Out," which I heard when I was ranching in the San Andreas Mountains, was written, I believe, by Gene Rhodes; but, as far as I know, Gene himself never said so.[26] "Hell in Texas" is a popular ballad describing a supposed deal between the Lord and the Devil by which the latter acquired some land so bad that the Lord

---

[24] Thorp's opinion differs from some others, notably J. Frank Dobie's. But whether the singing was for the benefit of the cattle or the singer is a debatable point. Nevertheless, musical convention has evolved a distinctive song type, the night-herding song, a slow, soft, and quiet song that exudes a kind of open-sky deism where the lone cowhand speculates on death, the hereafter, and other transcendental things. "The Grand Roundup," VI of this work, is a fine example.

[25] See "Educated Feller," XII of this work.

[26] Identity and authorship of "The Campfire Has Gone Out" is yet to be worked out. Lewis F. Crawford (*Rekindling Camp Fires*, Bismarck, N.D.: Capitol Book Co., 1926, pp. 309–10) gives under this title a poem ascribed to Ben Connor (Arnold) which begins "Through progress of the railroads our occupation's gone." The refrain concludes: "The cowboy has left the country/His camp-fire has gone out."

couldn't use it, but perfectly suited to the Devil's needs for a little hell on earth: he "put thorns on the cactus and horns on the toads . . . poisoned the feet of the centipede," and did more of the same—and called it Texas. At one time or another I picked up five versions of this song, each supposed to be by a different author; some of them say the place the Devil got hold of was Texas, others say New Mexico, depending on the writer's partisanship.[27] There was "Fightin' Mad," too, a ballad about a cowboy who was offered ginger ale to drink. This I got at the annual Colorado Springs Roundup from Jean Beaumondy. Jean was then the champion trick girl roper of the world—she's still good, according to accounts of a movie film in which she did her stuff less than a year ago.

"Did you write the song, Jean?" I asked her.

"Oh, I was around when it was written," she said. And that's all I ever could get out of her.[28]

Sometimes a song lost its author and even changed its name as it passed from mouth to mouth. Henry Herbert Knibbs once brought me a cowboy song from southern Arizona, known there under the title "High-Chin Bob." Actually the song was written by Charles Badger Clark, Jr., and the original version appeared in his book, *Sun and Saddle Leather*, under the title, "The Glory Trail."[29] A song of mine called "Nigger 'Lasses" had this four-line refrain:—

> Oh, dere ain't no horse what can't be rode,
> Dat's what de white folks say!
> En dere ain't a man what can't be throwed,
> *Oh, Mah!*—I finds it jest dat way!

---

[27] "Hell in Texas" has grown some since Thorp encountered his five variants. To date we have unearthed more than a score of texts and variants, the maligned areas being Texas, Arizona, New Mexico, the Rio Grande, and the Yukon. It was widely reproduced in newspapers through the late 1880's. A long narrative poem published in 1873 by J. H. Beadle (*The Undeveloped West*, Philadelphia: National Publishing Co., pp. 536–40) contains many of the images that contributed to the subsequent formation of "Hell in Texas."

[28] Except for Thorp's reference here and in Thorp and Clark (caption to photo of Jean Beaumondy, p. 33) we have never encountered the song.

[29] Charles Badger Clark's "Glory Trail" (in his *Sun and Saddle Leather*, Boston: R. G. Badger, 1915, pp. 39–41) is one of the greatest songs of the cowboy repertoire. Through the image of High-Chin Bob, mighty tall in the saddle, who threw his lasso on a mountain lion, Clark creates the transcendental image of man and his glorious but futile dreams of conquest. Thorp included it in *The Songs of the Cowboys* (1921), pp. 81–83.

J. Frank Dobie once heard this song at Eagle Pass, Texas, sung by a darky singer, and Frank asked him where he got it. The singer said: "Ah don' know, sah. A man named Mister Jack he wrote it—ah dunno."[30]

Authorship wasn't reckoned very important—nothing to fight over. But when you did discover a song's author, sometimes it was a surprise.[31] The second night after I threw in with Speckles and Tom, we penned the horses on the outskirts of Gainesville and later hunted up a pasture to put them in for the night. While we were cooking supper a great tall ganglin' swamp-angel moseyed into camp looking hungrier than a dieting deb. A swamp-angel was a fellow raised down in the swamp lands, maybe Louisiana or Arkansas. They all had chills and fever, ninety per cent of them chewed snuffsticks, and they generally looked like walking matches. This one seemed to be a fair sample of the breed. Seeing my little banjo lying on my bedroll, he asked if any of us could sing. No, we said, but sometimes we opened our mouths and noise came out.

"Want me ter sing you a song?"

"Sure!" we said. So he picked up my banjo. And what a banjo-picker he was! He sang "Bucking Bronco"—sang the whole song of five verses. What's more, he knew the author's name. Belle Starr, he said, wrote it.

I had met Belle several times in Dallas and Fort Worth. Now, I was told, she had a ranch at Younger's Bend. Belle was one of the most famous of the women outlaws of the Southwest. A beautiful brunette, well educated, she wore guns and had a bunch of desperadoes working for her. She was running a holdout stable in Dallas, where stolen horses were fenced. But the horses came from the Indian Territory, which made it all right; nobody in Texas would bother her. All the cowpunchers went there to put up their horses when they came to town. Belle sang in the church choir, played the piano, and was a "sassiety" lady in those days. That she was also a song writer was news and quite a surprise to me. But Belle was an original, a product of the time and the region; and her end, when it came, was tragically in keeping with her life. Returning

---

[30] For the full text see Thorp (1921) pp. 106–8. The pseudo-Negro dialect was too heavy to permit survival of this humorous song about a colored puncher's frustrated attempt to ride a wild bronco.

[31] Yet, when a song really took hold, especially when it began to earn money via recording and sheet music, claims to authorship got heaped up like sardines in a can, and almost as smelly!

from a trip to Fort Smith, she was two miles from her ranch at Younger's
Bend when she was shot in the back by one of her tenants with whom
she had quarreled, a man wanted in Florida on a murder charge but
afraid to meet Belle face to face. . . .[32]

I broke horses for old man Waggoner in Paul's Valley for some
time, picking up what songs I could; and when I felt I had enough cash
ahead to last a spell, I saddled up Gray Dog, packed Ample, and started
drifting and song-hunting again, south this time towards Dallas, Austin,
San Antonio, and points farther south and west.

IV

Cowboy songs did not always reach me through cowboys. I took
them where I found them, from all sorts and kinds of people. Walking
up Main Street in Fort Worth one morning, I heard the air of "My Old
Kentucky Home" through the doors of the Silver Dollar saloon. I went
in and found a girl singing a cowboy song for a drink. Her audience
soon left and she sat at a table with me. She know only one song, but
it was a good one for the notebook—"Buster Goes A-Courtin'." In Dallas
I camped in a pecan grove outside the Fair Grounds near a group of
Irish gypsies who drew crowds by fomenting horse races, and here I
picked up "My Pet Horse" and "Ridin' Jane"[33]—not quite cowboy songs,
but good enough to go into the notebook. "Buckskin Joe"[34] I first heard
in the public square of Waco.

South of Waco one night I rode in the dark. It was a night for
riding! I saw a city on fire below the edge of the world, and presently
the moon popped up and made the whole State of Texas so bright you
could read a newspaper. A campfire flickered, and I rode in where three
men were camped. They were dressed no differently than other mounted
Texans—no uniforms, no brass. They invited me to get down and camp.
I unpacked, unsaddled, hobbled out my horses. Seeing my banjo, they
asked me to play. I did. One of the three responded with a song, a new

---

[32] Three stanzas given here, which we omit. See XI of this work.

[33] We have never seen another reference to these three items.

[34] Thorp printed it in 1921 (pp. 15–18). It is one of a constellation of
western boasting songs in which a gambler, who has accused his adversary of cheat-
ing, cools off all too quickly when the adversary boasts that he is "wild and woolly
and full of fleas. . . ."

one to me. That there was such a song I knew, but this was my first hearing of it. "The Texas Rangers"[35] it was; and it was a ranger who sang it. These three were part of Captain Hughes's famous force, on their way to Fort McKavett, they told me, to investigate a report of trouble between sheepmen and cattlemen.

Followers of many trades were found in the cow country, many of them with songs on their lips. From San Antonio I headed into mesquite-and-cactus country. I reached Devil's River four miles south of the town of Juno, and found a strange assemblage of wagons, all manned by Mexicans. They invited me to get down and try a cup of coffee.

At this camp one of the younger Mexicans sang me four verses of a song in Spanish called "El Rio Rey"—"The River King." It was a ballad of a *palomino* stud that roamed the range uncaught, untamed. I never found anybody who knew more of the original than the four verses sung me by this Mexican. But some months afterwards I was lying in my bedroll at two or three in the morning, and words to complete the song suddenly came to me. I slid out of bed, got my little notebook out of my chaps pocket, and wrote four new verses in English. I translated the four from the Spanish, and in that way completed the ballad. Such was the mongrel ancestry of some cowboy songs.[36]

It was at Toyah near the New Mexico line, from another cow-country character, "Sally" White, that I got four verses of "The Great Roundup":—

> Where cowboys·with others must stand
> To be cut out by the riders of judgment
> Who are posted and know all the brands.

"Sally" was no girl despite his name, but was so called from his fondness for singing a song with that title. No, Mr. White was no girl. I remember the night he got drunk in Pecos town. They had a law against wearing six-shooters within the city limits. "Sally" tied his gun to the end of

---

[35] "The Texas Rangers" is, of course, one of the best known of western songs. It tells of a youthful recruit among the Rangers who will die before returning to home and mother. We have assembled more than two hundred texts. The song has many analogues and parodies. Though we encounter literary Ranger songs from the 1830's, our oldest text of this particular song was published by Francis Allen (*Lone Star,* p. 38) in 1878. Kenneth Goldstein has made field recordings of it among the folk of Scotland. See Goldstein, *Texas.*

[36] We have not encountered the song.

his rope, thus in his opinion complying with the law, and went all over town dragging the rope and yelling "Don't step on my tail, boys! Open the door an' let me an' my tail through!" His song, attributed to the father of a Captain Roberts of the Texas Rangers, ends up:—[37]

V

Cowboy songs, as I have said, were full of the vernacular of the range, and it wasn't always parlor talk. I vividly remember sitting in the ranch house on Crow Flat with old Jim Brownfield during the latter stages of my trip, and hearing him give the entire range version of "The Top Hand." The theme—ridicule of a cowboy too big for his boots— was a scorcher in itself, and the words of the song would have burned the reader's eyeballs if printed as Jim sang it. I expurgated it and had to change even the title, and the song has appeared exactly as I rendered it in all books of cowboy songs published since:—

> While you're all so frisky, I'll sing a little song:
> Think a horn of whiskey will help the thing along.
> It's all about the Top Hand when he's busted flat,
> Bumming round town, in his Mexicana hat.
> He's laid up all winter and his pocketbook is flat.
> His clothes are all tatters, but he don't mind that.[38]

The same is true of Belle Starr's "The Bucking Bronco" and of many other songs.

In fact, I have found that cowboy songs have their adventures after they get into print as well as before. I closed my first little paper-covered book with a ballad I wrote myself, called "Speckles." There were eight verses as I wrote it, but the printer lost part of the copy and printed only six. Some time later a very learned professor brought out a big book of cowboy songs which he claimed to have collected with great labor, and he printed my abbreviated "Speckles" (without credit), but changed the name to "Freckles" and called it a fragment that he had picked up.[39]

---

[37] Four stanzas given here, which we omit. See VI of this work.

[38] See V of this work.

[39] The "learned professor" was, of course, the now famous John A. Lomax, who did more than any one person to fix cowboy songs in the ethos of America. He did make liberal use of Thorp's booklet in his 1910 and later editions of

Another song of mine also had a rather checkered history. In 1898, nearly ten years after the trip I am writing about, I helped trail a herd of O cattle from Chimney Lake, New Mexico, to Higgins, Texas. There were eight of us in the crew. One night I sat by the campfire with a stub of pencil and an old paper bag and wrote the story of little Joe, the horse wrangler, a Texas stray who had left home, he told us, and struck out for himself because his daddy had married again and his new ma beat him. The boss "sorter liked the little stray somehow," and took him on as a hand. One night in a thunderstorm everybody turned out to check a stampede. The cattle ran a ways, but were headed, and when they were milling and kind of quieted down, one of the hands was missing—our little Texas stray. He was found next morning in a wash twenty feet deep, under his horse, Rockett. . . .[40]

I sang the song to the men who were with me on that trail trip. After our return I sang it for the first time in any man's hearing—save on that trip—in Uncle Johnny Martin's store and saloon at Weed, New Mexico. From that time on it was passed along by word of mouth. I led off my first little book with it, but didn't sign it; none of the songs in that book were signed, though five of the twenty-four were my own compositions. In the course of time "Little Joe, the Wrangler" became one of the most widely sung and best liked of cowboy songs. I have no idea how often it has been sung over the radio in the last few years. I do know that it has been put on phonograph records and more than 375,000 of them have been sold—and the author of the song not richer by a penny for having written it.

> Never a cent in our pockets,
> But what did a cowpuncher care?[41]

VI

A morning in March, 1890, just a year after I started out, found me back on my home range not far from the place where I had encoun-

---

Cowboy Songs and Ballads without giving credit. In his *Songs of the Cowboys* (1921) Thorp returned the compliment even to the point of abandoning some of his genuine 1908 texts in favor of "the learned professor's" synthetic specimens. For notes on "Speckles" see XXIII of this work.

[40] Five stanzas given here, which we omit. See I of this work.

[41] We have not been able to locate the couplet Thorp uses here to express the cowboy's (or his own?) scorn of money.

tered Nigger Add and his chuck-wagon camp. I had but twenty-five
miles more to go to the old Carrizozo ranch, better known as the Bar W.
I reflected on the miles I had ridden (more than 1,500 of them), the
handful of songs I had collected, the nights and days I had passed in
cow country new to me, the hands I had shaken, the men "good" and
"bad" I had come to know. I had spent some time with "Old Perk," who
once dug a pit to trap predacious bears, and when his dog fell into the
pit while it was occupied by a big trapped bear Old Perk followed feet
first with no weapon but a butcher knife to save his dog. A braver deed,
wholly without audience, it would be hard to find. Old Perk killed the
bear and saved the dog, but received terrible scars which he wore to the
end of his life; he was so sensitive about his appearance that he would
never come to town except for necessary grub and then only after dark.
I had eaten and bunked, too, with a man who made his home in a cave
in the Guadalupes. He was "wanted," whether for murder or horse steal-
ing I did not know, and he certainly rode horses with too many different
brands to be honest; but he was as likable a man as you could meet.

Cowboys didn't judge too harshly. The best of them would do to
ride with anywhere, and the worst weren't all bad. "Show me a perfect
man and I'll show you Christ" was their tolerant attitude. With such
men I had lived and would live, and the time did not seem to me ill
spent. Next spring, I thought as I jogged along, I'll go again: this time
through western New Mexico, and on through Arizona, Utah, Colorado,
Wyoming. . . .

You would ride those ranges in vain today to find men who ride
and make songs and sing them in the old free larruping spirit and under
like conditions:—

> What's become of the punchers
> We rode with long ago?
> The hundreds and hundreds of cowboys
> Who all of us used to know? . . .[42]

But the country, and the life as it was, survive authentically in the
balladry, crude though it may have been, that grew out of the very lives
the cowboys led and the troubles they had; and our literature is richer
for it.

---

[42] This comes to us only from Thorp's 1921 edition, pp. 162–64, under the
title "What's Become of the Punchers?" written by Thorp himself.

Late afternoon brought sight of the cottonwoods around the old Bar W. Ample, the pack horse, had been raised there. He recognized home, and passed me at a fast trot. Gray Dog, too, commenced fishin' at the bit. Hi, boss! Want an old hand for the roundup? Our dust is arrivin'.

I

Little Joe, the Wrangler

"LITTLE JOE" IS ONE OF a constellation of heroes who, as a group, make up the mythical image of the cowboy—in this particular case the image of an abused youth whose loyalty in the crisis of a cattle stampede leads to a hero's death.

The mood and style of the song fall just short of sentimentality. A boy with decrepit horse and gear rides into a cattle camp, explains that he has left home to escape a stepmother's abuse, asks for a job, though admitting he doesn't know "straight up about a cow." The boss puts him on, goes out of his way to train the kid: "He sorter liked the little stray somehow." Thunderclaps and lightning flashes incite a stampede. Little Joe is called out with the other riders to stop it. When the herd is quieted down Little Joe is missing: his horse has fallen into a ravine and Little Joe has been killed.

No overdrawn images, no nonessential words: style, rhythms, cadences converge to tell the essential facts and nothing else. The

28

language is correct, with enough, and just enough, cowboy "lingo" to give the stamp of authenticity.

In his 1921 edition, Thorp says he wrote "Little Joe, the Wrangler" "on trail of herd of O cattle from Chimney Lake, New Mexico to Higgins, Texas, 1898."[1] There being no evidence to the contrary, we accept Thorp's claim. In his autobiography he gives additional details: that it was "woven around an actual event on the trail" witnessed by himself; that he wrote it "on a paper bag beside the campfire"; that the song made its first public appearance "in Uncle Johnny Root's saloon at Weed, New Mexico"; that it was sung to the air of "Little Old Log Cabin in the Lane."[2]

"Little Joe" has appeared many times in print, especially during the 1930's. Most printings, regrettably, follow the defective Lomax text.[3] Variations are numerous but not of substantive nature: efforts to patch up the rhyme, defective meter, especially where the music is lacking, and new geographic localizations (often with a Texas bias: *Texas* kack for *Southern* kack, the Pecos, Brazos, or Pease rivers for Red River, etc.).

One test of the acceptance of a song in folk tradition is the number, variety, and quality of the parodies it has bred. "Little Joe the Wrangler's Sister Nell," "The Little Bunch of Cactus on the Wall," and "Texas Short, the Kid"[4] are not enough to make of "Little Joe" an epic, but they do confirm its full acceptance by the folk. There is also "Cowboy Jack's Last Ride,"[5] a servile parody which takes its theme from "Little Joe" and its melody from "Cowboy Jack," a well-known western song not printed by Thorp. "Little Joe" has spawned railroad songs also. There are three different songs, all known as "The Little Red Caboose Behind the Train." One tells of a brakeman killed in an act of heroism to stop a runaway train; another of the conductor whose bride, honeymooning with him in the little red caboose, is killed in a wreck. There is a railroad bum's satirical song about the privileged railroad hands who ride in the little red caboose while the bums are lucky to ride the rods (metal bars beneath the cars).

---

[1] P. 96; Thorp, *Banjo,* p. 202; *supra,* p. 25.
[2] See Thorp and Clark, pp. 16, 27, 42–44, 52; Thorp, *Banjo,* p. 202; *supra,* p. 25.
[3] See item two of bibliography of significant texts, *infra,* p. 36.
[4] Hendren 478.
[5] Hendren 475.

"Little Joe the Wangler's Sister Nell" comes from Clark, *Happy Cowboy,*[6] where the words are ascribed to Thorp, and from an unidentified newspaper clipping in the Hendren Collection. We also have it in a field recording of 1960 made in Canada, sung by Sam Campbell of Toronto; from Missouri, 1941, sung by Mrs. Lillian Short of Cabool; and from Bill Garlinghouse of Globe, Arizona, 1956. The melody is the same as for "Little Joe." The mood and style make Thorp's authorship seem plausible, though he seems never to have claimed it.

The melody for "Little Joe" and its descendents comes from an earlier frontier song, "The Little Old Log Cabin in the Lane," which also gave birth to "The Little Old Sod Shanty" and "The Little Adobe Casa."[7] The setting here follows the singing of Ray Reed, Albuquerque, New Mexico, which is done with a slow tempo and appropriately sad and tender mood. It has a harmonic structure consisting of both stanza and chorus, though all except the first stanza are sung to the chorus melody beginning, " 'Twas late in the evening." This structure appears often in cowboy and western songs. We have encountered singings where either the verse or the refrain melody is used throughout. However, in such cases the song leaves the listener unsatisfied, especially in the case of the chorus melody beginning on IV chord. The figure ♪♪. is very common in western singing style as a device to synchronize syllabic and melodic stresses. The melodic line of "Little Joe's" refrain appears in a "Holy Roller" hymn, "Lily of the Valley," as sung by Dr. George Meyer of Logan, Utah, 1964. He had memorized it in about 1904 in Ohio.

I–A.   THORP (1908) pages 9–11

1.   Little Joe, the wrangler, will never wrangle more;
            His days with the "Remuda"—they are done.
        'Twas a year ago last April he joined the outfit here,
            A little "Texas Stray" and all alone.

2.   'Twas long late in the evening he rode up to the herd
            On a little old brown pony he called Chaw;
        With his brogan shoes and overalls a harder looking kid
            You never in your life had seen before.

[6] Pp. 20–21.
[7] Number VII of this book.

3.   His saddle 'twas a southern kack built many years ago,
       An O. K. spur on one foot idly hung,
    While his "hot roll" in a cotton sack was loosely tied behind
       And a canteen from the saddle horn he'd slung.

4.   He said he'd had to leave his home, his daddy'd married twice
       And his new ma beat him every day or two;
    So he saddled up old Chaw one night and "Lit a shuck"
       this way
       Thought he'd try and paddle now his own canoe.

5.   Said he'd try and do the best he could if we'd only give
       him work
       Though he didn't know "straight" up about a cow,
    So the boss he cut him out a mount and kinder put him on
       For he sorter liked the little stray somehow.

6.   Taught him how to herd the horses and to learn to know
       them all
       To round 'em up by daylight; if he could
    To follow the chuck-wagon and to always hitch the team
       And help the "cosinero" rustle wood.

7.   We'd driven to red river and the weather had been fine;
       We were camped down on the south side in a bend
    When a norther commenced blowing and we doubled up
       our guards
       For it took all hands to hold the cattle then.

8.   Little Joe the wrangler was called out with the rest
       And scarcely had the kid got to the herd
    When the cattle they stampeded; like a hail storm, long
       they flew
       And all of us were riding for the lead.

9.   'Tween the streaks of lightning we could see a horse far out
       ahead
       'Twas little Joe the wrangler in the lead;
    He was riding "old Blue Rocket" with his slicker 'bove his
       head
       Trying to check the leaders in their speed.

10.   At last we got them milling and kinder quieted down
            And the extra guard back to the camp did go
            But one of them was missin' and we all knew at a glance
            'Twas our little Texas stray poor wrangler Joe.

11.   Next morning just at sunup we found where Rocket fell
            Down in a washout twenty feet below
            Beneath his horse mashed to a pulp his horse had rung
            the knell
            For our little Texas stray—poor wrangler Joe.

McConathy (p. 85) gives an apocryphal final stanza:

12.   And now Joe, the wrangler, will wrangle nevermore,
            For his wrangling days forever now are o'er.
            He has left his spurs and saddle for others here below
            So bid farewell to little wrangling Joe.

I–B.   "LITTLE JOE THE WRANGLER'S SISTER NELL"
            Sung by Bill Garlinghouse, Arizona, 1956. UAFA (FAC I 123).

1.   She rode up to the wagon, as the sun had moved along,
            A slender little pixie dressed in gray
            We told her to get down, of course, and pull up to the fire,
            For red hot chuck would soon be on its way.

2.   An old slouch hat with a hole on top was perched upon
            her head
            A pair of bullhide chaps, well-greased and worn,
            And her old stock saddle scratched and scored from a
            working in the brush
            And the slick maguey tied to her saddle horn.

3.   She said she'd rode from Llano, four hundred miles away,
            Her horse it was so tired it couldn't go,
            She asked to stop a day or two and kinda rest him up
            Then maybe she could find her brother Joe.

4.   We could tell that she'd been crying, her little face looked
            sad,

When she spoke her upper lip would tremble so,
She was the living image, we all saw at a glance,
Of our little Texas stray, poor wrangling Joe.

5.   We asked where Joe was a-working, if she knew the outfit's
          brand,
His letter said it was the Circle Bar,
It was mailed in Amarillo about four months ago
      While our trail herd headed north to the Cinnabar.

6.   I looked at Jim, he looked at Tom, and he looked back at me
          There was something in our hearts we couldn't speak.
But she got kinda worried when she never heard no more
      And things at home got tougher every week.

7.   "You see, my mother died," she said, "when Joe and I were
          born,
Joe and I were twins," the story ran.
"Then Daddy ups and marries and he gets another wife
      And then it was our troubles sure began.

8.   "She beat us and abused us and starved us most the time,
          You see she had no children of her own,
Nothing Joe or I could do would ever seem just right
      When Joe pulled out that leaved me all alone."

9.   I gave the kid my bed roll while I bunked in with Jim
          We planned and schemed and talked the whole night
              through
As to which of us would tell her the way that Joe was killed
      And break the news as gently as we knew.

10.   "I'll wrangle in the morning, boys," she said as she turned in,
          "I'll have the horses at the wagon 'fore it's day."
When the morning star was rising I saw that kid roll out
      Saddle up that grayhide horse and ride away.

11.   Soon we heard the horses coming, headin' into camp
          'Twas daylight and we could plainly hear the bell,
And then someone a-crying, coming round behind
      'Twas our little Joe the wrangler's sister Nell.

12.   We couldn't quite control her, she'd seen the horses' brand
                 As she drove them from the river's bank below,
             From the looks on our faces she seemed to realize
                 That she ne'er again would see her brother Joe.

I–C.   "THE LITTLE BUNCH OF CACTUS ON THE WALL"
         PNFQ 254. Date and source unknown.

1.   In my old bunkhouse tonight there's a spot that is so bright,
                 To my memory the time I can recall,
             It was little Joe the wrangler, my cowboy pal so true,
                 That hung that bunch of cactus on the wall.

2.   There never was a cowboy who could ride a bronc like Joe,
                 As true and dear a friend as he was brave;
             Now his bronc is in the stall and his chaps hang on the wall,
                 And his saddle lies a-moldering in his grave.

                                   (Yodel)

3.   Little Joe, his eyes were fading; on his face there was a smile,
                 He said: "My pals, I'm tellin' you goodbye.
             I can hear the Boss a-callin', 'Please come home, Joe, my boy,
                 For you're goin' to join the roundup in the sky.' "

4.   Little Joe, he passed away on one bright September day,
                 We buried him early in the fall,
             And I wouldn't take a fortune or nothing in this world
                 For that little bunch of cactus on the wall.

(The yodel suggests that we are dealing with a text from the 1930's.
Note the eternal folk theme of premonition of death, stanza 3. Tales
and anecdotes about "hunches" pervade popular literature.)

I–D.   "LITTLE JOE THE WRANGLER"
         Sung by Ray Reed, New Mexico, 1959. (FAC I 193).
         Reproduced by permission of the collector, Dean Emeritus John
         Donald Robb, University of New Mexico.

Then lit-tle Joe the wran-gler_ will wran-gle ne-ver more._ His
days __ with the re-mu-da __ now are o'er. __ 'Twas a
year a-go last A-pril__ he rode up to our herd, __ Just a
lit-tle Te-xas stray and all a-lone __ 'Twas
late __ in the eve-nin'_ He rode up to our camp_ On a
lit-tle Tex-as po-ny__ he called Chaw._ With his
bro-gan shoes and o-ver-alls, a tough-er look-ing kid __ as you
ev-er in your life be-fore had saw.

BIBLIOGRAPHY

Significant texts:

1898 Thorp (1908) pp. 9–11; (1921) pp. 96–98; Thorp and Clark, p. 43
      (omits stanzas 2–6).

1909   Lomax (1910) pp. 167–69; (1938) pp. 91–93. The defective texts of the Lomax editions cited here seem to derive from a handwritten text sent him November 7, 1909, by Mrs. M. B. Wight, Fort Thomas, Arizona (Lomax d. 5653: JL 224).

1916   Lomax d. 5560 contains a letter from a Mr. Armstrong of Jones County, Texas, dated October 20, 1916, transmitting text of a song entitled "Little Joe."

Other printed texts:

Allen, *Cowboy Lore*, pp. 65–68.
Clark, *Cowboy*, pp. 44–45; *Happy Cowboy*, p. 19.
Colorado II, pp. 35–36.
Davis, *Tip Top*, p. 27.
German (unpaged).
Hendren 603, unidentified newspaper clipping.
Hobo News, fol. 10, col. 2 = Thorp (1921) pp. 96–98.
Idaho Farmer, October 29, 1931 (FAC III 421).
Kincaid No. 7, pp. 20–21.
Larkin, pp. 119–122 = Thorp (1921) pp. 96–98.
Lee, *Cowboy* (1938) pp. 40–41.
Lomax (Lilly), pp. 24–29 (FAC III 742).
Lone Ranger, pp. 8–9.
McConathy, pp. 84–85.
Pack (unpaged).
Patterson and Dexter, pp. 27–29.
Randolph II, pp. 234–36.
Rhinehart, p. 41.
Roaming Cowboy, No. 2, p. 18.
Rogers, *Cowboy*, pp. 26–27.
Rogers' Favorite, p. 31.
Roundup Rangers, pp. 3–4.
Sherwin and Klickman, pp. 44–45.
Sires, pp. 48–49.
Sizemore, *Family*, p. 30; *Hearth*, p. 27.
Texas Centennial, p. 6 (FAC III 488).
Utah Cowboy's, pp. 17–18.
Williams Favorite, p. 24.
Newspaper clipping, unidentified, from V Stocks, Utah (FAC II 534).

Commercial recordings:

Bob Atcher: Columbia 20619, 6524, Album A90 (FAC III 1010).

Edward L. Crain: Crown 3239.
Jules Allen: Montgomery Ward 4344; Victor 21470 (FAC III 989).
Leon Chappalear (The Lone Star Cowboy): Champion 16497, 45068; Montgomery Ward 4850, 4950; Melotone 45068.
Marc Williams: Brunswick 269 (FAC III 1009).
Ranch Boys: Decca 2644, Album 65.
Texas Drifter: Melotone 12214 (FAC III 991).
Dance record: Banner 32146.

"Little Joe the Wrangler's Sister Nell"—Wilf Carter record in 1920's (according to Fowke, *American,* p. 250).

Manuscripts and field recordings:

Fife. *Maryland:* Frank Goodwyn, 1959 (FAC I 250). *Utah:* P. Stocks, 1953 (FMR 505A1).
Lomax. *Oregon:* d. 5653, "as learned from her mother who learned it in eastern Oregon," 1931 (JL 226). *Texas:* LC cylinder no. 22, Newton Gaines, 1908–10; LC 654A, 1936.
O'Bryant. *Arizona:* A. Bittick, 1958 (FAC I 95).
Robb. *New Mexico:* No. 199, R. Reed, 1949 (FAC I 196); No. 765, R. Reed, 1951 (FAC I 193); No. 633, J. Farris, 1951 (FAC I 195); No. 666, J. K. Plauche, 1951 (FAC I 194).
Todd and Sonkin. *California:* LC 4116B, 1940.
UAFA. *Arizona:* B. Garlinghouse, 1956 (FAC I 122).

Discussion:

Barrett, Chapter 7.
Craddock, p. 184.
Fowke, *American,* p. 250.
Gillis, pp. 103–5.
Laws, pp. 17, 46, 134.
Lomax (1938), p. 91.
Lomax d. 5639 (JL 501).
Lomax (Lilly), pp. 24–29 (FAC III 742).
Randolph II, p. 234.
Sires, p. 48.
Thorp, *Banjo,* pp. 202–3 (*supra,* p. 25)
Thorp and Clark, pp. 16, 27, 42–44, 52.
Wight, Jesse: interview with (FAC I 570).

II

Windy Bill

*R*OPING RANGE CATTLE, on horseback of course, was no job for amateurs. Yet in days before barbed wire it was a skill every puncher had to master: to ride full-tilt until you were less than two rods behind and a bit off the critter's right or left stern, to swing and throw your loop around the animal, to take a wrap (or "dally") around the saddle horn; stop that horse on all fours, hopeful of throwing the roped critter off his feet; to dismount, follow down the rope—your horse keeping it taut meanwhile to keep the steer down until you could tie the legs, and thus take him out of play long enough to brand and earmark. Then let him go. All this demanded strength, skill, and judgment beyond the ordinary.

Windy Bill's flaw, though he was one of the best, was that he made his dally so he could not release the rope when the black outlaw (or "snake" steer) proved too much. Being, no doubt, a bit too "windy," his prankster pals had knowingly turned him loose on a steer all had learned to respect. Thus there is a moral to the story over and above the one cited in stanza 6: when among cowboys don't claim more than you can deliver: you might have to eat crow.

"Windy Bill" has some elements in common with a Mexican *corrido* called "The Black Bull" (*El Toro Moro*),[1] yet not enough to imply direct influences: both end with the bull's victory, but in the Mexican treatment attention focuses upon the indomitable bull rather than upon the boastful cowboy and his relations with the other cow hands.

There are numerous variations, none of which alters substantially the basic idea, or even the form of the song. Authorship has been claimed by George B. German and by Ray Reed of Albuquerque, New Mexico.[2]

The song possesses a subtle humor set forth in typical western "lingo." There are several musical settings available, but the one which seems to match the humor of the text is the Larkin version. It possesses a light jaunty air, with the rhythm and melodic line carrying an undercurrent of good-humored laughter befitting the text. One interesting rhythmic variation is given by Kitty Lee, where it has a $\frac{6}{8}$ rhythm that gives the song another humorous twist,[3] although the standard setting seems to be a $\frac{2}{4}$ rhythm. It is sung by Frank Goodwyn to the well-known tune "Polly Wolly Doodle."

II–A.   THORP (1908) pages 11–12

1.   Windy Bill was a Texas man
         And he could rope you bet,
      Talk of the steer he could'nt tie down
         Had'nt sort'er been born yet;
      The boys they knew of an old black steer
         A sort of an old outlaw,
      Who ran down in the bottom
         Just at the foot of the draw.

2.   This slim black steer had stood his ground
         With punchers from everywhere
      The boys bet Bill two to one
         He couldn't quite get there

---

[1] See Goodwyn. He also gives a text and commentary of this *corrido* in PTFLS, XXVI (1954), pp. 147–50. Recorded in singing of Goodwyn himself, with commentary, FAC I 574.

[2] German (unpaged); FAC I 222.

[3] Lee, *Cowboy*, p. 34.

So Bill brought up his old cow horse
    His weathers and back were sore
Prepared to tackle this old black steer
    Who ran down in the draw.

3.   With his grazin' bits and sand stacked tree,
            His chaps and taps to boot,
        His old maguey tied hard and fast,
            Went out to tackle the brute.
        Bill sorter sauntered around him first;
            The steer began to paw
        Poked up his tail high in the air
            And lit down in the draw.

4.   The old cow horse flew at him like
            He'd been eatin' corn
        And Bill he landed his old maguey
            Around old blackies horns.
        The old time cow horse he stopped dead still,
            The cinches broke like straw
        Both the sand stacked tree and old maguey,
            Went driftin' down the draw.

5.   Bill landed in a big rock pile
            His face and hands were scratched;
        He 'lowed he always could tie a steer
            But guessed he'd found his match.
        Paid up his bet like a little man
            Without a bit of jaw
        And said old blackie was the boss
            Of all down in the draw.

6.   There's a moral to my song, boys,
            Which I hope that you can see
        Whenever you start to tackle a steer
            Never tie hard your maguey.
        Put on your dalebueltas
            'Cordin' to California law
        And you will never see your old rim-fires
            Driftin' down the draw.

II–B.   Larkin, pages 58–59. Reproduced by permission of Margaret Larkin
          and Oak Publications.

Wind - y Bill was a Tex - as boy, Said
he could rope, you bet   Said the steer he
could - n't tie, He hadn't met up with yet.   Us
boys we knew of an old black steer, A
sort of an old out - law, That ran down in the
Mal Pa - is at the bot - tom of the draw.

II–C.   Sung by Frank Goodwyn, Maryland, 1959 (FAC I 235). Published
          with Mr. Goodwyn's permission.

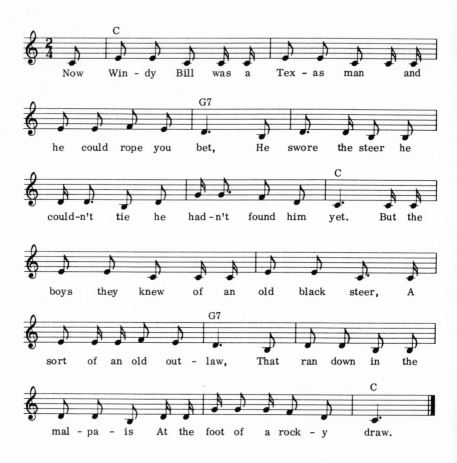

Now Win - dy Bill was a Tex - as man and
he could rope you bet, He swore the steer he
could-n't tie he had - n't found him yet. But the
boys they knew of an old black steer, A
sort of an old out - law, That ran down in the
mal - pa - is At the foot of a rock - y draw.

BIBLIOGRAPHY

Printed texts:

Allen, *Cowboy Lore*, pp. 140–42.
Big Round-Up, pp. 43–44.
Briegel, *All Star*, p. 28; *Souvenir*, p. 28.
Clark, *Cowboy*, pp. 50–51.
Felton, p. 54.
Frey, pp. 74–75.
German (unpaged).
Larkin, pp. 57–60.
Lee, *Cowboy*, pp. 34–35.
Lomax (1916) pp. 381–82; (1936) pp. 382–83; (1938) pp. 113–15.
Patterson and Dexter, pp. 40–41.
Sing 'em Cowboy, pp. 74–75.
Sires, pp. 28–29.
Thorp (1921) pp. 168–70.
Treasure Chest, pp. 46–47.

Commercial recordings:

Bill Bender: Varsity 5133.
Jack Lee: Bluebird 5298.

Manuscripts and field recordings:

Fife. *Maryland:* Frank Goodwyn, 1959 (FAC I 235).
Lomax. *Texas:* d. 5653, obtained at cattlemen's convention, 1910 (JL 175);
    d. 5653, Birdsell Brisco, 1916 (= Lomax [1916] pp. 381–82) (JL 177);
    d. 5653, unidentified (JL 176).
PNFQ 524. Unknown.
Randolph. *Arkansas:* LC 5402–1, B. Campbell, 1942.
Robb. *New Mexico:* No. 768, Ray Reed, 1951 (FAC I 222).

Discussion:

Laws, p. 249.
Thorp and Clark, p. 295.

III

The Tenderfoot

THE SONG IS A REALISTIC first person account of an amateur's first days in the employ of a rawhide-tough ranch foreman who is bent upon making or breaking new members of his outfit in the same way he breaks mustangs. The new man, starting as horse wrangler —the least prestigious job in a cow camp—finds herding the 160-horse "cavvy" beyond his skill. To top it off they give him an innocent-looking stove-up outlaw of a horse that pitches him fifty ways from Sunday. Brown is satisfied—pleased, even—with the new hand's valiant start— and offers him a new horse for the next day, or the choice of walking back to town.

Van Gennep[1] might well have used this song as a classical ex- ample of the rituals of acceptance. The initiate's reaction, witness the last stanza, has been proper. He is "duly impressed," ready for accept- ance by the new group. His stature among his peers will henceforth depend upon demonstrated valor.

This ballad "smells somewhat of the lamp." The rhyme scheme (AAAB/AAAB) is occasionally encountered in folk poetry but is not usual. Despite this, as the notes and discussion testify, the song is widely disseminated in popular literature, both oral and written.

Thorp must have gotten his 1908 text from an oral source: one stanza is displaced and the significant last stanza is lacking. By 1921

---

[1] Arnold van Gennep. *Les Rites de passage* (Paris: Nourry, 1909).

44

he had come into possession of a fuller and better text. We give the 1908 text plus the last double stanza of the 1921 edition. There is a great amount of variation among texts, especially when it comes to certain cowboy terms not universally understood, and to proper names. Examples: In stanza 2, line 2, *Palace* variously appears as *Plaza*, *Platter's*, *MacQueen*, *Inn*, *hotel*, *ranch*, and (most frequently) *saloon*. Stanza 5, line 1, *caballada* (the string of saddle horses used on trail or roundup) as *cavard*, *cavvy yard*, *cavyard*, *cavvy hole*, *Cavvy yard*, *covy yard*, *Coloreus yard*, *calf yard*, and *calfy yard*; in two places the wrangler is in charge of cattle rather than horses, and once *cavyard* is construed to mean a single horse. In stanza 9, line 1 , *hack* (a disreputable horse) appears as *hag*, *rack*, *tack*, *cack*, *true-born black*, and *screw-ball black*. In stanza 9, line 2, *three set-fasts* (saddle sores) appear as either *one*, *two*, or *a bunch*, *big set-parts*, and *two big sores*. Typically stanza 11, line 2, has the boss rolling the injured puncher down with a *stake-pin* (picket used to stake out a horse on a stake rope), *picket pin*, *pickin'-pin*, *iron stake-pin*, *tent pin*, or *rolling pin*. Thorp has a distinctive new line: "He bathed my head and commenced to grin." Stanza 14, line 3, has variously *Barlow knife*, *carving knife*, *butcher knife*, *old dull knife*, *dull jack knife*, and *bowie knife*.

"The Tenderfoot" is known under several titles: "The Tenderfoot Cowboy," "A Tenderfoot's Experience," "The City Cowboy," "The Greenhorn," "The Greenhorn Cowboy," "The Greenhorn's Experience," and "The Horse Wrangler," or "The D–2 Horse Wrangler."

Authorship and date of origin are under dispute. It was submitted to John A. Lomax by A. S. Jackson of Dickens, Texas, sometime after 1907, with this significant statement: "I am sending you a cowboy song which was composed by myself and another puncher during the summer of '79 while on a trip from Texas to Colorado."[2] Thorp gave nothing about provenance in 1908, but in the 1921 edition he says: "By Yank Hitson, Denver, Colorado, 1889. I got the song from old Battle Axe, whom lots of old punchers remember, at Phoenix, Arizona, 1899."[3]

D. J. O'Malley, who published the song in the *Stock Growers' Journal*, Miles City, Montana, February 4, 1894, is more precise and

---

[2] Lomax d. 5652 (JL 135, 168).
[3] P. 146.

emphatic about his claim in a letter dated April 4, 1932: ". . . The Tenderfoot's another (slightly changed) I called it the D2 Horse Wrangler. And this man R. D. Mack says he wrote it when the truth is I wrote it in 1893 probably before Mack was born and to prove it (as with my others) I have copies of the verse. . . ."[4]

Elsewhere O'Malley explains that it was published under the name of a friend, R. J. Stovall, as a surprise to Stovall's wife, and that his pay was a five-dollar hat—the only remuneration he ever received for any of his songs.[5] The tune, according to O'Malley was from "The Day I Played Baseball."[6]

J. Frank Dobie, after contesting some of O'Malley's other claims, says of "The Tenderfoot": "I don't know a thing about 'Horse Wrangler' except that it is old—certainly older than 1894."[7]

Following Thorp's 1908 text, we present three others which offer significant differences. "An Irish Trainman's Chant,"[8] an unmistakable though not servile railroaders' parody, is not given here.

However painful the occasion may be, one can at times laugh at one's self, although the laughter may come easier in retrospect. Such an occasion is here portrayed in song to a lilting $\frac{6}{8}$ rhythm, the standard version being most accurately and skillfully set down by Sandburg. Seven versions were found in print that correspond to this musical setting in nearly every way.

Jules Verne Allen gives a version of the song which, although similar in rhythm, is so different melodically that it bears printing here. Also of great interest is the singing of Kathy Dagel, to whom this work is dedicated. Although melodically her work is much like the Sandburg version, she sings it in a $\frac{2}{4}$ rhythm. Her style of singing is almost half spoken and half sung in a good-natured bantering way. The natural inflections of the words seem to dictate the rhythmic accents of certain notes. Unlike many western folk singers, her tone is not throaty or nasal but quite relaxed, although she does, in typical western style, place strong emphasis on some consonants rather than on the vowels.

---

[4] To John A. Lomax, d. 5567 (JL 6).

[5] O'Malley, p. 7 (FAC III 137, p. 4).

[6] *Ibid.*, p. 11 (FAC III 137, p. 9).

[7] Letter to John White, Westfield, N.J., February 26, 1934 (FAC II 126). See also Lomax (1938) p. 119, and Pollan, pp. 30–31 (FAC II 634).

[8] From R. S. Hasbrook, Michigan (LC files: FAC II 618).

III–A.   Thorp (1908) pages 13–14

1.   I thought one spring just for fun
        I'd see how cow-punching was done
        So before the roundup was begun
            I tackled a cattle king.

2.   Said he "my boss is down in town
        He's at the Palace, his name is Brown;
        I think to the ranch he'll take you down."
            "That's what I want," says I.

3.   We started to the ranch next day
        Brown augered me most all the way
        Told me cow-punching was just child's play
            It was no work at all.

4.   For all you have to do is ride
        Its only drifting with the tide
        Oh how that old cow puncher lied
            He surely had his gall.

9.   He saddled me up an old gray hack
        With three set-fasts upon his back
        Then padded him up with gunny sacks
            And used my bedding all.

5.   Put me in charge of the Caballada
        And told me not to work too hard
        For all I had to do was ride
            And keep the horses near.

6.   I had one hundred and sixty head
        Sometimes I wished that I were dead
        Brown's head would often get bright red
            If any got away.

7.   Straight to the bushes they would take
        As if they were running for a stake
        I've often wished their necks they'd break
            But they would never fall.

8.   Sometimes I couldn't head them all
        At other times my horse would fall
        And I'd roll on like a cannon ball
            Till earth got in my way.

10.   When I got on he gave a bound
        Sprung in the air and turned around
        Just then my head hit on the ground
            It was an awful fall.

11.2   He picked me up and carried me in
        He bathed my head and commenced to grin
        Says that's the way they all begin
            You're doing very well.

12.   To-morrow morning if you don't croak
        I'll give you another horse that's broke
        You'll not need a saddle or even a rope
            "No, I'll quit right here," says I.

From Thorp (1921) p. 148:

13.   I've traveled up and I've traveled down,
        I've traveled this country round and round,
        I've lived in city and I've lived in town,
            But I've got this much to say:

14.   Before you try cow-punching, kiss your wife,
        Take a heavy insurance on your life,
        Then cut your throat with a barlow knife,—
            For it's easier done that way.

III–B.   "THE TENDERFOOT"
         Lomax d. 5653, from Joe Harris, Westwater, Utah (JL 40).

1.1   I started out one summer for fun
        I bought a saddle and stole a gun
        And when the round-up it begun
            I tackled a cattle king.

2.   Says he, "My foreman is down town
      When he's out on the ranch his name is Brown
      If you'll go see him, he'll take you down."
          "Oh, it's just the thing," says I.

3.1   So to the ranch we started next day
      Old Brown, he argued me all the way
      About how long he thought I'd stay
          Until I fairly bawled.

4.   Says he, "Young man, there's nothing to do but ride
      And drift the cattle along with the tide."
      The son-of-a-bitch, oh how he lied!
          Oh, didn't he have his gall?

5.   He put me in charge of the covy-yard
      Says he, "Young man there's nothing to do
      But these horses to guard
          And keep them from getting away."

7.1   But now and then an old horse he'd break
      And out across the country he'd take
      He'd run just like he was running for a stake
          And head him I couldn't at all.

8.   And now and then my old horse he'd fall
      And I'd shoot on like a cannon ball
      I'd see the stars and the comets fall
          When the earth came in my way.

9.   They saddled up an old gray hack
      With two big set-fasts on his back
      They rubbed him down with a gunny-sack
          And used my bedding all.

10.   When I crawled on, I went up in the air
      And he whirled around
      And when I come to I found
          I'd had one hell of a fall.

11.1 They carried me in, rubbed liniment on
      Poured whiskey in

"You're doing quite well," says Brown,
"That's the way we all begin.

12.1   "And if you don't die we'll give you
            Another good horse to try."
            "Oh, it's may I walk?" says I.
            "Oh yes," says Brown, "it's back to town."

13 and 14. I've traveled up and I've traveled down
(fused)   I've traveled this wide world round and round
            If ever you try a cowboy life
            Get a heavy insurance on your life
            Go cut your throat with a dull jack knife
            You'll find it's the easiest way.

III–C.   "THE CITY COWBOY"
          From C. T. Dakin (Gordon 982).
          Reproduced by permission of Roberta Paul Gordon Nye.

1.   I thought last spring, just for fun,
            I'd go out and see how cow-punching was done;
            So I struck a cattle king.
2.   Said he, "my boy, 'tis a life of joy;
            It is the very thing.
4.   All you have to do is to ride
            An' that's like driftin' with the tide."
            The son-of-a-gun—how he lied!
            'Twas no such a thing.

9.   They roped me out an old gray "cack"
            Who had two setfasts on his back
            They padded him up with gunny sacks,
            It took my bedding and all.
10.   When I got on he left the ground,
            He went in the air and he turned around
            And when I came down I busted the ground
            It was one h—— of a fall.

11.   They picked me up. They carried me in.
            They rubbed me down with an old stake pin.
            Said the boss, "That's the way they all begin.

12.   An' in the mornin', if you do not die,
We'll give you another hoss to try."
Said I, "My friend, I've this to say,
I quit right here and I ask no pay.

13.   Next time I tire of city life,
I'll cut my throat with an old dull knife,
For I think it the easier way."

14.   Now my city friend with vision wild,
Just take this tip from one wise child,
Who's learned a thing or two.

15.   When you feel the call to ride,
Don't drift west with the drifting tide.
But stay at home in your own home town.
And ride a horse on the merry-go-round,
And save a fall of pride.

III–D.   Intruding in a text of "The Trail to Mexico" (PNFQ 478) we find
a variant of stanza 9 plus the following stanza, which should belong to "The Tenderfoot":

9.1   The next day they gave me an old gray
I'll remember him to my dying day
And if I had to swear to the fact
I believe he was worse off than the black.

III–E.   "The Tenderfoot"
Sandburg, pages 274–75.
Reprinted by permission of Harcourt, Brace & World, Inc.

III–F. "THE HORSE WRANGLER" or "THE TENDERFOOT"
Allen, *Cowboy Lore,* page 89.
Reprinted by permission of The Naylor Company.

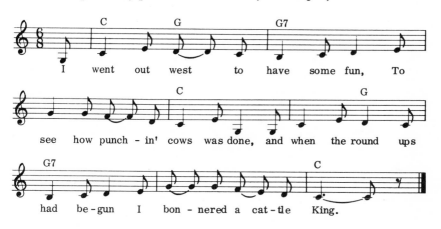

I went out west to have some fun, To see how punch - in' cows was done, and when the round ups had be - gun I bon - nered a cat - tle King.

III–G. "BRONCO BUSTER"
Sung by Kathy Dagel, Kansas, 1959 (FAC I 507).

One day I thought I'd have some fun and see how punch - ing cows was done so when the round - up

had be - gun I tack-led the cat - tle king. Says

he, "My fore-man's gone to town, he's in a sa - loon and his

name is Brown. If you see him he'll take you down. Says

1, 2.

(3) 3rd verse ending

I, "That's just the thing. (Stanza 4) They

picked me up and car - ried me in and they

rubbed me down with an old stake pin, That's the way they

all be - gin. "You're do - in' well," says Brown, "And

in the morn-ing if you don't die We'll give you an-oth - er

horse to try." "Oh say can't I walk?" says I. Says

he "Yes, back to town." I've tra-vel ed up, I've
tra-vel ed down, And I've tra-vel ed this coun-try round and round.
Lived in a ci - ty, I've lived in town but I've
got this much to say: Be-fore you try cow punch-ing,
Kiss your wife_____ Take a hea - vy in - sur-ance
on your life_____ Then cut your throat with a
Bar - low knife, It's eas - ier done that way.

BIBLIOGRAPHY

Significant texts:

1879? Lomax d. 5652, A. S. Jackson, Texas (JL 135). See authorship,
       supra p. 45.
1889   Thorp (1921) pp. 146–48.

1894   *Stock Growers Journal,* February 3, 1894 (from O'Malley, pp. 11–
        12) (FAC III 137, pp. 9–10). Lomax (1938) pp. 119–21.
1901   Gordon 1137, B. C. Kenyon, Texas.
1907   Lomax d. 5652, J. J. Green (JL 135), and A. S. Jackson (JL 168).
1910   Lomax (1910) pp. 136–38.
1913   *Farm and Ranch,* XXXII (April 12, 1913), p. 32. JAFL, XXVI
        (1913), p. 185, North Dakota (FAC III 164).
1916   Pollan, pp. 30–31, Clinton Gentry of Oklahoma, who learned it in
        Kansas (FAC II 634).
1930   Sutley, pp. 79–81 (FAC III 745). This is the best text yet made of
        this song: rhyme and meter are superior, yet none of its basic content
        has been altered.
 ?   Gordon 982, C. T. Dakin.
 ?   Lomax d. 5652, Harry Stephens (JL 135) (significant because of
        Stephens' importance in regard to other cowboy songs).
 ?   Lomax d. 5653, Joe Harris, Utah (JL 40).

Other printed texts:

Allen, *Cowboy Lore,* pp. 89–90.
Arkansas, pp. 54–55.
Big Round-Up, pp. 14–15.
Botkin, *Sampler,* pp. 548–49.
Browne, newspaper clipping (FAC III 799).
Carlson, p. 62.
Clark, *Cowboy,* p. 58.
Coolidge, *Texas,* pp. 126–27.
Davis, *Tip-Top,* p. 52.
Fowke and Johnston, pp. 96–97.
Frey, pp. 60–61.
German (unpaged).
Klickman and Sherwin, pp. 38–39.
Leakey, pp. 161–63.
Lindroth, p. 9.
Lomax (Lilly), pp. 24–29 (FAC III 742).
Lone Ranger, pp. 14–15.
Nebraska No. 1, pp. 1–3.
Pound, *American,* pp. 176–78 (FAC III 779); *Syllabus,* pp. 29–30; *Western,*
        pp. 28–29.
Sandburg, pp. 274–75.

Sing 'em Cowboy, pp. 13–15.
Sires, pp. 2–3.
SFQ III (1939) pp. 28–29.
Treasure Chest, pp. 28–29.
White, *Lonesome* (unpaged).
White and Shakley, pp. 46–48.

Commercial recordings:

Bill Bender: Varsity 5148/US 76 (FAC III 959).
Tony Kraber: Keynote 104, Keystone 506–B.

Manuscripts and field recordings:

Fife. *Kansas:* Kathy Dagel, 1959 (FAC I 507).
Gordon. No. 884, Henry S. Baker; No. 1036, E. T. Yardley, "sung by . . . a sailor and cowboy along the Pacific Coast who was also a sailor in England."
Hoffman. *Pennsylvania:* Hyrum M. Cranmer, 1958 (FAC I 555).
Lomax. *Idaho:* d. 5656, 1922 (JL 338). *New Mexico:* d. 5653, two texts, c. 1915. *Oklahoma:* d. 5653, S. Roy Hadsell. *Texas:* d. 5654, T. O. Midkeff, 1909; LC, F. Hight, 1942; LC, T. C. Richardson (FAC II 594); d. 5652, C. W. Heanenn, and T. O. Midkeff (JL 135); d. 5652, 5656, King Sloan (JL 341). *Unknown:* d. 5634, 5652, Lowell German (JL 135); d. 5652, three unidentified texts (JL 135); d. 5638, 5653, 5634, 5656, four texts.
PNFQ. Nos. 448, 449, 450, three texts; No. 478 ("Trail to Mexico" with one stanza of "Tenderfoot").
UAFA. *Arizona:* Ellen S. Murphy, 1959 (FAC II 424).

Discussion:

Barrett, Chapter 7.
Dobie, J. Frank: letter to John White, Westfield, N.J., February 26, 1934 (FAC II 126).
Lomax, d. 5567 (JL 6): from D. J. O'Malley, April 4, 1932; d. 5652 (JL 135), from D. S. Jackson, Texas.
Lomax (1938), p. 119.
O'Malley, pp. 7, 11 (FAC III 137, pp. 4, 9).
Pollan, pp. 30–31 (FAC II 634).
Stock Growers Journal, February 3, 1894 (from O'Malley, p. 11). We have been unable to verify this particular reference. This issue is not in the files of the Montana Historical Society.

IV

California Trail

*M*IGRATION INTO CALIFORNIA from the time gold
was discovered in 1847 to the completion of the transcontinental railroad
in 1869 is one of the great episodes in the story of the West. Indians,
space, isolation, hunger, breakdown, buffalo herds, coyotes, grizzly bears,
and other exotic fauna and flora; mirages, thirst, *mexicanos*, gold, buffalo
chips, jerked beef, rawhide, high adventure, rugged individualism,
treachery, religious zeal and its opposites—all these and a great deal more
—conspired to shake the imaginations of men to the very core. Occasionally their reaction was simply to give up and go home. More often
they took it in stride, or laughed and sang it all off in story or crisply
satirical songs like "California Trail." More popular but no less authentic
among these scores of overlander ballads are "Sweet Betsy from Pike,"
"Joe Bowers," "The California Stage," "Oh! California!" (from Foster's
"Oh Susannah"), "The Lonesome Roving Wolves," and many others.

Thorp is very specific about "California Trail." It was written by
Kate Childs, otherwise known as Montana Kate, in about 1869.[1] He
first heard it sung by Sam Murphy at Horse Head Crossing on the Peace
(or Pease?) River in 1900.[2] To this date we have found, other than in

---

[1] A letter from the Montana Historical Society dated January 30, 1964, states
that they know nothing about such a person (FAC II 640).

[2] (1921) p. 18.

58

Thorp, only three texts: Lomax, *Cowboy Songs*,[3] which is exactly like Thorp; dossier 5653 of the Lomax papers contains an undated student theme written by Madge Bayles, who learned part of the song "during Christmas vacation . . . from cowboys on my uncle's ranch in Western Colorado . . . the rest from my father's friend who had a large cattle ranch in the San Juan Country."[4] Her text is exactly like Thorp. Also, there is a complete text in the folk song files of the Pacific Northwest Farm Quad.[5] No melody has been encountered.

IV–A.   THORP (1908) pages 15–16

1.   List all you Californ'y boys
            And open wide your ears
        For now we start across the plains
            With a herd of mules and steers.
        Now bear it in mind before you start
            That you'll eat jerked beef not ham
        And antelope steak oh cuss the stuff
            It often proves a sham.

2.   You cannot find a stick of wood
            On all this prairie wide
        Whene'er you eat you've got to stand
            Or sit on some old bull hide.
        It's fun to cook with Buffalo Chips
            Or Mesquite green as corn
        If I'd once known what I know now
            I'd have gone around Cape Horn.

3.   The women have the hardest time
            Who emigrate by land
        For when they cook out in the wind
            They're sure to burn their hands.
        Then they scold their husbands 'round
            Get mad and spill the tea
        I'd have thanked my stars if they'd not come out
            Upon this bleak prairie.

---

[3] 1916 to 1935 editions, pp. 375–76.
[4] JL 228.
[5] PNFQ 54.

4.   Most every night we put out guards
          To keep the Indians off
       When night comes round some heads will ache
          And some begin to cough.
       To be deprived of help at night
          You know it's mighty hard
       But every night there's someone sick
          To get rid of standing guard.

5.   Then they're always talking of what they've got
          And what they're going to do
       Some will say they are content
          For I've got as much as you.
       Others will say I'll buy or sell
          And damned if I care which
       Others will say boy's buy him out
          For he doesn't own a stitch.

6.   Old rawhide shoes are Hell on corns
          While tramping through the sands
       And driving a Jackass by the tail
          Damn the overland.
       I would as lief be on a raft at sea
          And there at once be lost
       John let's leave this poor old mule
          We'll never get him across.

V

Top Hand

*T*HE COWBOYS COULD TOLERATE, even come to admire, a greenhorn, provided he showed the proper respect for the genuine article and provided he gave promise of redemption. But to the pure unadulterated phony—variously identified as a mail-order, Monkey-Ward, or skim-milk cowboy, a punk, savage, or shorthorn—they gave no quarter whatsoever. The "Top Hand'" was one of these.

Thorp got the song from Jim Brownfield at Crow Flat, New Mexico, in 1899, and says it has been attributed to Frank Rooney, about 1877.[1] The fact that we find it printed in Thorp's expurgated text, in the Lomax works, and in Dane Coolidge's *Texas Cowboys,* but not elsewhere, makes us feel that it has not had extremely wide circulation—in printable variants, that is. Moreover, a husband-wife collecting team is not apt to provoke a singer to give out with a text such "as would have burned up the paper on which it was written," to quote Thorp. He even felt obliged to change the title "because the old name . . . did not sound good in print." "Waddie Cow boy," appearing as a signature, leaves us intrigued and perplexed.

Although unmistakably the same song, "The Top Screw," as given by Coolidge, has such distinctive poetic structure and even basic content as to deserve presentation in full. These facts indicate what seems to be

---

[1] Thorp (1921) p. 156.

a typical device in the creation of folk poetry—the free use of poetic couplets where the sequence of their presentation is unimportant. We have not encountered field recordings, commercial recordings, or melody.

V–A.   THORP (1908) pages 17–18

1.   While you're all so frisky I'll sing a little song
        Think a horn of whiskey will help the thing along
        It's all about the Top Hand when he's busted flat
        Bumming round town, in his Mexican hat
        He'd laid up all winter and his pocket book is flat
        His clothes are all tatters but he don't mind that.

2.   See him in town with a crowd that he knows
        Rolling cigarettes an' a smoking through his nose.
        First thing he tells you, he owns a certain brand
        Leads you to think he is a daisy hand
        Next thing he tells you 'bout his trip up the trail
        All the way to Kansas to finish out his tale.

3.   Put him on a horse, he's a handy hand to work
        Put him on the branding pen he's dead sure to shirk.
        With his natural leaf tobacco in the pockets of his vest
        He'll tell you his Californy pants are the best.
        He's handled lots of cattle, has'nt any fears
        Can draw his sixty dollars, for the balance of his years.

4.   Put him on herd, he's a cussin all day
        Anything tries, its sure to get away.
        When you have a round up he tells it all about
        He's going to do the cuttin' and you can't keep him out.
        If anything goes wrong he lays it on the screws
        Say's the lazy devils were trying to take a snooze.

5.   When he meets a greener he aint afraid to rig
        Stands him on a chuck box and makes him dance a jig.
        Waives a loaded cutter, makes him sing and shout,
        He's a regular Ben Thompson, when the boss aint about.
        When the boss aint about he leaves his leggins in camp.
        He swears a man who wears them is worse than a tramp.

6. Say's he's not caring for the wages that he earns
    For Dad's rich in Texas 'n got wagon loads to burn
    But when he goes to town he's sure to take it in
    He's always been dreaded, wherever he has been.
    He rides a fancy horse, he is a favorite man
    Can get more credit than a common waddie can.

7. When you ship the cattle he's bound to go along
    To keep the boss from drinking and to see that nothing's
        wrong
    Wherever he goes, catch on to his game
    He likes to be called with a handle to his name.
    He's always primping with a pocket looking glass
    From the top to the bottom he's a bold Jackass.

                                        Waddie Cow boy.

V–B.   "The Top Screw"
        Coolidge, *Texas Cowboys*, pp. 128–30.
        Printed with permission of E. P. Dutton and Co., Inc. Copyright
        by them 1937, renewal © 1965 by Coit Coolidge and Mrs. Calvin
        Gaines Collins.

1.1   While you are all so frisky
        I will sing you a song.
        I will take a horn of whiskey
        To help the sing along.
        It is all about a top screw
        When he is busted flat
        Setting around town
        With his Mexican hat.

2.1   See him setting around
        With a crowd he thinks he knows
        He is smoking cigarettes
        And smoking through his nose.
        He will tell you in a moment
        That he owns a certain brand
        And he will lead you to believe
        That he is a daisy hand.

3.1   Put him on a pony
        He will do good work
        But down in the branding pen
        He is dam sure to shirk.
        With a natural-leaf tobacco
        In the pocket of his vest
        He will tell you that his eight
        Dollar pants is the best.

4.1   Put him on herd
        He will ring all day;
        If anything gets out
        It is sure to get away;
        If anything is missing
        He will lay it to the screws
        And he will swear the lazy devils
        Was trying to take a snooze.

5.1   When he strikes a greener
        He is dam sure to start a rig
        He will put him on the chuck-box
        And make him dance a jig.
        He will wave a loaded six-shooter
        And he will make him step about.
        He is a regular Ben Thompson
        When the boss is not about.

2.2/8. This is all about
        A trip up the trail
        I will lead you clean to Kansas
        To finish up my tale.
        He wants to be a top man
        With nothing much to do
        And he will tell you about him
        Chasing off the wild Sioux.

9./4.1   He is going to Montana,
            He is going to make a raise,
            He is good for a hundred dollars a month
            The balance of his days;
            Just to show you
            That he don't care for expense
            He tears down the bushes
            With his eight dollar pants.

BIBLIOGRAPHY

Printed texts:

Coolidge, *Texas,* pp. 128–30.
Lomax (1916) pp. 373–74.
Lomax (1938) pp. 72–73.
Thorp (1921) pp. 156–58.
Thorp, *Banjo,* p. 202 (*supra,* 24).

Discussion:

J. Frank Dobie's note in personal copy of Lomax, *Cowboy* (FAC II 748).
Thorp, *Banjo,* p. 202; *supra,* 24.
Thorp and Clark, pp. 41–42, 203.

VI

Grand Round-up

"IN THE SWEET BY AND BY" is a gospel hymn that was a part of the spiritual baggage brought west by many a pioneer. Its simple, transcendental mood was especially comforting during a two- to four-hour stint of night herding when a puncher could feel very small and more than a mite lonely. We're not sure the steers were edified, but the punchers were, and it just came natural to the poetic and literate among them, and especially to fundamentalist frontier preachers or their likes, to shape the old Christian ideas, as intoned in the hymns, to the new environment. Trail driving, cutting, branding, roping, tying, rounding-up, and such, became metaphors of the delicate condition of our own species once an obvious analogy had been made: man is to God and the eternal scheme of things as the dogies are to man and his society. This simple formula led to the production of many cowboy songs, the most popular of which is variously known as "The Grand (Great, Last) Roundup," "The Dim Narrow Trail"; "The Cowboy's (Cowgirl's) Sweet By and By" (Thoughts, Vision, Dream, Hymn).

Actually we may be dealing here with two songs, although their mood, melody, and content are intertwined. The one which typically begins "Last night as I lay on the prairie"[1] has endured in a very fluid

---

[1] Composite text, stanza 1, and texts A and C.

66

form, being sung variously with from four to a dozen stanzas, with or
without one or more of the three refrains given. The order of stanzas is
instable and, dependent upon their selection and order, the mood can
vary from a bittersweet but vapid deism to rigorous fundamentalism. The
second form of the song, "When I think of the Last Great Roundup,"[2]
is more stabilized, possibly through transmission in books of folk songs
and fundamentalist hymnals.

Origin, authorship, and dissemination of "The Grand Round-Up"
are an intricate web of claim and counterclaim, and to the extent that we
can unravel it we may be able to throw light upon some of the processes
of folk creativity. Nowhere does Thorp tell where he got the five stanzas
of his 1908 edition. In 1921 he had a new and expanded text (11
stanzas) under the title "The Cowboy's Dream," which he ascribes to
the "father of Captain Dan W. Roberts, of the Texas Rangers."[3] Meanwhile he adds a song, "The Great Round-Up," consisting of six double
stanzas of our Text B, which he got from Mr. "Sally" White at Toyah,
Texas, in 1909.[4] Sullivan also ascribes the song to White, though Captain Roberts, interviewed by J. Frank Dobie in 1926, had no knowledge
concerning his father's role in the composition of the song.[5] E. D. Smith
says that some have ascribed it to J. H. Nation, a cattleman living in El
Paso at the turn of the century.[6]

One account has it that J. W. Benham and another cowboy were
guarding a herd during a wild night of wind, rain, thunder, and lightning. Benham, restless and depressed, listened to the strong defiant voice
of his comrade swept by the wind across the herd as he composed and
sang, correcting and repeating as he vocalized, until at last he had
worked out one good stanza:

> Last night as I lay on the prairie
>   And gazed at the stars and the sky
> I wondered if ever a cowboy
>   Would drift to that sweet by and by.[7]

---

[2] Text B.
[3] Thorp (1921) pp. 40–41.
[4] *Ibid.*, pp. 75–77; Thorp and Clark, pp. 40–41.
[5] Sullivan, pp. 258–59 (FAC III 827); Dobie, *Ballads*, p. 46.
[6] Smith, pp. 582–84.
[7] *Arizona Graphic*, I, 8 (November 4, 1889), p. 8 (FAC III 627).

Benham went into business with Will C. Barnes, the writer, and later became an officer of the U.S. Forestry Service. Now Barnes had written the story of a cowboy who got religion, joined the Salvation Army, and wrote a hymn. Not being a poet, however, he got hung up on the hymn and appealed to his partner, Benham. Haunted all these years by the stanza he had heard composed on the wild night previously described, Benham added six more stanzas, which are very much like 3, 2, 4, 5.1, 9, and 8 of the Composite Text.[8] Barnes accepted Benham's song and published it in an eastern magazine.[9] Some months after its publication, Barnes, strolling up Washington Street in Phoenix, encountered a Salvation Army group singing "The Cowboy's Sweet By and By." Sharlot M. Hall says it was written by Barnes in 1893, that to Barnes's stanzas "every night-herding puncher from the Sonora line to the San Francisco mountains[10] has added a verse to suit himself."[11]

Barnes's story, as quoted by O'Malley, is quite different. He, O'Malley, had written in the mid-1880's a rough five-stanza poem sung variously to "Red River Valley" and "My Bonnie," which "furnished the idea for the more polished ballad generally known as 'The Cowboy's Dream' written by Mr. Will C. Barnes." Then he quotes the following as having been published by Barnes "In the *Saturday Evening Post* a few years ago" concerning the origin of *his* song:

> I first heard this song in 1886 or '87 on the Hash Knife range in northern Arizona. A half-breed Indian boy from southern Utah sang about four verses which he had picked up from some other singers. He knew nothing of their authorship. I wrote these four out in my calf-branding book one evening. Later on a boy from down the Pecos way drifted into our camp and sang the four with slight variations, adding two new stanzas, one of which he claimed as his own work. I wrote another and eventually picked

---

[8] *Infra.*

[9] Barnes, pp. 60–61 (FAC III 291).

[10] In Arizona.

[11] Hall, pp. 217–18 (FAC III 96). There are also two texts of this song in Sharlot Hall's personal papers at the museum that bears her name in Prescott, Arizona. Annotated in her own hand, "Will C. Barnes, Holbrook, Arizona, 1893." (FAC II 438).

up three more, until I finally had ten verses in all. With
the idea of using it as the motif for a cowboy story, I re-
wrote two or three verses, changed the words of several,
added the chorus, and cut the ten down to six verses.
These were published with one of my earliest Western
stories—Stampede on the Turkey Track Range.[12]

Nothing here of Benham or Captain Roberts' father, or others yet to be
mentioned!

But, getting back to O'Malley, let us note that he credits a fellow
puncher, Tom Phelps, who was always singing hymns, especially "The
Sweet By and By," with the idea for the original four stanzas![13] The
notable J. Frank Dobie questioned O'Malley's claims in a letter of February 26, 1934: Dobie's father, who quit trail driving, where he learned
his songs, in the 1880's, often sang "Cowboy's Sweet By and By." It was
already well known when Barnes heard it in '86 or '87.[14] Moreover, in
1930, a Mrs. M. N. Perkins sent Dobie a significant and distinctive text[15]
written by the Reverend C. A. Clark, pastor of a church south of Prescott, "written under the chuck wagon of the OX outfit on September 2,
1899," said that it was sung that night by him and a cowboy by the
name of Charlie Pyskin before seventy cowboys, and finally that it was
published by a Texas revivalist preacher known as " 'the clown cowboy,'
whose name . . . very Irish . . . I fail to remember."[16]

Finally, we add the name of Charlie Hart, formerly of Carrollton,
Mississippi, "a most cultured gentleman," who was "under necessity of
living far away from resuts [sic] and found surcease of sorrow on a ranch
in Clay County, Texas in 1868. . . . It was from '72 to '85 a very popular ballad, and the phraseology is purely cowboy originality. . . ."[17]

So what are the facts? Only these:

(a) More than one cowboy poet has had a hand in the creation of
this classic among night-herding songs, and

---

[12] O'Malley, pp. 6, 10 (FAC III 137, pp. 3, 8). See Barnes, *Cowboy*, p. 122.
Printed by permission of John I. White.

[13] *Ibid.*

[14] FAC II 126.

[15] Text C.

[16] FAC II 125.

[17] Lomax d. 5654 (JL 270): letter from I. P. Skinner.

(b) Several more have tried to crown themselves with the glory of its creation. *Quien sabe?*

The basic themes of "The Great Round-Up" have appeared frequently both in the cowboy era and later. The following prayer, composed by "Uncle Kin" Elkins in 1898, is said to have inspired "The Last Great Round-Up," written by C. W. Byron, W. L. Harris, and W. H. Harris.[18]

> Oh Lord, round us up in one great round up
> And rope us with the cords of love—
> Brand us with the iron of truth and mark us with the
> cross of Calvary—
> So when we start on the last great drive, Grant that there
> shall not be any cut-backs, as we appear before the Head
> Boss in the green Pastures of Eternal Reward.
>
> > Amen.

The prayer is followed by four stanzas of the well-known revival hymn "Rounded Up in Glory," copyrighted and popularized in the 1920's by Oscar J. Fox and John A. Lomax.

A song ascribed to Pat Hurley, politician and one-time Secretary of War, is also related to "The Grand Round-Up:"

> When my earthly trail is ended
> And my final bacon's curled
> And the last great round-up's finished
> At the home ranch of the world . . .[19]

"The Cowboy's Mother"[20] is a sentimental parody written by Tex Fletcher in the 1920's. It deserves a place here only to illustrate the influence of the marketplace on the evolution of popular songs. A better item from the same period comes to us from Idaho: "Home Corral."[21] We have no information on the source from which Mrs. Hendren got it. Several songs, of more recent vintage, extract other transcendental

---

[18] Letter from Mrs. L. B. Peckenpaugh, Corpus Christi, Texas, to J. Frank Dobie, July 4, 1937 (FAC II 124).

[19] *Kansas City Star*, January 25, 1934 (FAC III 104). This is actually one stanza of a poem by Badger Clark entitled "Ridin'."

[20] Text D.

[21] Text E.

images by conscious imitation of the "Grand Round-Up."[22] An example
follows as Text F.

Melodies are as varied as the texts, although, excepting for a few
cases, they seem to fall into one of two common patterns. The song is
commonly sung to "My Bonnie," which we give here in the singing of
Robert E. Voris, a former Congregational pastor reared and still living at
Globe, Arizona. Our second setting is transcribed from the singing of the
San Angelo Cowboy Quartet as recorded by John A. Lomax in 1934.
Finally, we offer a unique melodic treatment of the song by D. Price of
Taos, New Mexico, in 1953.

VI–A.   THORP (1908) page 19

          (Repeat last two lines of each stanza.)
          Air Bonnie Lies Over the Ocean.

    2.1   I hear there's to be a grand round up
                  Where cow-boys with others must stand
              To be cut out by the riders of judgment
                  Who are posted and know all the brands.

    3.   The trail to that great mystic region
                  Is narrow and dim so they say
              While the one that leads down to perdition
                  Is posted and blazed all the way.

    6.1   Whose fault is it then that so many
                  Go astray on this wild range and fail
              Who might have been rich and had plenty
                  Had they known of the dim narrow trail.

    4.2   I wonder if at the last day some cow-boy
                  Un-branded and un-claimed should stand
              Would he be mavericked by those riders of judgment
                  Who are posted and know all the brands?

---

[22] "The Four Sixes," Hendren 300; "Would He Ride on a Roundup in
Heaven?" Hendren 104; "A Cowboy's Best Friend is His Horse," Hendren 173;
"The Range is Heaven to Me," Hendren 454; and "What's It Like in the Prom-
ised Land?" Hendren 535.

6.   My wish for all cow-boys is this
        That we may meet at that grand final sale
    Be cut out by the riders of judgment
        And shoved up the dim narrow trail.

VI–Composite Text

1.   Last night as I lay on the prairie
        And looked at the stars in the sky
    I wondered if ever a cowboy
        Would drift to that sweet by and by.

1.1   Text F.

2.   They say there will be a great round-up
        And cowboys, like dogies, will stand
    To be mavericked by the Riders of Judgment
        Who are posted and know every brand.

2.1   Text A.

2.2   Text B.

3.   Text A.

3.1   The canyons and gorges are many
        And "dogies" go often astray
    But the pale-horse rider will gather
        Everyone to that great judgment day.

3.2   Text B.

3.3   Text B.

4.   I wonder if ever a cowboy
        Stood ready for that Judgment Day
    And could say to the Boss of the Riders,
        "I'm ready, come drive me away."

4.1   In the day of the great final judgment
        When we all come around the white throne

How happy will be every cowboy
To whom the Lord sayeth, "Well done."

4.11   Text F.

4.2   Text A.

4.3   Text B.

4.4   Text B.

5.   For they, like the cows that are locoed,
            Stampede at the sight of a hand
        Are dragged with a rope to the round-up
            Or get marked with some crooked man's brand.

5.1   For they're all like the cows from the "Jimpsons"
            That get scart at the sight of a hand
        And have to be dragged to the round-up
            Or get put in some crooked man's brand.

6.   I know there's many a stray cowboy
            Who'll be lost at the great final sale
        When he might have gone in green pastures
            Had he known of the dim narrow trail.

6.1   Text A.

7.   And I'm scared that I'll be a stray yearling—
            A maverick, unbranded on high—
        And get cut in the bunch with the "rusties"
            When the Boss of the Riders goes by.

7.1   Perhaps there will be a stray cowboy
            Unbranded by anyone nigh,
        Who'll be cut by the riders of judgment
            And shipped to the sweet by and by.

8.   They tell of another big owner
            Who's ne'er overstocked, so they say
        But who always makes room for the sinner
            Who drifts from the straight narrow way.

9.   They say he will never forget you
            That he knows every action and look
        So for safety you'd better get branded
            Have your name in his big Tally Book.

9.1   Oh, they say that the boss is a-coming
            To rope and to brand and earmark
        And will take all the cuts back to Judgment
            To be registered in his great Tally Book.

9.2   Text B.

9.3   Text B.

9.4   Text B.

10.   So 'haps there will be one stray cowboy
            Unspotted, unseen by an eye
        That'll be roped by the riders of justice
            And shipped to the sweet by and by.

11.   I watched and I waited for Jesus
            But then for the light could I see
        I wondered if Jesus, my redeemer
            Could save a poor sinner like me.

12.   Then my brother, let's come to the branding
            Our owner is calling today
        If he touches and blesses and owns you
            You'll be glad in that great judgment day.

13.   Text F.

14.   Text F.

Refrain 1.   Roll on, roll on,
                    Roll on, little dogies, roll on, roll on,
                Roll on, roll on,
                    Roll on, little dogies, roll on.

Refrain 2.   Oh, bring back, bring back,
                    Bring back my night horse to me

> Oh, bring back, bring back,
>> Bring back my night horse to me.

Refrain 2.1   Text C.

Refrain 3.   How sad as we come to that roundup
>> If our hearts do not have the right brand
> For no "maverick" or "stray" in the judgment
>> Will ever be able to stand.

Refrain 4.   Text F.

VI–B.   "Last Round-Up"
           James, pages 212–13 (FAC III 19). Dobie, *Ballads*, pages 47–48.

2.2   When I think of the last great round-up
>> On the eve of Eternity's dawn,
> I think of the host of cow-boys
>> Who have been with us here and have gone,
4.3   And I wonder if any will greet me
>> On the sands of the evergreen shore;
> With a hearty "God bless you, old fellow,"
>> That I've met with so often before.

4.4   I think of the big-hearted fellows
>> Who will divide with you blanket and bread,
> With a piece of stray beef well roasted,
>> And charge for it never a "red."
1.2   I often look upward and wonder,
>> If the green fields will seem half so fair;
> If any the wrong trail have taken
>> And fail to "be in" over there.

3.2   For the trail that leads down to perdition
>> Is paved all the way with good deeds;
> But in the great round-up of ages,
>> Dear boys, this won't answer your needs.
3.3   But the way to green pastures, though narrow,
>> Leads straight to the home in the sky;
> And Jesus will give you the passports
>> To the land of the sweet by-and-by.

9.2   For the Savior has taken the contract
                To deliver all those who believe,
           At the headquarters ranch of His Father,
                In the great range where none can deceive.
10.1   The Inspector will stand at the gate-way,
                And the herd, one and all must go by;
           The round-up by the angels of judgment
                Must pass 'neath His all-searching eye.

9.3   No mavrick or slick will be tallied
                In the great Book of Life in His home,
           For He knows all the brands and the ear-marks
                That down through the ages have come.
9.4   But along with the strays and the sleepers
                The tailings must turn from the gate;
           No road brand to gain them admission,
                But the awful sad cry "Too late!"

3.2   For the trail that leads down to perdition
                Is paved all the way with good deeds;
           But in the great round-up of ages,
                Dear boys, this won't answer your needs.
3.3   But the way to green pastures, though narrow,
                Leads straight to the home in the sky;
           And Jesus will give you the passports
                To the land of the sweet by-and-by.

VI–C.   "THE COWBOY'S VISION"
         In a letter from Mrs. M. N. Perkins, Perkinsville, Arizona, to
         J. Frank Dobie, May 21, 1930 (FAC II 125).

1.   Last night as I lay on the prairie,
                Looking up to the stars in the sky,
           I wonder if ever a cowboy
                Would get to that Sweet bye and bye.

2.   Oh yes there will be a great roundup
                Where cowboys like cattle will stand
           To be "cut" by the Rider of Judgment,
                Who is posted and knows every brand.

Refrain 2.1 Bring back, bring back,
      Oh bring back my cowboy to me.
      Bring back, bring back,
      Oh bring back my cowboy to me.

   3.1 The canyons and gorges are many
      And "dogies" go often astray
      But the pale-horsed rider will gather
      Everyone to that great judgment day.

   4.1 In that day of the great final judgment,
      When we all come around the white throne,
      How happy will be every cowboy,
      To whom the Lord sayeth "Well done."

Refrain 2.1 (repeated)

Refrain 3. How sad, as we come to that roundup
      If our hearts do not have the right brand,
      For no "Maverick" or "stray" in the judgment
      Will ever be able to stand.

   12. Then my brother, let's come to the branding
      Our owner is calling today
      If he touches and blesses and owns you
      You'll be glad in that great judgment day.

Refrain 2.1 (repeated)

VI–D. "THE COWBOY'S MOTHER"
    Fletcher, pages 22–23 (FAC III 822).

    Last night as I rode on the prairie, under the bright western sky
    I thought I heard mother a callin', from the land of the sweet by
     and by.
    It wasn't the moon in the valley, making her shadow so clear
    Twas only the mind of a Cowboy Thinking his mother was near.
    It sounded like I've heard her callin', like other times I have known
    Callin' as if she were guiding, my horse when I'm riding alone.

I wonder if up there in Heaven, she'll meet me when my life is o'er
And lead to the ranch of the Father. Who lives on the bright golden
   shore.

Chorus: I know that Old Paint will be happy, when our work on earth is done
To ride on the trail up to Heaven, at the set of the bright western sun.

VI–E.   "HOME CORRAL"
         Hendren 46.

Sometimes when on night guard I'm riding
And the stars are a gleam in the sky
Like millions of wee little candles
That glimmer and sparkle on high

I wonder if up there among them
Are streets that are shining with gold
And if its as pretty a country
As all the Sky Pilot's have told

And sometimes I wonder and wonder
If over that lone great divide
I'll meet with my pals who have journeyed
Across to that dim other side

If ever the great starry ranges
Someday in the future I too
Shall ride on a heavenly broncho
When earth's final roundup is thru

They tell us no storms nor blizzards
Blow over that moon scattered range
That is always and always like summer
A land where theres never a change

At night when I lay in my blanket
And the stars would cast over me a spell
I seem to look on the glories
That lie in that Great Home Corral.

VI–F.   "WILL THERE BE ANY COWBOYS IN HEAVEN?"
         Hendren 279.

1.1   Tonight as I ride over the prairies
         And gaze at the great western sky
         I wonder if ever a cowboy will drift
         To that sweet by and by
4.11   On the final day of Judgement
         When the range boss cuts out the strays
         Will he leave any hard shooting gunmen
         To go to that straight narrow way.

Chorus: Will there be any cowboys in Heaven
         And bad broncs or steers we may ride
         Will there be any campfires or cactus
         Over there on that great divide

4.31   When the cowboys are called to that roundup
         And the last great Judgement over
         Will I see my darling
         I know has gone on before.

4.32   She is praying that I'll be in that number
         After the roundup is over
         To be lead by the riders of heaven
         Across the bright happy shore.

VI–G.   "THE COWBOY'S DREAM"
         Sung by Robert E. Voris, Arizona, 1959 (FAC I 169).

Last night as I lay on the prai - rie____

Gaz - ing at the stars in the sky,____   I

VI–H.   "Roll on Dogies"
      Sung by San Angelo Cowboy Quartet, Texas, 1935 (LC 5438:
      FAC I 453).

VI–I.   "THE COWBOY'S DREAM"
Sung by D. Price, New Mexico, 1952 (FAC I 208).
Reproduced by the permission of the collector, Dean Emeritus John
Donald Robb, University of New Mexico.

BIBLIOGRAPHY

Significant texts:

1873?   Lomax d. 5654, letter claiming authorship (JL 270): see *supra*,
            p. 69.
mid 1880's O'Malley, pp. 6, 10 (FAC III 137, pp. 3, 8).
1889   *Arizona Graphic*, I, 8 (November 4, 1889), p. 8 (FAC III 627).
1890?   Smith, pp. 582–84
1893?   MS, Sharlot Hall Museum, Prescott, Arizona (FAC II 438):
            see *supra*, p. 68.
1893   James, pp. 212–13 (FAC III 19); Dobie, *Ballads*, pp. 46–48.
c. 1894   Guy Chambers, Oklahoma, who learned it from his father, who
            learned it . . . (FAC I 393).
1899   Letter to J. Frank Dobie claiming authorship for Rev. C. A.
            Clark (FAC II 125).
1908   Hall, p. 218 (FAC III 96).
1909   Sullivan, pp. 258–59 (FAC III 827).

Other printed texts:

Allen, *Cowboy Lore*, pp. 91–93, 148–50 = Lomax (1938) pp. 327–29.
Arkansas, pp. 6–7, 50–51.
Army, pp. 32–33.
Baber, p. 92 (FAC III 273).
Barnes, *Cowboy*, p. 125; *Tales*, pp. 60–61 (FAC III 291).
Big Round-Up, pp. 64–65.
Bosworth, pp. 134–35 (FAC III 333).
Branch, p. 161 (FAC III 601).
Bratt, p. 207 (FAC III 268).
Brown, pp. 573–74.
Clark, *Cowboy*, pp. 31–32; *Happy Cowboy*, pp. 8–9.
Colorado II, p. 29.
Cosmopolitan (undated, p. 440) (PC-F 34).
Davis, *Tip-Top*, pp. 41, 48, 49.
Delaney's IV, p. 21.
Dick, pp. 94–95 (FAC III 271).
Dobie, *Ballads*, pp. 166–68.
Farm and Ranch, XXXII (January 11, 1913), p. 36.
Felton, p. 72.
Finger, pp. 101–3.
Frey, pp. 84–85.

Fuld, p. 51.
Gard, p. 247.
Gaviana (unpaged).
Hudson, p. 227.
Hull, pp. 58–59.
Idaho Farmer, January 8, 1932 (FAC III 431).
JAFL 39 (1926), pp. 170–71.
Kansas City Star, January 25, 1934 (FAC III 104).
Klickman and Sherwin, pp. 43–45.
Larkin, pp. 100–2.
Lindroth, pp. 20–21, 36–37.
Lomax (1910) pp. 18–19; (1911) 282–83; (1938) pp. 45–48, pp. 327–29 =
    Thorp (1921) pp. 75–77; *Best Loved,* pp. 210–11; *USA,* pp. 210–11.
Lone Ranger, pp. 20–21, 31.
Moore, pp. 305–7.
Nebraska I, pp. 10–11.
Pound, *American,* pp. 166–67 (FAC III 777); *Western,* p. 26.
Randolph II, pp. 187–89.
Republic, pp. 2–3.
San Antonio Express, May 30, 1909 (Lomax d. 5652: JL 157).
Sealy News, n.d. (Lomax d. 5652).
SFQ III, No. 1 (March, 1939) p. 26.
Sing 'em Cowboy, pp. 56–58.
Sires, pp. 24–25, 36–37.
Song Hit I, No. 1, p. 4; II, No. 10, p. 12; V, No. 5, p. 31.
Sullivan, pp. 258–59 (FAC III 827).
Surprise Lake No. 87.
Texas Centennial, p. 13 (FAC III 488).
Texas Stockman's, n.d. (Lomax d. 5652; JL 157).
Thorp (1921) pp. 40–41, 75–77.
Treasure Chest, pp. 30, 38–39.
Weadick, pp. 34, 35, 38 (FAC III 790).
White, *Lonesome,* p. 32.
White and Shakley, pp. 32–35.
Wilgus, *Combs,* p. 134 (FAC III 1098).
Unidentified newspaper clipping from Katie Martin, Texas (Lomax d. 5652:
    JL 157).

Commercial recordings:

Arkansas Woodchopper: Columbia 15463D
Bing Crosby: Okeh 2879

Bradley Kincaid: Decca 5048A
Carl T. Sprague: Victor 20122
Chesley Shirley: Champion 45075
Ed McCurdy: Elektra EKL–205
Gene Autry: Okeh 04485
Marc Williams: Supertone S2054 (FAC III 948).
Masterpiece Male: Masterpiece 8602 (FAC III 1032).
McGinty's Oklahoma Cowboy Band: Okeh 45057
Merrick Jarrett: Oct 12
Ranch Boys: Decca 5017
Red River David: Sonoro 464
Texas Drifter: Champion 45194 (FAC III 1013).
Texas Jim Robertson: Victor P–84.
Thomas and Novak: Musicraft 300 and 300–A.
Vernon Dalhart: Romeo 2546 (FAC III 1004).
West Virginia Rail Splitter: Champion 15897 (FAC III 947).
Williams and Cowboys: Decca 03892.
Zeke Williams: Vocalion 3892.

Manuscripts and field recordings:

Cheney. *Idaho:* 1936, p. 114.
Fife. *Arizona:* Robert E. Voris, 1959 (FAC I 169). *Kansas:* Kathy Dagel, 1959 (FAC I 503). *Maryland:* Frank Goodwyn, 1959 (FAC I 248, 252).
Fowke. *Toronto, Canada:* Sam Campsell, 1960 (FAC I 501).
Gordon. Unknown: No. 189, James N. Boyd, 1923; Nos. 845, 1541, 1575.
Halpert. *Mississippi:* LC 3029A1, 1936.
Hendren 90. Unknown.
Lomax. *Arkansas:* d. 5652, Tom Hight. *California:* d. 5652, D. C. Lamereau (JL 156). *Colorado:* d. 5652, 5653, F. A. Brewer, (JL 157, 202); d. 5653 (JL 228). *Texas:* LC 57B2, Alex Moore, 1934 (FAC I 440); d. 5638, H. W. Thompson, 1910 (JL 82); d. 5652, W. S. Tolbert, 1910 (JL 157); d. 5653, Blanche House, c. 1910; LC 5438, 1935 (FAC I 453; II 588); LC 5642A2, Al Brite, 1941; d. 5652, six texts from D. L. Browning, H. K. Knight, L. M. Hargo, Julian G. Cooper, C. H. Amerman, H. J. LaBove (JL 157); d. 5653 (JL 192); d. 5654, Z. Hamilton. Unknown: d. 5654 (JL 46).
PNFQ. Unknown: Nos. 75, 77, 90, 177, 242, 245.
Robb. *New Mexico:* No. 669, J. Farris, 1951 (FAC I 206); No. 963, D. Price, 1952 (FAC I 208).
WKFA. *Kentucky:* Mrs. Lucille Tary, 1948 (FAC II 207).
WPA. *Arkansas:* LC W2651, 1936 (FAC II 49).

Discussion:

Arizona Graphic, I, 8 (November 4, 1889), p. 8 (FAC III 627).

Barnes, *Cowboy,* pp. 122, 125.

Barrett, p. 180 (FAC II 638).

Dobie, *Ballads,* pp. 166–68; *More Ballads,* pp. 168–69 (FAC III 50); letter from Mrs. M. N. Perkins, 1930 (FAC II 125); letter to John White about O'Malley, 1934 (FAC II 126); letter from Mrs. L. B. Peckenpaugh, 1937 (FAC II 124).

Fowke, *American,* p. 250.

Hall, p. 218 (FAC III 96).

Hinkle, p. 19.

Kansas City Star, January 25, 1934 (FAC III 104).

Lomax (1938) pp. 44–45; *Best Loved,* p. 196; *USA,* p. 196; letter to Carnegie Foundation, 1908; d. 5567, letter from D. J. O'Malley, 1932 (JL 6); d. 5654, 5672, letter from I. P. Skinner, 1910 (JL 155, 270).

O'Malley, pp. 6, 8, 10 (FAC III 137).

Pollan, pp. 75–76 (FAC II 629).

Pound, *Syllabus,* p. 27.

Sullivan, pp. 258–59 (FAC III 827).

Thorp, *Banjo,* pp. 201–2 (FAC III 803). See *supra* p. 23.

Thorp and Clark, pp. 40–41.

Weadick, p. 35 (FAC III 790).

VII

The Little Adobe Casa

"*S*od-busting" and raising cattle on the open range began to get in the way of each other in the early 1880's. Fences, essential to taking up homesteads and growing crops, made open-range grazing and trail driving increasingly difficult, ultimately impossible.

In "The Little Adobe Casa" Thorp gives us a New Mexico parody of our greatest "sod buster" ballad, "The Little Old Sod Shanty on My Claim,"[1] which is, in turn, based upon an earlier sentimental song, "The Little Old Log Cabin in the Lane," published in 1871 as the work of W. S. Hays. D. K. Wilgus traces Hays's melody to "Keep Your Feet Still, Geordie Hinny," which is credited to Joe Wilson (1841–1874), a Tyneside music-hall comedian. Yet to be explained is the juncture of the tunes for "Geordie Hinny" and the hymn "Lily of the Valley," previously cited in our treatment of "Little Joe, the Wrangler."[2]

---

[1] Claimed to have been written by Addison Bennet, who went to Kansas in 1879 and eventually owned a number of newspapers there that published final proof land notices. He is said to have written the parody at that time. After about a decade he went on to Oregon. See George S. Turnbull, *History of Oregon Newspapers*, Portland, 1939, pp. 395–96 (FAC II 704). Other claims to authorship have been put forth for Harry Cline, a Civil War veteran, and Dr. Oliver E. Murray, a song writer and music composer of South Dakota. See Coursey, pp. 258, 307–8.

[2] *Supra*, p. 30.

But, since meaning more than origins is to be the meat of this book, let's stay with "The Little Adobe Casa" long enough to see that it is filled with honest images of pioneering in the great American Southwest —the cactus roof, the coyotes, "Greasers," centipedes, *alacranes* (Spanish for "scorpions"), cockroaches, *frijoles* and *tortillas* stirred up in chili sauce, and especially the dark-eyed *mujer*—all conspire to make the image of the Southwest what it is today, and hence we thank Jack Thorp and Tom Beasley, who wrote this gem of western lyricism in 1887.[3]

"The Little Adobe Casa," by the way, is only one of several of the offspring of "The Little Old Sod Shanty." Not for treatment here are "The Little Vine-clad Cottage on the Claim"; the popular woman's "Reply to the Little Old Sod Shanty"; "The Little New Log Cabin in the Hills" of the poet-scout Jack Crawford;[4] "The Double-Breasted Mansion on the Square"; and even "The Little Red Caboose Behind the Train."

In "The Old Chuck Wagon" we see another genuine western parody whose setting is not at the *adobe casa* but at the cowboy's true range home, the chuck wagon. This rare but authentic item has come to us uniquely from the singing of C. S. Weir of Tucson, Arizona. The chuck wagon was the center of operations in the roundup and on the trail drive. Crew consisted typically of a stove-up cowboy who doubled as cook, and the adolescent wrangler who managed the *remuda* and assisted the cook. The chuck wagon—and in big outfits there were two or more—carried food, bed rolls, extra gear, and all the sundry supplies that had to be on hand. At roundup it moved, as necessary, from spot to spot so that the punchers didn't lose time riding back and forth for food or fresh mounts. On trail drives it moved out ahead of the herd to areas, preferably watering places, selected for chuck stops or camping. Hot coffee was available at almost any hour.

Strangely, John Lomax never used "The Little Adobe Casa" in his printed collections, although in his papers there is a manuscript copy that departs somewhat less from the original "Sod Shanty" than does Thorp.[5] His files also contain one manuscript and one printed copy of

---

[3] Thorp (1921) p. 93.
[4] Crawford, *Poet Scout*, p. 53.
[5] D. 5634 (JL 44).

a stanza which is clearly related to "The Old Chuck Wagon."[6] We offer also the sentimental but unique and more refined text of "The Little Adobe Shack Way Out West."[7]

We have encountered three significant musical treatments. The first, sung by C. S. Weir,[8] presents substantially the same melodic line as the one previously given for "Little Joe the Wrangler."[9] The same tune, given on p. 93, comes from the singing of an unknown informant from Missouri. Finally, we give words and music to "The Little Old Log Cabin by the Stream," which carries a lilting $\frac{6}{8}$ rhythm suggestive of the black-face musical tradition that is in direct contrast to the staid $\frac{2}{4}$ rhythm of the treatment previously mentioned.

VII–A.   THORP (1908) page 20

1.
    Just one year ago to-day,
    I left my eastern home
Hunting for a fortune and for fame,
    Little did I think that now,
    I'd be in Mexico
In this little adóbe casa on the plains.

Chorus.

2.
    The roof is ocateo,
    The coyotes far and near
The Greaser roams about the place all day
    Centipedes and Tarantulas
    Crawl o'er me while I sleep
In my little adóbe casa on the plains.

3.
    Alacranies on the ceiling
    Cockroaches on the wall.
My bill-of-fare is always just the same
    Frijoles and tortillas
    Stirred up in chili sauce
In my little adóbe casa on the plains.

---

[6] See text C.
[7] From the singing of James McGuire, Arkansas, 1958 (FAC II 486).
[8] Text B.
[9] *Supra*, p. 35.

4.   But if some dark eyed mujer
            Would consent to be my wife
       I would try to be contented and remain
            'Till fate should show a better place
            To settle down for life
       Than this little adóbe casa on the plains.

VII–B.   "I WILL TELL YOU MY TROUBLES"
         Sung by C. S. Weir, Arizona (FAC II 641).
         Reproduced by permission of the collector, Ray B. Browne of
         Purdue University.

1.   I will tell you of my troubles
            My ups and downs through life
            And I'll tell to you a story rather strange
            I will tell you of my boarding house
            A structure built on wheels
            And it's drawn by four black horses 'cross the plains.

2.   Oh, the wheels are made of [black oak?]
            The running gear white oak
            And the bed is made to haul our bedding, chuck, and grain
            In the rear there is a chuck box
            Where the cowboys get their chuck
            It's the XIT[10] chuck wagon on the plain.

3.   As the old chuck wagon rolls on
            You can hear the cowboys yell
            You can hear the dogies bawling all around
            You can see the bronco pitching
            Trying to shake his rider off
            But they seldom ever put one on the ground.

4.   You can hear the howling coyotes
            The barking prairie dog

---

[10] The XIT (sometimes read "Ten in Texas") Ranch was a two-million-acre spread granted as payment for the construction of the Texas State Capitol Building. It extended over or into ten counties in West Texas.

You can see the bronco buster holding to his rein
You can see a thousand white-face cattle
Grazing on the grass
'Round the XIT chuck wagon on the plains.

5.   Oh, my life's a poor cowpuncher
        And I daily ride the range
        While the irons is getting hot I ride my wild bronco
        When the rounding of the yearlings
        And the branding does begin
        From my roping horse I throw my long lasso.

6.   Oh, the boys go dog the yearlings
        To burn the XIT
        While on guard the boys are holding to the reins
        When our day's work is ended
        Then we all go into camp
        To the XIT chuck wagon on the plains.

7.   When the cook gets chuck all ready
        And he hollers, "Here it is,"
        To the chuck box there's a rush by all the crew,
        When our tins and cups are loaded
        With hot coffee, bread, and steak
        Then we all sit down upon the grass to chew.

8.   Oh, the beefsteak's brown and tender
        The bread is sour dough
        And the coffee's strong enough to float a barge of grain
        As we chew our [floury greeting?]
        There's a loco weed in bloom
        'Round the XIT chuck wagon on the plains.

9.   Oh, my associates are cowpunchers
        And their jewels are forty-fives
        We're there with smoking rifles when troubles occurs
        The only amusement is
        High Five and Seven Up
        And the music is the rattle of the spurs.

10.   Oh, our beds are made of tarpaulin
        Our blankets are Navajo

And we snap the [?] to keep out wind and rain.
When the boys are all through jesting
Then we all lie down to sleep
'Round the XIT chuck wagon on the plains.

VII–C.   "LITTLE OLD SOD SHANTY"
          Lomax d. 5634, from Loyal German, Texas, n.d. (JL 32). Also
          from Mrs. M. F. Dickey in *Dallas Semi-Weekly News*, August 5,
          1902 (Lomax d. 5652).

          You could see the tired cowboy as he is coming through the rain
          To the little old chuck wagon on the plains,
          You could hear the wild coyote sneaking by the side
          Of the little old sod shanty on the claim.

VII–D.   "LITTLE ADOBE SHACK, WAY OUT WEST"
          Sung by James McGuire, Arkansas, 1958 (FAC II 486).
          Reproduced by permission of the collector, James Ward Lee of
          North Texas State College.

   1.   I love to sit alone at night when the moon is shining bright
              And the stars in the heaven wink at me
            And to sing a dear old song that my mother used to sing to me
              When she cradled me upon her lovin' knee.

   2.   I can hear the whip-poor-will, he is calling for me still
              He sings a song to me of peace and rest,
            Seems to say to me, "Come back to your used to be
              Back to your little adobe shack way out West."

   3.   I will soon be coming back for a debt that I can't pay
              To that little adobe shack where I was born,
            Where the roof is fallen in and it lets in the rain
              But it shelters me from every wind and storm.

   4.   Can you hear the whip-poor-will? They are calling for me still
              They sing a song to me of peace and rest,
            Seems to say to me, "Come back to your used to be,
              Back to your adobe shack way out West."

VII–E. "LITTLE OLD SOD SHANTY"
LC 3199B1: unknown informant, Missouri, 1936 (FAC I 287).

1, 3, 6

I'm look - in' rath - er see - dy now while

hold - ing down my claim, And my vit - als are not

al - ways served the best, _____ And the mice play shy - ly

round me as I nes - tle down to rest, In my

lit - tle old sod shan - ty on my claim. _____ The

2, 4, 5, 7 sung to Chorus melody

hing - es are of leath - er and the win - dows have no

glass, _ While the board roof lets the howl - in' bliz - zard

in _____ And I hear the hun - gry coy - ote as he

slinks up through the grass, Round the lit - tle old sod

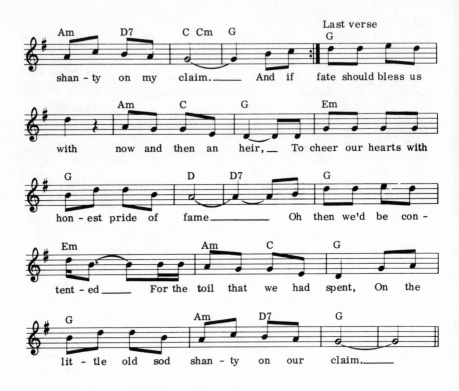

VII–F.   "Little Old Sod Shanty"
          LC 8421A–1: L. A. Coffee, Illinois, 1946 (FAC I 290).

There was a happy time to me not many years ago
    When the darkies used to gather on the green
And the fiddle and the banjo, they would make the forest ring
    In that little old log cabin by the stream.

Then hang up the fiddle and the banjo on the wall
    And we'll lay aside the bones and tambourine
Since death has called away my rose, the only flower that blows
    In that little old log cabin by the stream.

The footpath's all grown over now that leads around the hill
    And the fences am a goin' to decay
And the brook am all dried up where I used to go to swim
    For in time it's changed its course another way.

The chimbley tumbled down and it killed a brindled cow
And I 'spects it'll break my head if I remain
But the angels they watch o'er me while I lay me down to sleep
In that little old log cabin by the stream.

There was a hap - py time to me not man - y years a - go, When the dark - ies used to gath-er round the green,___ And the fid - dle and the ban - jo, they would make the for - est ring, In that lit - tle old log cab - in by the stream.___ Then hang up the fid - dle and the ban - jo on the wall, And we'll lay a - side the bones and tam - bour - ine,___ Since death has called a -

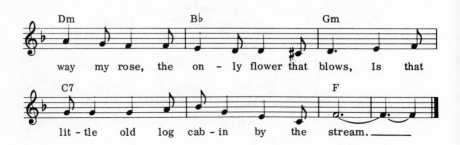

way   my rose,   the   on - ly flower that blows,   Is   that

lit - tle   old   log cab - in   by   the   stream._____

Discussion:

Clark, N. M., letter to A. E. Fife, September 6, 1964 (FAC II 699).
Lomax: letter to Carnegie Foundation, 1908.
Pound, *Pedigree,* pp. 30–31; *Syllabus,* pp. 24–25, 63.
Thorp and Clark, p. 215.

VIII

The Texas Cowboy

*T*HE BOOM IN MINING and other settlement activity in Montana coincided with the fencing and the breaking up of the open ranges farther south. To the east the sod busters had fenced so much of the land and subjected it to the plough that cattle drives north and east had become impossible—unnecessary too, because iron horses puffed across the land, and railroad corrals were often only a few miles distant from the cattle ranges. Drives did continue, however, from the ranges of western Texas to western Montana under contracts to supply beef to "Uncle Sam's Indians," and the needs of a growing population in the state of the last frontier.

"The Texas Cowboy" was written in this historic setting. It is a serio-comic treatment of the themes of geographical displacement and culture shock typical of the whole era of our national development: Europe to the eastern seaboard, the eastern seaboard over the Appalachians and into the Ohio Valley, the Ohio Valley on to the Great Plains, and finally all the way into the Rockies, the Northwest, and the Pacific Coast.

Thorp's 1908 text is unified, vigorous, and satisfying. It is a pity that in 1921 he felt constrained to abandon it for the longer but synthetic

97

text that Lomax fabricated, using stanzas from three or four of several
texts that he had encountered before 1910.

Two printed texts have accompanying music. The Larkin setting[1]
is most interesting because it offers rich rhythmic, chordal, and melodic
variety suggesting four or five accompanying chords and carrying a
snappy well-regulated rhythm. By contrast, "The Arkansaw Woodchopper"[2] is lacking in dotted notes, requires only chords I and V. We
give the music here as sung by Kathy Dagel, whose keen insight into
the meaning of the song and whose artful interpretation make for a
delightful listening experience.

VIII–A. THORP (1908) pages 21–23

    1.1   Come all you Texas cow-boys
              And warning take of me
          Don't go out in Montana
              For wealth or liberty

    2.   But stay home here in Texas
              Where they work the year around
          And where you'll not get consumption
              From sleeping on the ground.

    3.   Montana is too cold for me,
              And the winters are too long
          Before the round-ups have begun,
              Your money is all gone.

    4.   For in Montana the boys get work
              But six months in the year
          And they charge for things three prices
              In that land so bleak and drear.

    5.   This thin old hen-skin bedding,
              'Twas not enough to shield my form
          For I almost freeze to death,
              Whene'er there comes a storm.

---

[1] Larkin, pp. 54–55.
[2] *Arkansas*, pp. 42–44.

6.   I've an outfit on the Mussleshell
      Which I expect I'll never see
  Unless by chance I'm sent
      To represent this A R and P T.[3]

7.   All along these bad lands,
      And down upon the dry
  Where the cañons have no bottoms
      And the mountains reach the sky.

8.   Your chuck is bread and bacon
      And coffee black as ink
  And hard old alkali water
      Thats scarcely fit to drink.

9.   They'll wake you in the morning
      Before the break of day
  And send you out on circle,
      Full twenty miles away.

10.   With a "Tenderfoot" to lead you
      Who never knows the way
  You're pegging in the best of luck
      If you get two meals a day.

11.   I've been over in Colorado
      And down upon the Platte
  Where the cow-boys work in pastures
      And the cattle all are fat.

12.   Where they ride silver mounted saddles
      And spurs and leggin's too
  And their horses are all Normans
      And only fit to plow.

13.   Yes I've traveled lots of country,
      Arizona's hills of sand
  Down through the Indian Nation
      Plum to the Rio Grande.

14.   Montana is the bad-land
      The worst I've ever seen
  Where the cow-boys are all tenderfeet
      And the dogies are all lean.

---

[3] Lomax d. 5652 (JL 138) has a text with "the Circle R D T."

VIII–B. "THE TEXAS COW BOY"
        Glendive Independent, March 31, 1888, page 4.

1.   I am a Texas cow boy, and I am far away from home,
         If I ever get back to Texas, I never more will roam.
4.1   Montana is too cold for me, and the winters are too long,
         Before the round-ups do begin your money is all gone.

5.3   Now, to win these fancy leggings you will have enough to do;
         They cost me fourteen dollars the day that they were new.
5.2   And this old hen skin bedding too thin to keep me warm,
         I nearly freeze to death my boys, whenever there comes a
             storm.

11.1   I have worked down in Nebraska, where the grass grows
             ten feet high;
         Where the cattle are such rustlers they hardly ever die.
11.2   I have been up in the sand hills, and down upon the Platte,
         Where the punchers are good fellows and the cattle always
             fat.

13.   I have traveled lots of country, from Nebraska hills of sand,
         Down through the Indian Nation and up the Rio Grande.
14.   But the Bad Lands of Montana are the worst I ever seen,
         Where the punchers are all tenderfeet and the doggies are
             so lean.

9.   They will wake you in the morning before the break of day,
         And send you on a circle a hundred miles away.
8.   Your grub is bread and bacon, with coffee black as ink,
         And the water so full of alkali that it isn't fit to drink.

11.3   If you want to see some bad lands just go over on the Dry,
         Where you will bog down in the coulies and the mountains
             touch the sky,
10.   With a tenderfoot to guide you who never knows the way,
         And you are playing in the best of luck if you eat three
             times a day.

2.1   Up along the Yellowstone it is cold the year around,
You will surely get consumption if you sleep upon the
ground.

4.2   And the wages almost nothing for six months in the year.
When you pay up all your outside ⸗ bts you have nothing
left for beer.

1.2   Now all you Texas cow boys this warning take by me,
Don't come up to Montana to spend your money free,

2.   But stay at home in Texas where there is work all the year
around,
And you will never get consumption by sleeping on the
ground.

—M. S. W., REDWATER POET.

VIII—OTHER STANZA VARIANTS

5.1   And take this old tarpoleon
Too thin to shield my frame
I got it down in New Mexico
A-dealin' a Monte game.

5.3   Now to win these fancy leggin's
I'll have enough to do
They cost me twenty dollars
The day that they were new.

13.1   All along these bad lands
And down upon the Dry
Where the canyons have no bottoms
And the mountains reach the sky.

13.2   If you want to see some bad lands
Go over on the Dry
You will bog down in the coulees
Where the mountains reach the sky.

VIII–C. "TEXAS COWBOY"
Sung by Kathy Dagel, Kansas, 1959 (FAC I 508).

Oh, I'm a Tex - as cow - boy far a - way from home, If ev - er I get back to Tex - as I nev - er more will roam. Mon -

Last two lines sung from here.

tan - a is too cold for me, And the win - ters are too long, Be - fore the round - ups do be - gin___ Our mon-ey___ is all gone.___

BIBLIOGRAPHY

Printed texts:

Arkansas, pp. 42–44.
Botkin, *Sampler,* p. 548 = Larkin, pp. 54–55.
Branch, pp. 173, 254, 255 (FAC III 601).
Clark, *Cowboy,* p. 64 = Lomax (1910) pp. 229–32.
Felton, p. 48.
Glendive Independent, Glendive, Montana, March 31, 1888, p. 4 (FAC III 765).
Hobo News, fol. 6.
Hudson, pp. 227–28.
James, *Smoky,* p. 35.
Larkin, pp. 54–55.
Lee, *Range,* p. 36.
Lomax (1911) pp. 229–32; (1938) pp. 22–24.
Nebraska XI, pp. 2–4.
Thorp (1921) pp. 148–51.

Manuscripts and field recordings:

Fife. *Kansas:* Kathy Dagel, 1959 (FAC I 508).
ISUHM. *Idaho:* Mrs. Addie Hawes (FAC II 688).
Lomax, *Colorado:* d. 5653, Madge Baylus, c. 1930 (JL 228). *North Dakota:* d. 5638, James B. Goldsbury (JL 106). *Texas* or *Oklahoma:* LC cylinder 36, 1908–10. Unknown: d. 5654, 5656, 3 variants; d. 5652, 5653, A. D. Edsall (JL 138, 172).
PNFQ 452, 453. Unknown.

Discussion:

Barrett, Chapter 7.
Clark, N. M., letter to A. E. Fife, September 6, 1964 (FAC II 699).
Kansas City Times, May 17, 1938 (FAC III 823).
Lomax d. 5638, A. D. Edsell (JL 172).

IX

Mustang Gray

THE CHARM OF MAIDENS from "south of the Border" has warmed the blood of Anglo-American men ever since that August day of 1821 when Stephen F. Austin arrived at Bexar, Texas, to take up land under a charter granted to his father. Shortly there was to emerge a moving theme in American folk song, that of a wild and adventurous Anglo-American who provokes the undying love of a Mexican maiden who will deny her ties of family, country, and even her religion, if need be, to serve her cowboy hero. John Hill Hewitt (1801–1890), composer, and son of one of America's first composers, was among the first to capitalize this romantic image in our national popular music. "Mustang Gray," more correctly known as "The Maid of Monterey," evolves from an aria in a musical of the 1840's composed by Hewitt. The aria was published in sheet music in 1851. It has floated in oral tradition for more than a century. Dark-eyed mantilla- (or serape-) toting maidens have also made hay in popular fiction. *The Volunteer, or The Maid of Monterrey,* a novel written by Ned Buntline, was published in 1847. Another romantic and readable novel in this vein was, precisely, one about the loves and adventures of Mayberry G. ("Mustang") Gray, written by Jeremiah Clemens and published by J. P. Lippincott of Philadelphia in 1858.

For his 1908 edition, Thorp used a somewhat defective text first learned, he says, from a man named Sanford, saloon keeper at La Ascensión, Mexico, in about 1888.[1] It lacks stanzas 6 and 7 and has

---

[1] Thorp (1921) p. 102.

stanzas 2 and 3 transposed. Obviously by 1921 he had seen a better text.[2] From Paul Kelso, Denton, Texas,[3] and a manuscript of Winnie Allen of Austin, Texas,[4] we get additional stanzas that have floated in oral tradition.

The song takes two quite distinct forms. In Hewitt's original aria interest is focused on the *señorita* and her heroic deed. The texts most current in western American oral tradition, however, bring the American soldier-cowboy into central focus, attenuate the theme of feminine devotion, and centralize attention on the heroic soldier and his love for his native land—Texas, of course.

J. Frank Dobie says his mother recalled that "Mustang Gray" was sung to her by her mother down on the Nueces in the '70's: "In high quavering tones that carried above rattling hocks and clacking horns, and in low monotone that harmonized with the sleeping herd all stretched out on the ground, it was sung to longhorns on range and trail from the Gulf of Mexico to the Canadian Rockies. . . ."[5]

From *The Flag of Freedom,* published by the American army of occupation at Puebla, Mexico (December 11, 1847), Dobie also supplies the fragment of a ballad entitled "El Niño, or the Soldier Child," which seems related:

> She bore him to her Indian home
> Upon her matted bed
> She spoke,—O soothing was her tone—
> And pressed his weary head,
> She look'd and cried in accents wild
> *El niño que?* the soldier child.[6]

Despite the strong case for J. H. Hewitt, authorship has been ascribed to Tom Grey of Tularosa, New Mexico,[7] and to James Lytle, "a Texas Ranger."[8]

---

[2] Possibly in Lomax (1910) pp. 79–80.

[3] FAC II 478.

[4] Sent to Lomax in 1942 (p. 5654, JL 263).

[5] Dobie, *Mustang,* p. 121.

[6] Dobie, *More Ballads,* pp. 160–63; photostat of original item in FAC III 798. From his early childhood on an Idaho ranch Mr. Fife recalls a vulgar jingle that evokes this stanza: " 'Alas!' she cried in accents wild/'If I take this I'll have a child!' " Strange, indeed, are the processes of the folk imagination!

[7] Thorp (1921) p. 102.

[8] Dobie, *More Ballads,* pp. 160–63; *Mustang,* p. 122; *Tone,* p. 122.

IX–A.   THORP (1908) pages 23–24

1.   There was a brave old Texan
         They called him Mustang Gray
     He left his home when quite a boy
         And went roaming far away.

Refrain 1.

     He'll go no more a-rangering
         Those savages to affright
     He has heard his last war-whoop
         He fought his last fight.

3.   When our country was invaded
         By the Indian warriors train's
     He used to mount his noble charger
         And scout the hills and plains.

2.   He would not sleep within a tent
         No pleasures did·he know
     But like a brave old frontiersman[9]
         A-scouting he would go.

4.   Once he was taken prisoner
         And carried far away
     Had to wear the yoke of bondage
         Through the streets of Monterey.

5.   A señorita loved him
         And with a brave woman's pride
     She opened the gates and gave him
         Her father's horse to ride.

8.   And when this gallant life was spent
         This was his last command
     Pray bury me in old Texas soil
         On the banks of the Rio Grande.

9.   And when the weary treveller
         Is passing by his grave
     He may sometimes shed a farewell tear
         O'er the bravest of the brave.

---

[9] "Tex-i-an."

IX–B.   "THE MAID OF MONTERREY"
MS from Paul Kelso, Texas, 1959. Mr. Kelso said he got the text
from Dobie, *More Ballads,* pp. 162–63, but he modified it to suit
his own needs.

4.1   Once he was taken prisoner, bound in chain upon the way
        He wore the yoke of bondage through the streets of
            Monterrey
5.   A senorita loved him and followed by his side
        She opened the gates and gave to him her father's steed to
            ride.

5.1   God bless the senorita, the belle of Monterrey
        She opened wide the prison doors and let him ride away
5.2   Our guns had hushed their thundering, our drums in
            silence lay
        Then came the senorita, the maid of Monterrey.

7.   She gave the thirsty water, she dressed the bleeding wounds
        Her gentle prayer she uttered for those who groaned around
8.1   And when the bugle sounded just at the break of day
        All blessed the senorita, the maid of Monterrey.

IX–C.   "THE MAID OF MONTEREY"
Lomax d. 5654, from Winnie Allen, Texas, 1942 (JL 263).
"Written after the battle of Monterey in 1848 by Colonel Theodore
O'Hara."

4.2   The moon was shining brightly upon the battle plain,
        The breeze was passing lightly o'er the faces of the slain,
5.2   The guns had hushed their thunder and the drums in
            silence lay
        When there came a senorita, the Maid of Monterey.

6.1   She said she loved her country and prayed that it might live
        Yet for a dying soldier she had a tear to give
7.   She gave the thirsty water and dressed their bleeding wounds,
        And gentle prayers she uttered for those who moaned around.

8.2   And when the dying soldier for one bright gleam did pray
        He blessed the senorita, the Maid of Monterey

9.1   And here's to that bright beauty who drove death's pangs
away
The meek-eyed senorita, the Maid of Monterey.

IX–D.   "THE MAID OF MONTERREY"
Dobie, *More Ballads,* pages 162–63.
Reproduced with permission of the Texas Folklore Society.

The first two stanzas are the same as IX–C, 4.2 and 5.2. Then:

6.2   She cast a look of anguish
On dying and on dead;
Her lap she made a pillow
For those who groaned and bled;

8.1   And when our bugle sounded
Just at the break of day,
All blessed the *senorita,*
The Maid of Monterrey.

Next are two stanzas that are very nearly the same as IX–C, 7 and
8.2.

6.1   Although she loved her nation
And prayed that it might live,
Yet for the dying foeman
She had a tear to give.

9.1   Then cheers to that bright beauty
Who drove death's pangs away,
The meek-eyed *senorita,*
The Maid of Monterrey.

IX–E.   "THE MAID OF MONTEREY"
By J. H. Hewitt, published by F. D. Benteen, Baltimore; W. T.
Mayo, New Orleans, 1851.

4.2   The moon was shining brightly,
Upon the battle plain;
The gentle breeze fann'd lightly
The features of the slain;

5.2   The guns had hush'd their thunder
The drum in silence lay;

When came the Senoretta,
    The maid of Monterey.

(repeat stanza 5.2)

6.2   She cast a look of anguish
        On dying and on dead;
    Her lap she made the pillow
        Of those who groan'd and bled.
8.2   And when the dying soldier
        For one bright gleam did pray,
    He bless'd the Senoretta,
        The maid of Monterey.

7.   She gave the thirsty, water,
        And dress'd the bleeding wound;
    And gentle prayers she uttered,
        For those who sigh'd around.
8.1   And when the bugle sounded,
        Just at the break of day;
    We bless'd the Senoretta,
        The maid of Monterey.

6.1   For, tho' she lov'd her nation,
        And pray'd that it might live;
    Yet—for the dying foeman
        She had a tear to give.
9.1   Then, here's to that bright beauty,
        Who drove death's pang away
    The meek-eyed Senoretta,
        The maid of Monterey.

IX–E.   Music

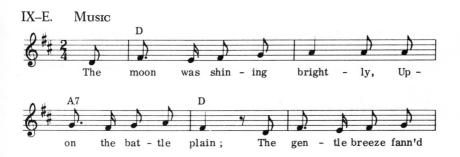

The moon was shin - ing bright - ly, Up -
on the bat - tle plain ; The gen - tle breeze fann'd

light - ly the fea - tures of the slain; The
guns had hush'd their thun - der, The drum in si - lence
lay; When came the Se - no - ret - ta, The
maid of Mon - te - rey, The guns had hush'd their
thun - der, The drum in si - lence lay, When
came the Se - no - ret - ta, The maid of Mon - te - rey.

BIBLIOGRAPHY

Printed texts:

Botkin, *Western,* pp. 775–76 = Dobie, *Toll,* pp. 122–23 = Thorp (1921)
   pp. 102–4.
Clark, *Happy Cowboy,* pp. 48–49.
Dick, pp. 93–94 (FAC III 271) = Siringo, *Song,* pp. 12–13 = Thorp
   (1921) pp. 102–4.
Dobie, *More Ballads,* pp. 160–63 (FAC III 781); *Mustang,* pp. 122–23;
   Tone pp. 122–23.
Hewitt, J. H., *The Maid of Monterey.* Baltimore: F. D. Benteen, 1851.
Lomax (1910) pp. 79–80; (1938) pp. 362–64; *American,* pp. 395–96 =
   Dobie, *More Ballads,* pp. 160–63.

Moore, pp. 311–12.
Siringo, *Song,* pp. 12–13.
Sowell, p. 76.
Thompson, pp. 134–35.
Thorp (1921) pp. 102–4.

Commercial recordings:

Bill Bender (The Happy Cowboy): Varsity 5135 (FAC III 917).
Bill Bender, Clayton McMichon and Dance Orchestra: ASCH 410.

Manuscripts and field recordings:

Fife. *Texas:* Paul Kelso, 1959 (FAC II 478). *Utah:* Clara W. Stevens, c. 1930 (FAC II 652).
Hendren 271.
Hoffman. *Pennsylvania:* Shoemaker MS (FAC II 677).
Lomax. *Texas:* d. 5634, Mrs. M. Tuggle; d. 5654, Winnie Allen, 1942 (JL 263); LC 916A1, D. W. Preece, 1937 (FAC I 450).
WPA. *Texas:* Travis Meeks (FAC II 309).

Discussion:

Angell, pp. 33–39.
Barker, p. 709.
Barrett, pp. 41–43, 172–74.
Botkin, *Western,* pp. 775–76 = Dobie, *Toll,* pp. 122–23.
Bradford, p. 569.
Dick, pp. 93–94 (FAC III 271).
Dobie, *Longhorns,* pp. 230–31; *More Ballads,* pp. 160–63 (FAC III 781); *Mustang,* pp. 109–23; *Tone,* pp. 122–23; notes in his personal copy of Lomax, *Cowboy* (FAC II 755).
Flag of Freedom, I, 15 (December 11, 1847), (FAC III 798).
Gard, p. 246 = Dobie, *Mustang,* pp. 109–23.
Laws, p. 247.
Lomax, letter to Carnegie Foundation, 1908.
Lynn, p. 322.
Sacks, pp. 17–18 (FAC III 802).
Siringo, *Riata,* p. 150.
Thompson, pp. 133–34.
Thorp (1921) pp. 102–4.

X

Sam Bass

THE BALLAD OF "SAM BASS" is a forthright piece of frontier realism written by a man very close to the historic events, sympathetic to the outlaw gang, and hostile to the Texas Rangers and other law enforcement agencies.

Stanza by stanza it treats the essential facts that led to the tragedy of Sam's death on July 21, 1878: his arrival in Denton, Texas, aged seventeen; his interest in horse racing and successes with the famous Denton mare; his generosity and love of classical frontier pleasures (cards, women, and horses); his drive of Texas cattle to Deadwood, Montana, in the company of Joel Collins; carousal there of the Collins's punchers, which left them broke; the successful and rewarding robbery of the Union Pacific train; return of the outlaws by twos to Texas, including the apprehension and killing of Joel Collins and Bill Heffridge; Bass's generosity, flamboyance, dash, and daring as he organized a robber band that assailed trains and banks in open defiance of the law; panic among the law enforcement agencies; the shooting of "Arkansas" by a "dead-beat" Texas Ranger named Thomas Floyd; success of the Bass band in out-maneuvering, out-riding, and out-shooting the Rangers; and finally the ultimate demise of Bass through the treachery of a Judas, turncoat, and stooly named Jim Murphy, planted by the Rangers in Sam's band.

Although our earliest printed text is of 1906, there is plenty of evidence that composition of the ballad goes right back to the weeks following Sam's death. Thorp first heard it at a dance hall in Sidney,

Nebraska, in 1888. He says it was composed by John Denton, Gaines-ville, 1879.[1] C. F. McCarty wrote Robert Gordon that he was around Texas, Kansas, and the Indian Territory "in '79 or '80, maybe '81" when "the song was sung night after night around the cattle, in the gambling halls, saloons, and other places where the boys and girls congregated."[2] Lomax, who recorded it on a cylinder (No. 51) in Oklahoma or Texas between 1908 and 1910 said that it was composed at Forth Worth by a friend of the outlaw himself.[3] Later, he also ascribes it to John Denton.[4]

Both Sam and his ballad have accumulated their myth. Several different people have proudly claimed Sam as a relative. In his copy of Lomax's *Cowboy Songs,* J. Frank Dobie wrote in longhand that near Bolton there is a mott of live oaks supposed to have been used as targets by Sam Bass and his gang. Once when riding at full speed Sam is sup-posed to have shot his initials into one of the trees. "They can be seen yet," Dobie's informant said, "though not very plainly."[5] Thorp knew personally the Joe Jackson of the eleventh stanza.[6] Lomax in his reminis-cences says that the song "was known by every cowboy from 1868 to 1892." Following a lecture Lomax gave at Coe College, Iowa, a student told him his mother was Sam Bass's sister.[7]

Hinkle says it was the one song known on every range in the South-west: ". . . there must have been two thousand verses, according to the variations of the cowpunchers." He offers unique variants.[8]

The melody for "Sam Bass" is supposed to come from a frontier ballad that precedes the Civil War, "The Range of the Buffalo." Like the good vehicle for folk satire that it is, it has also been transmitted to a rare western railroad song, "Way Out in Idaho." Numerous melodic transcriptions have been printed and innumerable field and commercial recordings made. Yet nearly all of them have similar internal direction and chordal outline. Rhythmic structures range from a square-cut $\frac{4}{4}$ with undotted notes through a swinging $\frac{6}{8}$ with a strangely accented rhythm

[1] (1921) p. 135.
[2] Gordon 934.
[3] FAC II 749.
[4] Lomax, *Best Loved,* p. 284.
[5] FAC II 750. See also published account in Dobie, *Tales,* p. 82.
[6] Thorp and Clark, pp. 138–39.
[7] Lomax, *Ballad,* pp. 56–58.
[8] Stanzas 16.1 and 17 of the composite text, from Hinkle, p. 19.

as in Randolph.[9] The subdivision of one count into four parts exemplifies the implied inner strength of Sam Bass despite his apparent weakness. The setting of Jules Verne Allen carries a rhythmic structure that is slow and plodding by comparison.[10]

We have, of course, given Thorp's own tune, the only one he ever recorded.

X–A.   THORP (1908) pages 24–26

1.   Sam Bass was born in Indiana, it was his native home
      And at the age of seventeen, young Sam began to roam.

2.   He first went down to Texas, a cow-boy bold to be
      A kinder-hearted fellow, you'd scarcely ever see.

3.   Sam used to deal in race stock, had one called the Denton mare
      He watched her in scrub races, took her to the County Fair.

4.   She always won the money, wherever she might be
      He always drank good liquor, and spent his money free.

5.   Sam left the Collins ranch in the merry month of May
      With a herd of Texas cattle the Black Hills to see

6.   Sold out in Custer City[11] and all got on a spree
      A harder lot of cow-boys you'd scarcely ever see.

7.   On the way back to Texas, they robbed the U. P. train
      All split up in couples and started out again

8.   Joe Collins and his partner were overtaken soon
      With all their hard earned money they had to meet their doom.

9.   Sam made it back to Texas all right side up with care
      Rode into the town of Denton his gold with friends to share

10.   Sam's life was short in Texas 'count of robberies he'd do
      He'd rob the passengers coaches the mail and express too.

11.   Sam had four bold companions, four bold and daring lads
      Underwood and Joe Jackson, Bill Collins and Old Dad

---

[9] Randolph II, p. 70.
[10] Allen, *Cowboy Lore*, pp. 112–13.
[11] One text reads: "Sold out and cursed the city."

12.   They were four of the hardest cow-boys that Texas ever knew
        They whipped the Texas Rangers and ran the hoys [*sic*]
          in blue.

17.   Jonis borrowed of Sam's money and didn't want to pay
        The only way he saw to win was to give poor Sam away
18.   He turned traitor to his comrades they were caught one
          early morn
        Oh what a scorching Jonis will get whem Gabriel blows his
          horn.

19.   Sam met his fate in Round Rock July the twenty-first
        They pierced poor Sam with rifle balls and emptied out his
          purse
20.   So Sam is a corpse in Round Rock, Jonis is under the clay[12]
        And Joe Jackson in the bushes trying to get away.

X–B.   Thorp (1921) pages 135–38

(The first twelve stanzas of the 1908 text were used, followed by:)

13.   Sam and another companion, called Arkansas for short,
        Was shot by a Texas Ranger by the name of Thomas Floyd;
14.   Oh, Tom is a big six-footer and thinks he's mighty fly,
        But I can tell you his racket,—he's a deadbeat on the sly.

15.   Jim Murphy was arrested and then released on bail;
        He jumped his bond at Tyler and then took the train for
          Terrell;
16.   But Mayor Jones had posted Jim and that was all a stall,
        'T was only a plan to capture Sam before the coming fall.

(Here occur stanzas 19 and 20 of the 1908 text.)

17.   Jim had borrowed Sam's good gold and didn't want to pay,
        The only shot he saw was to give poor Sam away.
18.1   He sold out Sam and Barnes and left their friends to
          mourn,—
        Oh, what a scorching Jim will get when Gabriel blows his
          horn.

---

[12] Some texts read: "Oh Sam is a corpse and Piper's in the Quay," or "Poor Sam a corpse now lies, they pitched him in the clay."

18.2   And so he sold out Sam and Barnes and left their friends to
         mourn,—
         Oh, what a scorching Jim will get when Gabriel blows his
         horn.

21.   Perhaps he's got to heaven, there's none of us can say,
         But if I am right in my surmise he's gone the other way.

X–Composite text

15.1   They were carried to the city
             And there locked up in jail
         With all their gold and silver
             They couldn't get out on bail.

16.1   Jim had used Sam's money
             And didn't want to pay
         He thought his only chance
             Was to give poor Sam away.

17.   But the man that plays the traitor
             Will feel it by and by
         His death was so uncommon
             'Twas poison in the eye.

19.1   In an unmarked shallow grave
             They laid him down to rest
         His saddle for a pillow
             And his gun across his breast.

20.1   Now Sam is a decaying corpse
             Down on the Round Rock's clay
         And Jack was on the broder [sic]
             Trying to get away.

20.2   Bass is in his coffin
             And six feet under clay
         A few are in the bushes
             A-trying to get away.

20.21   Now Sam lies at his trifles,
             His trifles in the clay
         While Jackson in the bushes
             Trying to get away.

20.22   It was on a Sunday morning
          They were hanged at break of day
          And that was the end of young Sam Bass—
          There's nothing more to say!

X–C.   THORP, *Banjo,* p. 198.

Sam used to deal in race - stock, ___ one
called the Den - ton mare; ___ He matched her in scrub
rac - es ___ and took her to the fair. ___ Sam
used to coin the mon - ey, ___ and
spent it just as free; ___ He al - ways drank good
whis - key where ___ ev - er he might be.

BIBLIOGRAPHY

Significant texts:

1906   Belden, p. 400, G. W. Bollinger, Missouri.
c. 1907   Stanley, p. 30 (FAC III 68).

Other printed texts:

"Allan's" Hillbilly, p. 20.
Allen, Cowboy Lore, pp. 112–14.
Barnes, Cowboy, p. 15.
Belden, pp. 399–400.
Big Round-Up, pp. 74–75.
Botkin, Sampler, pp. 549–60 = Larkin, pp. 162–64.
Branch, pp. 82, 139–44, 175 (FAC III 601).
Brown, Bass, pp. 141–42.
Burt, pp. 198–200.
Clark, Cowboy, pp. 32–33.
Colorado II, pp. 28–29.
Davis, Tip-Top, p. 35.
Dick, p. 93 (FAC III 271).
Finger, pp. 65–71.
Fox, Three.
Frey, pp. 52–53.
Friedman, pp. 375–77, 467.
Frontier Times, October 1924, p. 11; February 1926, p. 40.
Gard, p. 246.
Gordon, Adventure Magazine, December 20, 1924 (FAC III 352).
High, pp. 17–18.
Larkin, pp. 161–64
Lee, Cowboy, pp. 22–23.
Lindroth, pp. 40–41.
Lomax (1910), pp. 149–53; (1938) pp. 150–52; American, pp. 126–28;
    Best Loved, pp. 298–99; USA, pp. 298–99.
Lone Ranger, p. 46.
Luther, p. 204.
McIntosh, pp. 6–7.
Moore, pp. 343–45.
Nebraska, No. 11, pp. 6–7.
Owens, pp. 122–24.
Parker, p. 4 (FAC III 370).
PFLST III, pp. 226–30.
Pound, American, pp. 149–52 = Lomax (1938) pp. 150–52.
Randolph II, pp. 70–72.
Ridings, pp. 293, 338–40 (FAC III 71, 72).
Roaming Cowboy, p. 45.

Rogers' Favorite, p. 34.
Sandburg, pp. 422–24.
Shay, *Pious*, pp. 27–29.
Sherwin, *Bad Man*, pp. 36–37 (FAC III 476).
Sing 'em Cowboy, pp. 85–86.
Siringo, *Song*, pp. 16–18.
Thorp (1921) pp. 135–38.
Treasure Chest, pp. 32–33.
White and Shakley, pp. 22–23.

Commercial recordings:

Carl Sandburg: Decca A-356.
Harry McClintock: Victor 21420 (FAC III 1052).
Marc Williams: Brunswick 304.
Paul Clayton: WFM 12″.

Manuscripts and field recordings:

Dorson. *Michigan:* Mrs. Homer Andrews, 1950 (FAC II 147).
Gordon 120, 180, 312.
IU: AFPM 359.10, Gaspare Balvor (FAC III 986).
Larson. *Idaho* (FAC II 15).
LC. Misc. texts: Phoebe Blood.
Lomax. *Oklahoma* or *Texas:* LC cylinder 51, William Davis, 1908–10. *Kentucky:* LC 1462A, 1937. *Missouri:* two texts, d. 5654, Elwood Adams, A. N. Belden (JL 272). *Nebraska:* d. 5654, Goldie Fowler (JL 272). *Texas:* d. 5654, Ola Cunningham, 1910 (JL 272); LC 2637A1, 3806A1, 3808A1, 1939; LC 5643B1, Al Brite, 1941; d. 5638, Roy Bedishek; three texts, d. 5654, Bud Montgomery, H. J. Labouve, J. P. Arnold (JL 272); d. 5653, H. B. Labouve (JL 184); d. 5656, J. P. Arnold (JL 333). Unknown: three texts, d. 5638, H. L. Perry, Alice Lomax, no source; d. 5652; two texts, d. 5656.
PNFQ 417.
Randolph. *Arkansas:* LC 5340A2, W. Bishop, 1941.
Robb. *New Mexico:* No. 967, D. Price, 1952 (FAC I 197).
Robertson. *Missouri:* LC 3222B1, 1937.
Sackett. *Kansas:* Mary Ellen Muller, 1958 (FAC I 70).
Todd-Sonkin. *California:* LC 5115B–3, Bill Jackson, 1941.
WPA. *Arkansas:* LC W 12289, 1936–37 (FAC II 57). *Missouri:* LC W7362, 1938–39 (FAC II 72).

Discussion, "Sam Bass" (the song):

Angell, pp. 16–26.
Barrett, Chapter 7.
Belden, p. 399.
Dobie, J. Frank, note in his personal copy of Lomax, *Cowboy* (FAC II 750).
Gard, pp. 245–46 = Siringo, *Riata,* p. 101.
Gordon 312, 536, 934
Haley, pp. 198–204 (FAC III 156).
Hinkle, p. 19.
Laws, pp. 21, 57, 71, 172.
Literary Digest, February 21, 1914 (FAC III 464).
Lomax, *Ballad,* p. 56; *Best Loved,* pp. 284–85; *USA,* pp. 284–85; d. 5559,
    correspondence with William A. Dunn, 1913 (FAC II 751); in letter to
    Carnegie Foundation, 1908; letter from Oscar Fox giving date of their joint
    publication of this song as 1928 (JL 122).
Owens, p. 122.
Price, p. 93.
Randolph II, p. 69.
Ridings, p. 340, n. 3 (FAC III 72).
Rush, p. 131 (FAC III 599).
Siringo, *Riata,* p. 101.
Thorp (1921) pp 135–39; *Banjo,* pp. 197–98 (*supra* p. 17).
Thorp and Clark, pp. 27–28, 138–39.

Discussion, Sam Bass's life:

Breihan, p. 159.
Dobie, *Tales,* pp. 78–90.
Gard, *Law,* pp. 275–78.
Gillett, *Rangers,* p. 181.
Gordon 536.
Randolph II, p. 69.
Thorp and Clark, pp. 138–39.
Webb, *Sam Bass; Texas* XVII, pp. 371–91.

XI

Bucking Broncho

*I*F VARIATION IN CONTENT AND MELODY is a mark
of folk song, then "The Bucking Broncho" competes for highest honors
in the cowboy vein. There is a text for every taste—from those "that
would have burned the reader's eyeballs if printed" (to use Jack Thorp's
words),[1] to the circumspect but provocative ten stanzas that he gives in
his 1908 edition. Warned as we are in Thorp's 1921 edition that we are
dealing with a text willfully bowdlerized by himself,[2] it is not too hard
to re-create the symbols of prurience merely by forcing the meaning of
certain key words to some of their most elemental metaphoric possibil-
ities: riding, bucking, and bucking broncos, the gift of a ring, or of a
young maiden's heart, rawhide, gun, and so on. The remarkable thing
about Thorp's text, of course, is that the song, *sans* metaphor, gives an
enchanting image of the cowboy hero through the eyes of any and every
girl caught up with a strong masculine image: his pride, his energy, his
candid sensuality, his dash, daring, and swagger. Like "The Chisholm
Trail," the song has such a simple rhythmic pattern that the improvisa-
tion of couplets on prurient or romantic themes is not beyond the skill
of any cowboy poet.

John Lomax did much to popularize the song, though his text[3]

---

[1] Thorp and Clark, pp. 41–42.
[2] Thorp (1921) p. 14.
[3] Lomax (1916) pp. 367–68.

seems to be little more than a clumsy insertion in Thorp's text of two vulgar stanzas probably borrowed from White,[4] one of which introduces an image of male impotence not in keeping with the finished product, as Thorp wanted it. From the many recent texts and field recordings that we have examined, the song regrettably persists more often than not with these stanzas included.

But "The Bucking Broncho" has other faces in the popular tradition of the West: the rollicking slap-dazzle of a Katie Lee's "Johnny Ringo";[5] the genuine masculine slant of the remarkable text which Dobie got from James Hatch;[6] unabashedly vulgar texts, which still are heard from Idaho sheep camps all the way to Ivy League smokers, or the traveled cowboy Don Juan of the *Hobo News Song Book*. The song appears under multiple titles: "My Love (Lover, True Love, Sweetheart) Is a Cowboy"; "Cowboy's (White) Hat"; "The Bronco Buster"; "Johnny Ringo."

Assertions of authorship are multiple, though we venture that authors of the most basic texts haven't pushed their claims. Thorp ascribes it to the notorious Belle Starr and dates it 1878.[7] Dobie defends the claim of James Hatch and Billy Davis, 1882, for one of his texts,[8] and Charlie Johnson of Charco, Texas, for another.[9] Hull rallies a song published in 1855 as a possible ultimate progenitor,[10] if ultimate progenitors there are for the stuff of which myth and prurience are made.

Two texts of "The Cowboy with the White Hat" differ sufficiently to merit publication. Both are direct parodies of "The Bucking Bronco." The woman who supplied a version to a WPA field worker says it was sung around Roswell and Three Rivers, New Mexico, in the 1890's.[11]

There are several melodies for "The Bucking Bronco," although common elements prevail. The music typically reveals tendencies that support the texts they accompany. Whatever the melodic direction or interval relationship, there is a frequent and consistent return on the strong beats of the measure to the same note. Such a melodic structure could easily suggest the rhythmic, stiff-legged bucking of a bronco.

[4] White, *Arizona*, pp. 321, 322, 325 (FAC III 592).
[5] See bibliography, p. 134.
[6] Text C.
[7] Thorp (1921) p. 14.
[8] Dobie, *More Ballads*, pp. 170–72. (FAC III 12).
[9] *Ibid.*
[10] Text G.
[11] WPA, LC, Mrs. J. S. Watson, New Mexico, 1937 (FAC II 73).

Dobie's tune[12] is very significant, though not conforming to the statement above. Also important are the Hull[13] and Larkin[14] texts, the latter being the best setting of the most usual melody.

Three of the field recordings have outstanding characteristics. Kathy Dagel's rendition[15] has a melodic line similar to Larkin's except that at the close of each phrase it falls beautifully into a minor key; it is very much like Randolph's melody.[16] The song as sung in two different manners by Gaspare Balvor is noteworthy, but we have been unable to trace the source of this recording and hence to get permission for its use.[17] Katie Lee's "Johnny Ringo," though based upon 'The Bucking Bronco,' comes near being a new song.[18]

XI–A.   THORP (1908) pages 26–27

1.   My love is a rider, wild bronchos he breaks
       Though he's promised to quit it, just for my sake
2.   He ties up one foot,[19] the saddle puts on
       With a swing and a jump he is mounted and gone.

3.   The first time I met him 'twas early one spring
       Riding a broncho a high headed thing
4.   He tipped me a wink as he gaily did go
       For he wished me to look at his bucking broncho.

5.   The next time I saw him, 'twas late in the fall
       Swinging the girls at Tomlinson's ball
6.   He laughed and he talked, as we danced to and fro
       Promised never to ride on another broncho.

7.   He made me some presents, among them a ring
       The return that I made him was a far better thing

---

[12] Text B.
[13] Text G.
[14] Text H.
[15] Text I.
[16] Randolph II, p. 229.
[17] IU–AFPM 359.7.
[18] See bibliography, p. 134.
[19] Allusion to practice of tying up one leg of an unbroken horse to control him while being saddled and while the bronc buster gets his stance. The prurient overtone should be obvious.

8.   'Twas a young maiden's heart, I'd have you all know
            He'd won it by riding his bucking broncho.[20]

1.11   Now all you young maidens, where'er you reside
            Beware of the cow-boy who swings the rawhide
2.3   He'll court you and pet you and leave you and go
            In the spring up the trail on his bucking broncho.[21]

---

[20] Because they have become standard, despite their vulgarity, we give here four stanzas from Lomax (1910) p. 251, and (1916) p. 367. Reproduced with permission of Alan Lomax.

9.   My love has a gun, and that gun he can use,
            But he's quit his gun fighting as well as his booze;
11.   And he's sold him his saddle, his spurs, and his rope,
            And there's no more cow punching, and that's what I hope.

9.1   My love has a gun that has gone to the bad,
            Which makes poor old Jimmy feel pretty damn sad;
10.   For the gun it shoots high and the gun it shoots low,
            And it wobbles about like a bucking broncho.

[21] We give here some stanzas from an anonymous singer who learned the song "from a man I herded sheep and cattle for in Idaho in about 1955." It is unabashedly vulgar. The lady gave her "maidenhead," not her heart. The last six stanzas are substantially new. The melodic line is usual.

12.   'Twas near the arroya [sic] he first laid me down
            He was dressed for the round-up, and I wore a gown
13.   And he wiped off his chaps so the stain wouldn't show
            And he turned and rode off on his bucking broncho.

9.2   My love had a gun that was dirty and long
            But he wore it to visit the lady gone wrong
10.1   Though once it was strong and it shot straight and true
            Now it wobbles and buckles and it's red, white and blue.

1.11   Young maidens, take warning, where'er you reside
            Beware of a cowboy who swings the rawhide
2.3   He'll love you, he'll lay you, then one day he'll go
            In the spring up the trail on his bucking bronco.

Also, from the William L. Alderson papers in the University of Oregon Library (FAC II 736), we have this handwritten postscript stanza dated 1945:

            Lie still ye young bastard
            Don't bother me so
            Your father's off bucking
            Another bronco.

XI–B.   "The Cowboy's Hat, or The Bucking Broncho"
         Dobie, *More Ballads*, pages 170–72. Gives text and tune for four
         stanzas said to have been composed by Charlie Johnson (see *supra*,
         p. 122). Their rough form suggests the kind of materials Thorp used
         to create the excellent text of his 1908 edition. Reproduced with
         permission of the Texas Folklore Society.

1.3   My love is a vaquero,
             He rides on the Platte,
         Has a sunburnt moustache
             And a broad-brimmed hat.

2.5   He will treat you so clever
             With honest respect,
         That you never will regret
             Meeting his broad-brimmed hat.

3.   The last time I saw him
             It was early in spring;
         He was riding a bronco,
             A high-headed thing.

1.31   Now, all you gay ladies,
             Wherever you are at,
         Beware of the cowboy
             With a broad-brimmed hat.

XI–B.   Music

My love is a va-que-ro, He rides on the
Platte, Has a sun-burnt mus-tache And a broad-brimmed hat.

XI–C.   "The Bucking Bronco"
         James Hatch text from Dobie, *More Ballads,* pages 170–72.
         Reproduced with permission of the Texas Folklore Society.

1.13   Beware, all fair maidens
             Who live on the Platte,
         Beware of the cowboy
             Who wears the white hat.

2.31   He will toss you a kiss,
             Then away he will go,
         Recrossing the plains
             On his bucking bronco.

14.   He has a sweet heart in Texas,
             Depend upon that,
         Who worked the bright star[22]
             For the cowboy's big hat.

15.   She awaits his coming
             All anxious to know
         Just how he has dared
             With his bucking bronco.

16.   He holds off the marshal
             While having his fun.
         If crowded too closely
             He swaps ends with his gun.

2.32   Swinging into his saddle,
             Away he will go
         While hanging big spurs
             Into his bucking bronco.

17.   The cowboy is generous,
             His courage oft tried;
         A path seeming dangerous
             He surely will ride.

----

[22] An embroidered star often ornamented hat, boots, gauntlets, saddle, and other accoutrements of the "Lone Star" cowboys. A favorite western quilt pattern is known as the "Texas" or "Lone" Star.

18.   But he squanders his money
            Wherever he may go,
        While he shoots up a town
            On his bucking bronco.

19.   The bronco's his treasure
            In which he takes pride.
        That range has no limit
            O'er which he will ride.

20.   Most honest and truthful,
            To friend or to foe,
        Bold knight of the plains
            On his bucking bronco.

XI–D.   "BUCKING BRONCO"
        Lomax d. 5620, from "a cowboy in Cheyenne" (JL 19).

1.1   My love is a cowboy, wild horses he rides
        Away down in Texas my lover resides
3.   The first time I saw him, 'twas early in spring
        A-ridin' a bronco, a high-headed thing.

5.   The next time I saw him 'twas late in the fall
        Swinging the pretty girls at Flannigan's ball
6.1   'Twas there while dancing at night to and fro
        He wanted to ride on my bucking bronco.

7.   He gave me some presents, among them a ring
        I gave him a present, a far better thing
8.1   This present I gave him I want you to know
        'Twas the pride of all maidens, my bucking bronco.

1.11   Now come all ye fair maidens where'er you reside
        Beware of the guy that throws the rawhide
2.1   He will rope you and throw you and when you're fast tied
        Down on your bare belly, Lord God how he'll ride!

2.2   He'll not ride you bare and he'll not ride you slow
        But he'll spur a big hole in your bucking bronco.

XI–E.   "BEWARE OF A COWBOY WHO WEARS A WHITE HAT"
         Hobo News, folio 28.

    1.31   Come all you fair ladies,
            Where'er you are at,
       Beware of a cowboy
            Who wears a white hat.

    2.4   Today he may greet you;
            Tomorrow he may be
       In Cheyenne or Denver
            Like an Irishman's flea.

    2.33   With his false fickle heart
            And his flattering tongue
       He courts all the ladies,
            The old and the young.

    2.34   He'll tell you that he loves you,
            But he's only in fun.
       Beware of the cowboy
            And his flattering tongue.

    2.41   On a big bucking broncho
            The cowboy you'll see,
       And then up in Cheyenne
            This cowboy will be.

    2.43   In Chicago's art gallery
            You'll find him enthroned;
       Then back on the plains,
            The white hat he has donned.

    21.   With his great big sombrero
            And chaparajos to match,
       The ladies all think;
            "Now we'll have a great catch."

    22.   But I dare you to try it!
            He'll not stand for that;
       Beware of a cowboy
            Who wears a white hat!

XI–F.   "The Cowboy with the White Hat"
          WPA, LC, Mrs. J. S. Watson, New Mexico, 1937 (FAC II 73).

1.31	All ye young ladies wherever your at
	Beware of the cowboy that wears a White Hat,
2.4	For today he will woo you and tomorrow will be
	In Cheyenne or Denver like an Irishman's flea,[23]
2.42	It's first in your parlor this young man will be
	And then in Cheyenne this young dandy you'll see,
2.431	In Chicago's Art Gallery you'll find him in scorn,
	But out on the plains his White Hat he adorns,
23.	Now a Lion White Hat was not made to be beat,
	But a Statson white hat is this cowboy's conceit
24.	As he sits in his saddle with his most princely air
	You'd think his White Hat a most gorgeous affair;
21.	With his great big sombrero with leggin's to match
	Now all the young ladies think, "Here's a great catch,"
22.1	But he dares you to try it
	You ne'er can do that;
	He's surely no dude, tho' he wears a White Hat.
1.32	He reaches heart fate and for future cares not
	So beware of the rider that wears a white hat.

XI–G.   "My Lover's a Rider"
          Hull, pages 56–57. ". . . the following song, which my mother,
          Mrs. Eliza Sinclair Hull, brought West with her from Ohio, in
          1866."* Reproduced with permission of Kansas State Historical
          Society.

---

[23] This Irishman's flea has been too elusive for the editors. If a reader should find it we should appreciate being informed. Is the reference to a con game, a vaudeville act, a practical joke, or some specimen of popular literature?

* Note 29, p. 56: ". . . 'My Lover's a Rider' appeared in William B. Bradbury's *New York Glee and Chorus Book*, 1855. Since this was one of the most popular singing school books during the 1860's, it might well have been seen by Belle Starr, or the resemblance between the two songs may be accidental. The author's name is not given, but it was translated by C. M. Cady. (The original language is not mentioned, but the song has all the earmarks of the "tra-la-la" Swiss songs of which William Bradbury was so fond.)"

1.2   My lover's a rider, a rider so fine;
        The steed is his sov'reign; the rider is mine.
        La-la-la-la-la-la-la-la-la-la,
        La-la-la-la-la-la-la-la-la-la.

25.   Blue eyes and brown hair, and right noble in mien;
        Oh, charming and fair is my lover, I ween.

26.   My heart is a castle well-bolted and grim;
        My love is the pass-key; it opens to him.

27.   My lover's away; he is over the sea;
        I need not be told he is thinking of me.

28.   If you have a lover so noble and true;
        I'll finish my song and then listen to you.

XI–G. Music

XI–H.   "My Love Is a Rider"
Larkin, pages 46–47.
Reproduced with permission of Margaret Larkin and Oak Publications.

My love is a rid - er, wild hor - ses he

breaks, But he's prom - ised to give it up

just for my sake, One foot he ties

up and the sad - dle puts on, With a

leap and a jump, he is mount - ed and gone.

XI–I.   "BUCKING BRONCO"
Sung by Kathy Dagel, Kansas, 1959 (FAC I 509).

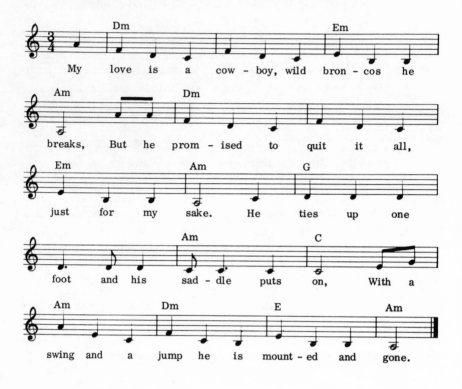

My love is a cow - boy, wild bron - cos he breaks, But he prom - ised to quit it all, just for my sake. He ties up one foot and his sad - dle puts on, With a swing and a jump he is mount - ed and gone.

BIBLIOGRAPHY

Printed texts:

Allen, *Cowboy Lore*, pp. 157–58.
Arkansas, pp. 29–30.
Barnes, *Cowboy*, pp. 15, 122.
Big Round-Up, pp. 89–90.
Blue Grass, pp. 32–33.
Buck Jones, p. 5.
Caldwell, pp. 45–46 (FAC III 270) = Dobie, *More Ballads*, pp. 170–72.
Clark, *Cowboy*, p. 7.
Cowboy Songs, p. 16.
Cowboy Tom, p. 33.
Davis, *Tip-Top*, p. 10.
Dobie, *More Ballads*, pp. 170–72 (FAC III 12).
Frey, pp. 82–83.
Hendren 542: unidentified-newspaper clipping.
Hobo News, fol. 28.
Larkin, pp. 46–47.
Lee, *Cowboy*, pp. 42–43.
Lomax (1916) pp. 367–68; (1938) pp. 267–68; *American*, pp. 417–18.
Lone Ranger, p. 33.
Luther, pp. 209–11.
Randolph II, pp. 229–30.
Roaming Cowboy, p. 38.
Rogers' Favorite, pp. 46–47.
Sing 'em Cowboy, pp. 62–63.
Sires, pp. 40–41.
Thorp (1921) pp. 14–15 = Dobie, *More Ballads*, pp. 170–72.
Treasure Chest, p. 22.
White, *Arizona*, pp. 321, 322, 325 (FAC III 592); *Rawhide*, pp. 175–76.

Commercial recordings:

Dick Deval: LC 20.
Girls of the Golden West: Bluebird 5752 (FAC III 990); Montgomery Ward 7204.
Jack Lee: Bluebird 5298-A; Sunrise 3379.

Manuscripts and field recordings:

Fife. *Kansas:* Kathy Dagel, 1959 (FAC I 509).
Halpert. *Texas:* 1934 (FAC II 469).
IU-AFPM 359.7. Unknown: Gaspare Balvor (FAC I 72).
Lomax. *Wyoming:* d. 5620, "Cowboy in Cheyenne" (JL 19). *Texas:* d. 5638
    (JL 83); d. 5653, Betty Filcher, 1931 (JL 227); d. 5654, W. H. Thomp-
    son, 1910 (JL 281); d. 5557, H. V. Benedict, 1907.
Meredith: *Wyoming:* Burton S. Hill, 1963 (FAC II 571).
PNFQ. *Idaho:* Lowell Miles (No. 38); *Oregon:* H. T. Beachler (No. 304).
    Washington: Jo Hoffman (No. 39). Unknown: No. 33.
UAFA. *Arizona:* Katie Lee (FAC I 73).
WPA. *Arkansas:* LC W354, 1936–37 (FAC II 47). *New Mexico:* LC, Mrs.
    J. S. Watson, 1937 (FAC II 73).

Discussion:

Barrett, Chapter 7.
Dobie, *More Ballads,* pp. 170–72 (FAC III 12).
Gard, *Law,* pp. 278–79.
Hull, pp. 56–57 = Larkin, pp. 45–47.
Idaho Farmer, January 29, 1942 (FAC III 824).
Larkin, pp. 45–47.
Laws, p. 140.
Randolph II, p. 228.
Thorp (1921) p. 14; *Banjo,* p. 200. (*supra,* p. 21).
Thorp and Clark, pp. 34–36, 42.
UAFA, Katie Lee (FAC I 73).
Wilgus, pp. 160, 252, 274.

XII

Educated Feller

THAT "EDUCATED FELLER" is the stuff of which
legend is made is witnessed by the following story of its origin given in
the words of a puncher who sang it for the University of Arizona Folklore Archives:

> A rancher who was pretty well fixed sent his boy back
> east to college. When he came back home, to get to the
> ranch he had to get off the train at a little stop-over near
> the Mexican side where he caught a ride with a freighter.
> When he came riding through a cow-camp on this freight
> wagon in his fancy city clothes they just thought him as
> green as could be and got to making fun of him. Well, he
> kinda played along with them, saying, "This wagon's awful
> slow. I'd sure like to get along faster," and so on, so at last
> they offered him a horse.
> "Well," he said, "I don't have no saddle."
> "We'll lend you a saddle."
> "Well, a feller couldn't make out without boots, could
> he?" So they got him a pair of boots.
> "Don't you have to have spurs to ride a horse?" he
> asked.
> "I guess maybe you do!" they said, and gave him
> some spurs.

135

Well, they got him all fixed up and went down there and roped out this old outlaw horse that had been throwing everybody off. Of course this kid was really a bronc rider. Well, he jist gathered his legs around that horse and lets him know somebody's a riding him. And after he rode him he just bucked out across the country, circled him around, came a running back around—even borrows a hat off somebody. Then he rides right down through the middle of the camp and he says, "Thanks for the horse, boys!"[1]

A variant of the tale says it was Con Price, a Montana cowboy who "of late years had lived in California." He'd been back east with a shipment of cattle and, having had some of his clothes stolen, on his return he arrived in the cow-camp "with a hard-boiled hat on and was looking for a job." So, he fooled all the boys of the Circle-S outfit of New Mexico. Con is supposed to have been a friend of the artist Charlie Russell and "an all around bronc twister."[2]

Stories (and ballads) of the trickster tricked are as old as anecdote itself. "Educated Feller" develops an instance thereof in flamboyant proportions: the presumptive victim is an outsider; he senses hostility from the very start and capitalizes thereon by a bombastic show of naïveté and arrogance; step by step he leads the tricksters to bait the trap that he is only too ready to spring; then in a dramatic demonstration of skill and showmanship he proves that "he was a thoroughbred and not a gent from town."

Thorp's 1908 text is the first printing we have found. If he first heard it (as he says in his 1921 edition)[3] in 1890, then the song was significantly enriched and expanded during and after the Spanish American War. Following the text from the 1908 edition we shall give the stanzas added in his 1921 edition. Significant stanzas and/or variants that are in neither of the Thorp texts will also be given.

"Bow-Legged Ike" may well have been the "Educated Feller's" sire. Printed in 1899, in a book having the significant title *Cattle Ranch to*

---

[1] Mr. Lockett, of Williams, Arizona (FAC I 143).
[2] Lee, *Cowboy*, p. 33.
[3] Thorp (1921) p. 171.

College,[4] the song was first heard in Montana about 1875 from a horse wrangler named Curran.

The description of Curran re-inforces the myth of the trickster tricked: ". . . of medium height, stoop-shouldered, and rather bow-legged from long contact with a horse's round body. He was awkward and stiff when afoot, an appearance accentuated by the suit of canvas and leather that he wore. In the saddle he was another being, graceful, supple, strong —seemingly a part of the beast he rode. His skin was tanned and seamed by long years of exposure to the sun. He might be the very hero himself to the song."[5]

Among the "Educated Feller's" progeny we cite at least three parodies: "A Tenderfoot and the Bronco,"[6] "Preacher Dunn, The Outlaw,"[7] and the "Skewbald Black."[8]

"Educated Feller" is known under several titles: "The Zebra Dunn," "The Z-Bar Dun," "The Tenderfoot," "The Cowboy Victimized," "The Stranger and That Dun Horse." Authorship is uncertain. J. Frank Dobie had written the following in his personal copy of Lomax's *Cowboy Songs*: "John Custer, trail driver, told me that while he was on the Z-Bar-L ranch north of Big Spring in 80's a 'slim fellow wearing a little hat' and not looking anything like a cowboy came into camp, asked for a job, and was given an outlaw to ride—one of the Z-L horses. 'Rode him to a fare-you-well.' Then the song started."[9]

Lomax listed it in a letter to the Carnegie Corporation in 1908.[10] Elsewhere he says: "Said to be composed by Negro Jake working for George W. Evans and John Z. Means, Valentine, Texas,"[11] Dane Coolidge ascribes it to Sam Roberts.[12]

Among the available printed sources there is little melodic variation, although in meter there are substantial differences. In a song such as this,

---

[4] Doubleday, *Cattle*, pp. 227–28.
[5] *Ibid*; Dobie, *Ballads*, pp. 163–64.
[6] Ellard, *Ranch*, pp. 42–44 (FAC III 115).
[7] Lee, *Cowboy*, pp. 44–45; *West*, pp. 81–83. PNFQ 368.
[8] Hendren 229. Lee, *Cowboy*, p. 71. Lomax (1911) p. 243; (1938) pp. 14–15; d. 5654, c. 1910 (JL 299); d. 5656, D. L. Browning (JL 332).
[9] FAC II 752.
[10] Lomax papers, University of Texas.
[11] Lomax d. 5662 (FAC II 753). See also Laws, p. 140, and Randolph II, p. 244.
[12] Coolidge, *Cowboy*, pp. 509–10 (FAC III 462).

a narrative in which a good-natured joke backfires upon those plotting the downfall of the "dude," the outcome is a happy one for all. The typical melodic treatment carries within its outline the suggestion of a faint chuckle, a suitable commentary on the humorous set of circumstances. This melodic insinuation is best furthered by the lilt of a $\frac{6}{8}$ rhythm, rather than the choppier feeling of dotted 8th notes within a $\frac{4}{4}$ time. Note the even flow of $\frac{6}{8}$ ♩ ♪ ♩ ♪ | ♩. ♩ ♪ | as opposed to

the more rigid $\frac{4}{4}$ ♫ ♫ ♩ ♫.

These qualities are all encountered in the singing of Ray Reed of Albuquerque. It has enough melodic and rhythmic similarities to nearly all the printed versions to represent them adequately.

Also from the J. D. Robb Collection comes a rather unusual version, sung by True Benton of Taos, New Mexico. It is sung without accompaniment and lacks a uniform rhythmic structure. The unique aspect of this version is the singer's constant return to the tonic of the key—the pattern being a repeated leap from this note and then a return.

XII–A.   THORP (1908) pages 27–29

1.	We were camped upon the plains near the Cimarron
	When along came a stranger and stopped to argue some
7.	He was a well educated feller his talk just come in herds
	And astonished all the punchers with his jaw breaking words.
8.	He had a well worn saddle and we thought it kind'er strange
	That he didn't know much about working on the range
9.	He'd been at work he said, up near the Santa Fe
	And was cutting cross country to strike the 7 D.
9.1	Had to quit an outfit up near Santa Fe
	Had some trouble with the boss, just what he didn't say
9.3	Said his horse was 'bout give out would like to get another
	If the punchers wouldn't mind and it wasn't too much bother.
11.	Yes we'll give you a horse, he's just as sound as a bun
	They quickly grabbed a lariat and roped the Zebra Dun.

12.   Turned him over to the stranger
              Then they waited to see the fun.

14.   Old Dunny stands right still not seeming to know
              Until the strangers' ready and a fixing up to go
15.   When he goes into the saddle old Dunny leaves the earth
              He travels right straight up for all he was worth.

18.   But he sits up in his saddle just pullin his mustach
              Just like some summer boarder a waitin for his hash
16.   Old Dunny pitched and bauled and had wall eyed fits
              His hind feet perpendicular his front ones in his bits.

18.2   With one foot in the stirupp, he just thought it fun
              The other leg around the saddle horn the way he rode old
              Dun.
18.3   He spurred him in the shoulder and hit him as he whirled
              Just to show these flunky punchers the best rider in the
              world.

21/22   The boss says to him, you needn't go on
              If you can use the rope like you rode old Dun.
22.1   You've a job with me if you want to come
              You're the man I've been looking for since the year one.

24.   I can sling the rope, an' I'm not very slow
              I can catch nine times out of ten for any kind of dough
28.   Now there's one thing and a sure thing I've learned since I
              was born
              That all these educated fellows are not green horns.

XII–B.   ADDITIONAL STANZAS FROM THORP (1921) pages 171–74

2.   He looked so very foolish that we began to look around,
              We thought he was a greenhorn that had just 'scaped from
              town.

3.   We asked if he had been to breakfast; he hadn't had a smear;
              So we opened up the chuck-box and bade him have his share.

4.   He took a cup of coffee and some biscuits and some beans,
And then began to talk and tell about foreign kings and
queens,—

5.   About the Spanish War and fighting on the seas
With guns as big as steers and ramrods big as trees,—
6.   And about old Paul Jones, a mean-fighting son of a gun,
Who was the grittiest cuss that ever pulled a gun.

10.   He just kept on talking till he made the boys all sick,
And they began to look around just how to play a trick.

11.1   This tickled all the boys to death; they laughed 'way down
in their sleeves,—
"We will lend you a horse just as fresh and fat as you
please."

13.   Old Dunny was a rocky outlaw that had grown so awful wild
That he could paw the white out of the moon every jump
for a mile.

17.   We could see the tops of the mountains under Dunny every
jump,
But the stranger he was growed there just like the camel's
hump;

20.   When the stranger ·had dismounted once more upon the
ground,
We knew he was a thoroughbred and not a gent from town;

21.   The boss, who was standing round watching of the show,
Walked right up to the stranger and told him he needn't go,—
22.   "If you can use the lasso like you rode old Zebra Dun,
You are the man I've been looking for ever since the year
one."

XII–OTHER SIGNIFICANT STANZAS

1.1   Down on the foot of the plains, down on the Cimarron,
A boy came riding by and stopped to argue some.

1.2   We were settled round the fire one solemn afternoon
         When up there rides a stranger with a face all in gloom.

1.3   We were camped out on the Balley on the eighteenth day
              of June
         When a dudish looking feller came a-riding in at noon.

3.1   We asked him if he'd had his breakfast, he hadn't had a sniff
         So we up and opened up the chuck-box and bid him help
              himself.

6.1   He spoke of old Dewey down on the Santa Fe
         Where gun barrels are big as wagon wheels and ramrods
              big as trees.

8.1   When he had finished eating and put his plate away
         He rolled a cigarette and asked the time of day.

8.11   After he had finished eating he rolled a cigaret
         The very first puff started him you bet.

4.1/8   He talked about the weather, the elections and such things
         But didn't seem to know much about the workings on the
              range.

9.2   He didn't say how come it, some trouble with the boss
         But said he'd like to borrow a nice fat saddle horse.

11.2   This tickled all the punchers clear down to their boots
         And Shorty grabbed a lasso and began to make a loop.

11.11   The boss says, "You can have a horse as fresh as you please"
         This tickled the boys 'way down deep in their sleeves.

12.1   Shorty grabbed a lariat and roped the Zebra Dunn
         And turned him over to the stranger and waited for the fun.

16.   A-pitching and a squealing, a having wall-eyed fits
         His hind feet perpendicular, his front ones in the bits.

16.1   When his hind feet were perpendicular and fore ones on the bits
He spurred him on the shoulders till old Dunny had wall-eyed fits.

14.1/16 The saddle went upon him, it was screwed down tight
The front feet in the stirrups and his hind ones in the bits.

16.2   Old Dunny booed and bawled just like a jersey calf
While the stranger began to quirt his flanks and we began to laugh.

18.1/16 The stranger turned in the saddle and rolled a cigarette
His hind feet in the stirrups and his front ones in the bit.

18.31   He sat upon him and spurred him as he whirled
Says: "I'm educated cowboy, a wolf of the world."

19.   Old Dun he throwed his head up and concluded to let him ride
I don't know why he done it for I knowed he'd rather died.

21.1   The Bossman then said, "Stranger, do you want a job?"
He asked him what his name was and he said his name was Bob.

21.2   The Bossman said, "Stranger, you had better stay,
Unsaddle that Dun horse and start right in today."

23.   He said "You need not leave the camp unless you want to go
For I will give you a good long job and pay you with my dough.

24.1   Oh, he could twirl the lariat and he didn't do it slow
He could catch them four feet nine out of ten for any kind of dough.

25.   And when the herd stampeded he was always on the spot
And set them to milling like the stirrings of a pot.

26.   The stranger unsaddled old Dun and led him to the pen
He still was sorter rocky so he give him the rope's end.

27. He started in a-working and now he is the boss
  That's the reward the stranger got for riding that old Dunn
   horse.

28.1 And there is one thing (and a sure thing too) that we've
   learned out of school
  That all educated towns-men aren't damn fools.

28.2 And now my little lesson I will not soon forget
  Every man you meet with a white shirt on is not a greenhorn yet.

XII–C. "Bow-Legged Ike"
  Doubleday, *Cattle*, pages 227–28 = Dobie, *Ballads*, pages 163–64.

1. Bow-legged Ike on horseback was sent
  From some place, straight down to this broad continent.

2. His father could ride and his mother could, too,
  They straddled the whole way from Kalamazoo.

3. Born on the plains, when he first sniffed the air
  He cried for to mount on the spavined gray mare.

4. And when he got big and could hang to the horn
  'Twas the happiest day since the time he was born.

5. He'd stop his horse loping with one good, strong yank,
  He'd rake him on shoulder and rake him on flank.

6. He was only sixteen when he broke "Outlaw Nell,"
  The horse that had sent nigh a score men to—well!

7. He climbed to the saddle and there sat still,
  While she bucked him all day with no sign of a spill.

8. Five years later on a cayuse struck the trail
  Whose record made even old "punchers" turn pale.

9. He was really a terror; could dance on his ear,
  And sling a man farther than that stump—to here!

10.   A man heard of Ike; grinned and bet his whole pile
         His sorrel would shake him before one could smile.

11.   So the crowd they came round and they staked all they had.
         While Ike, sorter innocent, said: "Is he *bad?*"

12.   And durin' their laugh—for the sorrel, you see,
         Had eat up two ropes and was tryin' for me—

13.   Ike patted his neck—"Nice pony," says he,
         And was into the saddle as quick as a flea.

14.   That sorrel he jumped and he twisted and bucked,
         And the man laughed, expectin' that Ike would be chucked.

15.   But soon the cayuse was fair swimmin' in sweat
         While Ike, looking bored, rolled a neat cigarette.

16.   And then from range to range he hunted a cayuse
         That could even *in-ter-est* him, but it wasn't any use.

17.   So he got quite melancolic, wondering why such an earth,
         Where the horses "had no sperrits," should have given
         himself birth.

XII–D.   "ZEBRA DUN"
         Sung by Ray Reed, New Mexico, 1951 (FAC I 217).
         Reproduced with permission of the collector, Dean Emeritus John
         Donald Robb, University of New Mexico.

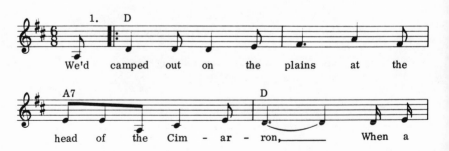

We'd camped out on the plains at the head of the Cim - ar - ron, When a

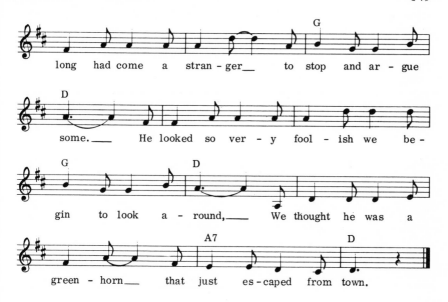

long had come a stran - ger___ to stop and ar - gue

some.___ He looked so ver - y fool - ish we be -

gin to look a - round,___ We thought he was a

green - horn___ that just es - caped from town.

BIBLIOGRAPHY

Significant texts:

1910   Lomax (1910) pp. 154–57.
1912   Coolidge, *Cowboy*, pp. 509–10 (FAC III 462).
1917   Gray, pp. 98–101 (FAC III 246).
1924   *Cattleman*, February 1924, p. 33 (FAC III 730).
  ?   Larkin, pp. 35–38.

  "Bow-Legged Ike"
  1899   Doubleday, *Cattle*, pp. 227–28 = Dobie, *Ballads*, pp. 163–64.
  1925   Gordon 376, Roland Guyer.

Other printed texts:

Allen, *Cowboy Lore*, pp. 159–61.
Big Slim, n. p.
Clark, *Cowboy*, pp. 68–69 = Lomax (1910) pp. 154–57.
Felton, p. 30.
Frey, pp. 62–63.
Friedman, pp. 427–29.

German, n.p.
Gray, pp. 98–101
Ken Maynard, pp. 28–30.
Kincaid No. 7, pp. 8–9; No. 8, pp. 52–53.
Landeck, p. 40.
Lee, *Cowboy,* pp. 32–33.
Loesser, p. 202.
Lomax (1938) pp. 78–81.
Lone Ranger, p. 44.
McConathy, pp. 82–83.
Patterson and Dexter, pp. 56–57.
Pound, *Western,* pp. 29–30.
Randolph II, pp. 244–45.
Rhinehart, p. 16.
Round-Up Rangers, pp. 56–57.
SFQ III (1939), pp. 29–30.
Sherwin and Klickman, pp. 54–56.
"*Tex,*" n.p.
Thorp (1921) pp. 171–74.
Treasure Chest, p. 45.
Utah Cowboy's, pp. 24–25.
Williams Favorite, pp. 26–27.

Commercial recordings:

Frank Luther Trio: Decca 1428
Jules Allen: Victor 40022, Montgomery Ward 4464 (FAC III 938).
Tex Fletcher: Decca 5302 (FAC III 937).

Manuscripts and field recordings:

Fife. *Maryland:* Frank Goodwyn, 1959 (FAC I 238).
Gordon 577. Unknown: W. E. Curtis.
Lomax. *Missouri:* d. 5662, Elwood Adams (JL 422). *Texas:* LC, Alex Moore,
   1919 (FAC II 573); LC 2616A1, 1939; LC 5675B2, 5677B, S. Matthews,
   1942. *Wyoming:* d. 5654, D. P. Lamereaux. Unknown: d. 5653; d. 5662,
   5654 (JL 296, 421); d. 5662, Mary Burt (JL 423); d. 5685, L. A. Lawhon
   (JL 471).
O'Bryant. *Arizona:* Al Bittick, 1958 (FAC I 90). *Arkansas:* Otis Byrd (FAC
   I 80).
PNFQ 536. Unknown.

Robb. *New Mexico:* Ray Reed, 1951, No. 763 (FAC I 217); True Benton, 1957, No. 1476 (FAC I 430); R. Newcomb, 1951, No. 678 (FAC I 218).
Todd-Sonkin. *California:* LC 4140A2, 1940.
UAFA. *Arizona:* Lockett, 1956 (FAC I 143); Ch. Shreeves, 1956, No. 122; Ellen S. Murphy (FAC II 425).

Discussion:

Barrett, Chapter 7.
Coolidge, *Cowboy,* pp. 509–10 (FAC III 462).
Craddock, p. 184.
Dobie, note in his personal copy of Lomax, *Cowboy Songs* (FAC II 752).
French, pp. 210–15.
Laws, p. 140.
Lee, *Cowboy,* p. 33.
Lomax, d. 5654, two items, one from D. P. Lamereaux (FAC II 754); d. 5662 (FAC II 753); listed in letter to Carnegie Foundation, 1908.
Randolph II, p. 244.
Thorp and Clark, pp. 31–33.

XIII

Cow Boy's Lament

IT WAS IN THE 1880's that a rough bunch of cow-
boys had taken their seats around a card table at Dodge City—possibly
in that very Tom Sherman's barroom touted as the setting for the shooting of the cowboy whose death gave rise to the most famous of all cowboy songs. Mysterious Dave was always a bit vague about how it came
about, but it seems he raised his eyes to look at his adversary across the
card table, only to receive on his forehead the glancing blow of a bullet
from a little .22 pistol. Before the badman could get in a second shot,
Mysterious Dave's own powerful persuader released a charge that drilled
the badman plum through, continued its deadly course on through the
potbellied stove, and entered the body of Miss Flora, the saloon keeper's
favorite hound.

Small differences of opinion like this being quite normal at Dodge
in those days, the card game was resumed and things were peaceful for a
spell—but not after someone noticed that Miss Flora was dead.

Now "Dog" Kelly, the saloon keeper, was a genuine dog lover, as
his nickname testifies. He owned about a hundred canine critters, all
trained variously to chase jack rabbits, antelope, coyotes, and sundry
other varmints that had no business roaming the prairie now that red-
blooded Yankee Americans had arrived on the scene. Naturally, Miss
Flora just happened to be the best in his whole durned pack!

Well, Kelly walked back, took a look at Miss Flora's carcass, took the Lord's and sundry other names in vain, and swore he'd bury Miss Flora with military honors. Moreover, he specified that if there was a single adult male in Dodge who failed to show up at the funeral, he would hunt him down with his trusty gun and give him free passage to the same place Miss Flora had just been sent.

So next day a funeral cortege was formed, headed by Dodge City's famous Cowboy Band,[1] spiked with fire-fighting vehicles, and a company of mounted police. Fearful that Dodge might otherwise be subjected to a whole epidemic of burials, the mayor had even declared a holiday. There being no hearse—burials in Dodge at that time not ordinarily being accompanied by such pomp and circumstance—they rigged up a dray, and then dolled up "Dog" Kelly's old white horse to follow the caisson, dead jack rabbits and coyotes tied across his saddle to remind the citizenry of Miss Flora's unparalleled accomplishments.

At the graveside on Boothill, the coroner, voice husky and eyes tearful, allowed it was fit and proper that a few words be said for the departed. A cow puncher twisted his sombrero nervously in his hands and said that Miss Flora could run down any jack rabbit on the plains. Another said there wasn't a coyote on the prairie she couldn't catch in half an hour. A third stepped forward, laid his right hand on his heart and tried to speak, but his words were silenced by sobs and tears.

Then the coroner requested the Lord's Prayer. While the casket was being lowered, the cowboys turned their backs to it. An old musket was planted as a headboard.

"Now, let's give her 'The Cowboy's Lament'," the coroner demanded. So in a grand finale of devotion Miss Flora was lowered to her last resting place as the whole male population of Dodge City sang:

> Once in the saddle I used to go dashing,
>   Once in the saddle I used to go gay.
> First took to drinking and then to card playing
>   Got shot in the neck and now here I lay.
>
> Beat the drum slowly, play the fife lowly,
>   Play the Dead March as you bear me along.

---

[1] Organized at Dodge City as the Stockman's Band in 1881; later, as the Cowboy Band, with a pair of horns from a Texas longhorn as an emblem, it became famous throughout the land. It may have made the first use of cowboy dress as a symbol: its members wore cowboy hats and bandannas.

Take me to Boothill and throw the dirt over me
I'm but a poor Cowboy, I know I done wrong.[2]

"Cow Boy's Lament" comes about as near to supplying the elements
of an epic of the American West as any other single song. It has been
sung throughout North America and in many parts of the remaining
English-speaking world. There are hundreds of texts, with variants so
numerous that no scholar will ever assemble and analyze them all. The
numbered stanzas that we offer as a composite text[3] have been selected
from several hundred possible choices. We do believe, however, that
they represent a great many of the elements commonly found in cowboy
treatments of this song.

A careful reading of these stanzas will reveal, we think, the qualities
that make of the "Cow Boy's Lament" a classic of its kind. The song
deals with the death of a sinner: sin, remorse, death—note these words
carefully for they are all of deep concern to man, and especially to the
kind of men who pioneered America. The cowboy, dying in a street or
on a barroom floor, captures the ear of a fellow cowboy to purge his soul
for the Last Ride. At this crucial moment he is concerned with human
beings most near and dear—wife or sweetheart, mother, sister, father,
brother—and not with their physical well being, but rather with remorse
for the anguish brought upon them by the cowboy's dishonorable life. At
the threshold of death, the cowboy also wants the death ritual that ties
man not so much to eternity and God but rather to mankind as he knows
it—hence the sixteen gamblers, the six pretty maidens, the thrown lasso,
the brandy sprinkled on his coffin, the whiskey to assuage the pall-
bearers' thirst, the dashing horse, even the fife and drum, which are like
mementos of the precowboy origins of our American culture. The cowboy also harbors an underlying Christian faith that forces him to admon-
ish his own kind into paths of righteousness. Yet this is secondary to his
deep surge towards oneness with men of his own breed. In this desire
the cowboy is rewarded, for, quite oblivious to the cowboy's "sinful" life,
his friends rally to his procession with love and affection, despite (or
should we say "because of"?) his self-assigned wrongdoings. Within this
broad frame, each of the scores of texts of "Cow Boy's Lament" makes
its own specific choices and embroiders its own details like the inter-
woven motifs of a Bach fugue or a patchwork quilt.

---

[2] Callison, pp. 155–58 (FAC III 315).
[3] *Infra.*

Several scholars have concerned themselves with the origins and dissemination of the "Cow Boy's Lament." It has been traced back to the early 1700's through a battery of songs popular in the United States, Canada, and Great Britain: "Saint James Infirmary," "The Bad Girl's Lament," "The Trooper (Soldier, Sailor, Young Man, Young Girl, etc.), Cut Down in His (Her) Prime," "The Whore's Lament," "The Unfortunate Rake," etc. Specific stanzas or lines have shown up in a host of similar songs: "The Dying Ranger," "The Kansas Line," "The Dying Cowboy," "Caris Viron," "The Dying Nun's (Girl's) Message," "Rosin the Beau." Its influences have been felt in a score of obvious, or not so obvious, parodies and analogues: "The Wild Lumberjack," "The Ballad of Bloody Thursday," "The Teacher's Lament," "Dugway Lament," "The Dying Lineman," "The Feathery Passage," "Git Along Little Dogies," "I Once Was a Carman," "Jack Combs' Murder," "The Ballad of Sherman Wu," "A Sun Valley Song (Dying Skier)," "The Streets of Hamtramck"—even a "Professor's Lament," especially designed as a kind of autosuggestion for ballad scholars who have belabored the poor dying cowboy too much and too often!

For his 1921 edition, Thorp abandoned the 1908 text for Lomax's longer and smoother synthetic text, which has had much more influence upon the twentieth century singing of the song than it deserves. The seven stanzas of 1908 have a stamp of authenticity and realism that Lomax's bowdlerization loses. Let us recall that our dying cowboy's literary progenitors, "The Unfortunate Rake" and "The Bad Girl's Lament," were grim songs about the ravages of venereal disease and the ills of indulgence in cards, whiskey, and women. It is true that in most of the cowboy forms of the song these unpalatable images are attenuated, even replaced in some texts, by a namby-pamby transcendentalism compatible with Victorian mores. Still, there ought to be a place left in the musical heritage of the frontier era for a few texts that come to grips with reality. Without vulgarity, Thorp's text does, nevertheless, remind us that men were men, that women can be treacherous, and that some of life's lessons can't be learned in school or church.

The problems of authorship in the case of "Cow Boy's Lament" are extremely complex. In its earliest forms the song almost stanza by stanza shows its dependency upon "The Unfortunate Rake." Not one but several attempts at parody seem to have taken place at different times and places based upon more than one of the pre-"Cow Boy's Lament" songs. Lomax himself made a collation of several texts for his 1910 edition, and in so doing suppressed or softened distasteful stanzas. One of our sources, exaggerating somewhat, says that there were originally seventy stanzas, sixty-nine of which had to be whistled.[4] Thorp credits the song to Troy Hale of Battle Creek, Nebraska; he first heard it sung in a barroom at Wiser in 1886.[5] Elsewhere we find it attributed to Henry Herbert Knibbs,[6] and to F. H. Maynard of Colorado Springs, Colorado.[7] Another source says Maynard wrote it at Dodge City in Tom Sherman's Saloon, July 1872.[8] This claim is based on very meager evidence.

One of the mysteries of this song is its localization. We have tabulated this for one hundred and fifty texts.

TEXTS

Laredo (also spelled Larado, Loredo, Lerado, Lareda) 39
Tom Sherman's (Shurman, Lo Therman, Tom Sheridan, John
    Sherman, Ben Sherman, Sam Sherman, Tom Shedon) 37
Lafferry, Laden, Lake Erie, Landen, Larden, Laterin in barin, Latern
    in Barringer Co., Latherio Barn, Leonards, Letharic, Letherian,
    Letheric Barren, Lock, London, Lukman's, Luke Indians, Luth
    Indian's, Lutherin (1 to 4 times each) 25
Anthony Borrow, Austin's fair city, Boston Tavern, Captain's, Cathe-
    lina, Catholic, Chapman's, Curis Viron, Erin's, Grecian's fair
    home, Joe Jones Hospital, Jordan's, Kearin's, Montana, Old In-
    diana, Rosie's, Saint James Infirmary or Hospital, Tavern Berry,
    Ten Jordan's, Tom Canians, Zeithels (1 to 4 times each) 31
Cases where localization vanishes in favor of a common noun or
    phrase: *streets of the city, ranges, lane, over there, one morning*
    in May, the theater, the prairie, walking, the tavern, alone, on the
    ranches, early one morning, etc. (1 to 3 each) 18

In this study we have limited ourselves to forms of the song that are essentially cowboy and western, or to parodies and analogues closely

---

[4] Paul L. Anderson in a letter to Robert Frothingham, *Adventure Magazine,* (March 10, 1922) pp. 179–80 (FAC III 825).

[5] Thorp (1921) p. 41.

[6] WPA, LC 12273, Wyoming (FAC II 223).

[7] Sires, p. 4; Gordon 1572.

[8] Heinie Schmidt, *The Dodge City Journal,* December 9, 1948 (FAC III 117).

tied to these cowboy and western manifestations of the song. Even with the subject thus circumscribed, there is raw data left over for a Ph.D. dissertation or two.

Texts and musical settings abound. Notwithstanding, most of the cowboy and western tunes fall into one of two camps. To illustrate the first we have selected the Barry music published in *Bulletin of the Folk Song Society of the Northeast*. The second is from the singing of Harry McClintock. Ironhead Baker's rendition reflects a style to be encountered again in "The Buffalo Skinners" where strict form and rhythm are abandoned. It is reminiscent of Negro singing styles out of the South, or even the Caribbean. Hull gives a setting resembling the usual "Laredo," which carries a minor harmonic implication almost throughout, even at the end where one ordinarily expects a cadence. The last line of the lyrics ("Got shot in the breast; I am dying today") underscores the feeling of suspense that is also carried by the tune.

We have also transcribed the song in two quite unusual renditions from the singing of L. Henson and an unnamed singer, both of Texas. Readers with a flare for ethnic music may wish to compare the musical settings printed here with the renditions of an equal number of texts of the whole constellation of songs to which "Cow Boy's Lament" is central.[9]

XIII–A. THORP (1908) pages 29–30

10. 'Twas once in my saddle I used to be happy
      'Twas once in my saddle I used to be gay
      But I first took to drinking, then to gambling
      A shot from a six-shooter took my life away.

7.6   My curse let it rest, let it rest on the fair one
      Who drove me from friends that I loved and from home
      Who told me she loved me, just to deceive me
      My curse rest upon her, wherever she roam.

7.7   Oh she was fair, Oh she was lovely
      The belle of the Viliage the fairest of all
      But her heart was as cold as the snow on the mountains
      She gave me up for the glitter of gold.

---

[9] Kenneth Goldstein, "The Unfortunate Rake." Folkways Records FS 3805.

5.1   I arrived in Galveston in old Texas
        Drinking and gambling I went to give o'er
But, I met with a Greaser and my life he has finished,
        Home and relations I ne'er shall see more.

6.5   Send for my father, Oh send for mother
        Send for the surgeon to look at my wounds
But I fear it is useless I feel I am dying
        I'm a young cow-boy cut down in my bloom.

8.1   Farewell my friends, farewell my relations
        My earthly career has cost me sore
The cow-boy ceased talking, they knew he was dying
        His trials on earth, forever were o'er.

2.1   *Chor.* Beat your drums lightly, play your fifes merrily
        Sing your dearth march as you bear me along
Take me to the grave yard, lay the sod o'er me
        I'm a young cow-boy and know I've done wrong.

XIII–Composite text

1.   Text E.

1.1   As I passed by Tom Sherman's barroom
        Tom Sherman's barroom quite early one morn
I spied a young cowboy all dressed in his buckskins
        All dressed in his buckskins and fit for the grave.

1.2   Text G.

1.3   Text E. See also Text D.

1.4   Text J.

1.x   Text H.

(2 to 2.3 are typical refrains:)
2.   Texts E, J.

2.1   Texts A, B.

2.2   O, beat the drum loudly and play the fife proudly
             And scare the devil off as you carry me along
         Then chase him o'er the hillside and beat him o'er the
                 meadow
             For I'm a poor cowboy and know I've done wrong.

2.3   Hi yi, a poor lonesome cowboy
             Hi yi, list' to my song
         Hi yi, about a poor cowboy
             About a poor cowboy who knew he'd done wrong.

2.4   Oh, muffle your drums, then play your fifes merrily,
             Play the Dead March as you bear me along
         And fire your guns right over my coffin
             There goes an unfortunate boy to his home.

3.   "I see by your outfit that you are a cowboy,"
             These words he did say as I boldly stepped by.
         "Come sit down beside me and hear my sad story;
             I was shot in the breast and I know I must die."

3.1   "Oh, I see by your outfit that you are a cowpuncher,"
             This poor boy said from his lips of flame red
         "They done gunned me down, boys, and run off and left me
             Here in the back street just like I was dead."

3.x   Text H.

3.xx   Text H.

4.   "Let sixteen gamblers come handle my coffin,
             Let sixteen cowboys come sing me a song.
         Take me to the graveyard and lay the sod o'er me
             For I'm a poor cowboy and I know I've done wrong."

4.x   Text H.

5.   Text E.

5.1   Text A.

5.2   Well, I was born in southeast Texas
            Where the jumpson weed and the lilac does bloom
        I long ago left there for to go far a-rangin'
            I've traveled from Canãdia to Old Mexico.

5.3   Text F.

5.x   Text H.

6.   Texts B, C. D, J.

6.1   Text F.

6.2   Oh, write me a letter to my gray-haired mother
            And break the news gently to my sister so dear
        But not one word of this shall you mention
            When a crowd gathers round you my story to hear.

6.3   Text E.

6.4   Says, "Come dear mother, mother, an' seat yourself nigh me
            Come dear father too, and sing me a song
        Tell them to bring 'long a bunch of them sweet-smellin' roses
            So they can't smell me while they drive me along.

6.5   Text A.

6.6   Oh, write me a letter to my gray-haired mother
            And break the news gently to my sister so dear
        But not one word of this shall you mention
            When a crowd gathers round you my story to hear.

6.7   Tell them I loved them all through my wild wanderings
            And that nobody here knows my name
        I got in a battle while playing stud poker
            And I don't want my people to share in my shame.

6.x   Text H.

7.   And then there's another more dear than a sister
            O, how she will weep when she hears I am gone
        But there will be another to gain her affection
            For I was a wild cowboy and I know I done wrong.

7.1   Text F.

7.2   Text F.

7.3   The last letter I had from dear little Emma
            Begging me so kindly to come to my home
        Lord! If I had gone and married this lady
            Quit all my wild ways and done as she bid!

7.4   Go send for the minister to cry and pray o'er me
            Go send for a doctor to cure me or try
        Go send for that pretty girl who's the cause of my ruin
            So that I can forgive her before I must die.

7.5   I left the barroom to do his bidding
            I walked very slowly with his downcast head
        I sent for his mother, his sister and sweetheart
            But before I got back the cowboy was dead.

7.6   Text A.

7.7   Text A.

7.x   Text H.

8.   Texts B, C.

8.1   Text A.

8.2   Go bring to my bedside a class of bold rangers
            Who shoot fast and straight
        And give them a warning to stop the gold gambling
            To stop the gold gambling before it's too late.

8.3   Text F.

8.4   Text F.

9.   Oh, bury beside me my knife and six-shooter,
             My spurs on my heel, my rifle by my side,
          And over my coffin put a bottle of brandy
             That the cowboys may drink as they carry me along.

10.   Texts A, B, C, D, E.

10.1   Text G.

10.2   My home's in Montana, I wear a bandanna,
             My spurs are silver, my horse is a bay
          I took to card playing in the house I was staying
             Got shot through the bowels and you see where I lay.

10.22   Text I.

10.23   Text I.

10.24   Text I.

10.3   My lasso I used to throw with perfection
             Roping wild cattle for me was great fun,
          To cattle I always gave satisfaction
             With a band of wild cowboys, but now I'm done.

10.4   The sun is fast sinking, the stars are fast rising
             And I shall never see morning again
          Come stand ye around me; my breath is expiring
             I'll soon be ready to enter the tomb.

10.5   I've missed life eternal, I'm bound for destruction
             But God was willing that I should do so
          Grieve not while thinking of my condition
             I'm a vile sinner, and now I must go.

11.   Get six jolly cowboys to carry my coffin,
             Get six pretty girls to carry my pall;
          Put bunches of roses all over my coffin,
             Put roses to deaden the clods as they fall.

11.1   Get six jolly fellows to carry my coffin,
             And six pretty maidens to bear up my pall
         And give to each of them bunches of roses
             That they may not smell me as they bear me along.

11.2   I want four good gamblers to carry my coffin
             And four pretty maidens to sing me a song
         Go line my coffin with green and red roses
             And play the dead marches and carry me on.

11.3   Over my coffin put handfuls of lavender,
             Handfuls of lavendar on every side,
         Bunches of roses all over my coffin,
             Saying, "There goes a cowboy cut down in his pride."

11.4   Get four wild cowboys to carry my body
             And two little girls to follow along
         A golden trumpet to sound in the morning
             To let my friends know that I am gone.

12.   Then swing your rope slowly and rattle your spurs lowly,
             And give a wild whoop as you carry me along;
         And in the grave throw me and roll the sod o'er me
             For I'm a young cowboy and I know I've done wrong.

12.1   Then drag your rope slowly, and rattle your spurs lowly
             And give a wild whoop as you carry me along
         And take me to Boot Hill and cover me with roses
             I'm just a young cowboy and I know I done wrong.

13.   Texts C, J.

13.1   "Go bring me a glass of cold water
             To cool my hot temples," this cowboy he said,
         But when I had returned he had gone to his Giver
             This once handsome cowboy lay senseless and dead.

13.x   Text H.

14.   We beat the drum slowly and played the fife lowly
             And bitterly wept as we bore him along;

>   For we all loved our comrade, so brave, young, and handsome
>   We all loved our comrade although he'd done wrong.

XIII–B.   "THE COWBOY'S LAMENT"
Bulletin, Northeast, VII, pages 16–17. From Barry Collection, contributed by Mr. and Mrs. H. J. Fligg, Massachusetts, 1913, as sung in eastern Kansas twenty-five or thirty years previously. Melody is almost identical to the Balvor recording, IU-AFPM 359.4, which would have been a somewhat better selection, but regrettably we have been unable to get permission for its use.

1.11   As I rode to the tavern so early one morning,
           To the tavern and barroom so early I came;
           And there I espied a handsome young cowboy
           All robed in white linen and clothed for the day.

3.01   He knew by [my] outfit that I was a cowboy,
           And smilingly said unto me:
           "Come sit down beside me and hear my sad story,
           For I'm shot through the heart and I know I must die.

10.   "Once on my broncho I used to go dashing,
           And once in my saddle I used to look gay,
           But I first took to drinking and then to card-playing,
           Got shot through the heart and I go to my grave.

6.   "Write a letter to my dear old mother,
           Break the news gently to my sister so dear;
           And there is another more dear than a mother,
           Who would bitterly weep if she knew I was here."

6.1   ". . . . .
           . . . .
           But not one word of this do you mention
           Of those who gather round you my story to hear."

8.   "O gather around you a crowd of gay cowboys,
           And tell them the story of a comrade's sad fate,
           Give each one and all of them timely good warning
           To mend their wild rovings before it's too late."

13.01   "A glass of cold water—a glass of cold water—
         A glass of cold water!" the poor fellow said;
         But ere I returned, the spirit had left him,
         And gone to its Maker; the cowboy was dead.

Refrain:

2.1   "Beat the drum slowly, play the fife lowly,
         Play the sad march as you carry me along;
         Take me to your graveyard and lay the sod o'er me,
         For I'm a young cowboy, and I know I've done wrong."

XIII–B. Music. (Reproduced as in our source.) Though apparently in $\frac{3}{8}$
         time, there are six measures which do not have the proper count.
         Stanzas and refrain are sung to the same melody.

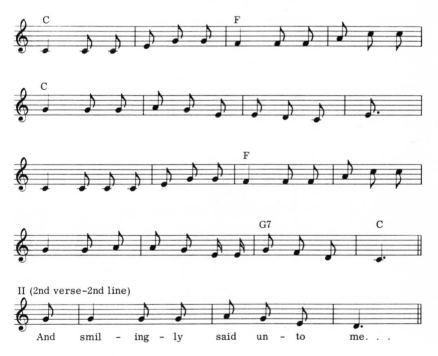

And smil - ing - ly said un - to me. . .

XIII–C. "The Cowboy's Lament"
          Hall, page 217 (FAC III 79).

1.   As I rode out to Latern in Barin
              As I rode out so early one day,
            'Twas there I espied a handsome young cowboy
              All dressed in white linen and clothes for the grave.

Chorus:
2.   Then play your fife lowly and beat your drum slowly,
              And play the Dead March as you bear me along;
            Take me to the graveyard and lay the sod o'er me,
              I am a poor cowboy and I know I've done wrong.

10.   'Twas once in the saddle I used to go dashing,
              'Twas once in the saddle I used to be gay;
            But I first took to drinking and then to card playing,
              Got shot in a fight, and now I must die.

Chorus.

8.   Go gather around you a crowd of young cowboys,
              And tell them the story of this my sad fate;
            And tell them to stop all their gambling and drinking,
              And all their wild ways before it's too late.

Chorus.

6.   Go write a letter to my gray-headed mother,
              And break the news gently to my sisters so dear;
            And then there's another dearer far than a mother,
              Who'll bitterly weep when she knows I am here.

Chorus.

13.   Go bring me a cup of pure cold water,
              A cup of cold water, the poor fellow said;
            But when I returned, the spirit had departed,
              And gone to the Giver—the cowboy was dead.

Chorus.

XIII–D. "THE YOUNG COWBOY"
WKFA, from Mrs. J. D. Tobin, Kentucky, 1956 (FAC II 138).

1.3   So early one morning as I rode
aloin [sic]
So early one morning I rode over there
I met a young cow boy all dress in
white linen.
With sparkling eyes and dark wavy
brown hair.

2.   *Cho:*
Beat the drum loudly and play
the fife sadly
Play the dead an arch [sic]as they
carry me on
Take me to ghe [sic] grave yard
and throw the sod oer me
For I am a young cow boy
And know Ive done wrong.

6.   Go bear the sad news to my
gray haird mother
Go bear the news to my sister
so dear
For there is another more dearer
than brother
If she only knew I was dying to
day

10.   Once in my saddle I use to
go dashing
Once in my saddle I use to go
gay
But now Ive took drinking then
card playing
God shorten my breath
For I am dying to day.

(Compliments to Flora from Laura)

D. K. Wilgus: Ballet on tablet paper. Originally the property of Mrs. Nannie Anderson Tobin (1886–1951), mother-in-law of Mrs. J. D. T. Ballets seem to date from about 1902.

XIII–E.   "THE DYING COWBOY"
          WKFA, Josiah H. Combs Collection (FAC II 188).

1.   As I walked out on the streets of Laredo,
              As I walked out in Laredo one day,
          I saw a poor cowboy all wrapped in white linen,
              All wrapped in white linen as cold as the clay.

          Chorus:

2.   Then beat the drums slowly and sound the fife lowly
              And play the Dead March as you carry me along,
          Take me down to the graveyard and throw the sod o'er me
              For I'm a young cowboy and I know I've done wrong.

5.   My home and my relation I left them in Boston,
              My parents knew not where their poor son had gone,
          I first came to Texas and hired to a ranchman,
              Now hell is my doom for I know I've done wrong.

6.11   Go write a letter to all of my brothers,
              And one, also, to my sister dear,
          But not one word of this do you mention
              As you gather around the sad story to hear.

6.3   Don't write to my mother, oh please don't inform her
              Of the wretched condition that death caught me in,
          I know it would grieve her at the loss of her darling,
              Oh, could I return to my childhood again!

1.3   So early one morning I rode to the Catholic [*sic*]
              So early one morning I rode over there,
          I met a young cowboy all dressed in white linen
              With dark sparkling eyes and black waving hair.

10.   Oh, once in my saddle I used to go dashing,
              Oh, once in my saddle I used to go gay,

> I first took to drinking and then to card playing,
> Got shot in the breast and am dying today.

XIII–F. "THE COWBOY'S LAMENT"
          Lomax d. 5656, from Slim Critchlow (JL 320).

1.11   As I was passing by Tom Sherwin's bar room
         Tom Sherwin's bar room so early one day
         Who should I see but a handsome young cowboy
         Stretched out on a blanket and all pale and gray.

5.3   Oh his eyes were fast glazing, and death was approaching
         His white lips were curled and tortured with pain
         As he spoke in a whisper of a scene far behind him
         Of his home in the East which he'd ne'er see again.

6.61   "Oh tell my old father I've tried to live honest
         Tried to shoot square and give all men their due
         But I first took to drinking and then to gambling
         Which brought me to trouble, and now I am through.

6.71   "Oh tell him I wish I had heeded his warning
         But now it's too late, and I bid him adieu
         Got shot in the breast by a Dodge City gambler
         Who dealt from the bottom and I'm dying today.

8.3   "Please gather up my last hand of poker
         The one that I dropped when I got my death wound
         Send it and my six gun home to my brother
         After you've buried me deep in the tomb.

8.4   "Tell him these things are what ruined his brother
         And never to part with the last fatal hand
         But carry it always just as a reminder
         If e'er he should drift to this wild cattle land.

6.1   "Oh, write me a letter to my gray-haired mother
         And break the news gently to my sister so dear
         But not one word of this shall you mention
         When a crowd gathers round you my story to hear.

6.21   "Tell them I loved them all through my wild wanderings
        And that nobody here knows my name
        I got in a battle while playing stud poker
        And I don't want my people to share in my shame.

7.1   "Oh there is another as dear as my sister
        Lovely and pure as the dew on a rose
        Tell her to wait for her lover no longer
        For he sleeps where the prairie wind smoothly blows.

7.2   "Tell her that her image has always been with me
        Carry me up through the long, lonely days
        And that I'm taking it down through the valley
        Locked in my heart to be with me always."

XIII–G. "ST. JAMES HOSPITAL"
        Lomax d. 5656, from Ironhead Baker (JL 342) = Lomax (1938)
        pages 420–21.

1.2   It was early one morning as I passed St. James Hospital
        It was early in the mornin', mornin' month of May
        When I looked in the window, and I spied a dear cowboy
        When wrapped up in white linen he was as cold as the clay.

6.41   Says, "Come, dear Mother, Mother, and seat yourself near
            me
        Come, dear Father, too and sing me a song
        For my knee bones am achin' and my poor heart am breakin'
        Well, I know I'm a poor cowboy, father, and I know I've
            done wrong.

11.11   "Six young gamblers, papa, to balance my coffin
        Sixteen young whore gals for to sing me a song
        Tell 'em to bring along a bunch of them sweet smellin' roses
        So they can't smell me as they drive me along.

10.1   "Well in my saddle, father, I used to go dashing
        Father, in my young days I used to look gay
        Down round some church house carryin' some handsome
            young ladies—
        While the women ought to carry me, follow me to my grave.

XIII–G. Music from Lomax (1938), page 420

Freely, with intense feeling (♩=69)

It was ear-ly one morn-in' as I passed St. James Hos-pit-al. It was ear-ly one morn-in' morn-in' month o' May, When I looked in the— win-dow And I spied a dear cow-boy— Wrapped— up in white lin-en He was cold as the clay.—

Collected, adapted and arranged by John A. Lomax and Alan Lomax.
© Copyright 1938 Ludlow Music, Inc., New York, N.Y. Used by permission.

XIII–H. *"Fran Sveas vänner, en döende 'cowboy'"*
Ragnar, Minneapolis, Minnesota (PC-F 124).

1.x   En morgen jag gick ner till värdshuset Boston
         En stralande varmorgon, klar och sa skön
         Da faglarne sjongo sa herrligt i skogen
         Och jorden sig klädt i en varmantel grön.

3.x I värdshuset var det en "cowboy" nyss skjuten.
    Pa pannan r'n döden sin stämpel har satt.
    Han hviskade sakta: "Kom, sitt vid min sida!"
    Han andades tungt, och hans röst var matt.

4.x "När frigjorda anden fran jordiska banden
    Har svingat sig upp til det eviga land,
    Sa göm mig i mullen deruppe pa kullen,
    En "cowboy," som dött för en mördares hand.

3.xx "Jag ser af din rustning, att du är en "cowboy,
    Kom sitt vid min side! "Han sade till mig.
    "Kom, lyssna och hör hvad jag har att dig säga,
    Min leinadschistoria vill jag ge dig.

6.x "Jag hade ett hem och en älskande moder;
    Jag hade en syster sa god och sa mild.
    Men bada jag lemnat. Jag ville se verlden,
    Nu maste jag dö, och sa langt fran dem skild.

5.x "Jag öfvergaf hemmet, jag ville se verlden,
    Jag styrde, min kosa till vestern hit ut.
    Jag började dricka och derpa att supa,
    Blef skjuten i bröstet. Mitt lif är snart slut.

6.1x "O, bringa ett bud til min älskade moder,
    En helsning, den sista, till syster sa kär,
    Och bed dem förlata, hvad jag mot dem brutit,
    Ty aldrig jag mera far möta dem här.

7.x "Men der är en annan, mer dyr än en moder,
    O, bringa en helsning till henne, min vän;
    Säg, att hon ej grater, ty vi skola ater
    En gang bortom dödsfloden mötas igen.

13.x "Vill nagon mig bringa ett glas med kallt vatten,
    Att svalka min feber! Den bränner som glöd."
    Han hviskar. Jag skynder att hemta friskt vatten,
    Men när jag kom ater, han redan var död.

4.x "När frigjorda anden fran jordiska banden
    Har svingat sig upp till det eviga land,

Sa göm mig i mullen deruppe pa kullen,
En "cowboy," som dött för en mördares hand."

XIII–H. TRANSLATION:

1.x   One morning I went down to the tavern Boston
        A glorious spring morning clear and bright
        The birds sang so lovely in the woods
        And the earth was clad in a spring mantle green.

3.x   In the tavern a cowboy had just been shot
        On his forehead death his stamp has put.
        He whispered slowly, "Come sit by my side."
        He breathed heavily and his voice was dull.

4.x   When the liberated soul from the earthly bond
        Has swung itself up to the eternal land
        Then hide me in the mound out there on the hill—
        A cowboy who died at the murderer's hand.

3.xx   "I see by your armour that you are a cowboy
        Come sit by my side," he said unto me.
        "Come listen and hear what I have to tell you
        My life story I wish to give you.

6.x   "I had a home and a loving mother,
        I had a sister so good and so gentle,
        But both I left, I wanted to see the world,
        Now must I die and so far from them separated.

5.x   "I gave up the home, I wanted to see the world,
        I steered my course out here to the West.
        I began to drink and then to sip [souse]
        Was shot in the breast, my life is soon done.

6.1x   "And carry a word to my loved mother,
        A last greeting to the sister so dear.
        And ask them to forgive what I have sinned against them,
        For never again will I meet them here.

7.x   "But there is another more gracious than mother
        Oh, bring a message to her, my friend

Tell her not to weep for we shall again
Meet each other beyond the river of death.

13.x   "Will someone bring me a glass of cold water
To soothe my fever, it burns like fire."
He whispers, I hasten to fetch the water,
But when I returned he is already dead.

4.x   "When the liberated spirit from earthly bonds
Has swung itself up to the eternal land
Then hide me in the mound up there on the hill,
A cowboy who died at the murderer's hand."

XIII–I.   "MY HOME'S IN MONTANA"
U-Ill. Campus. Sung by Glenn Ohrlin.
Three distinctive stanzas occur although melodic treatment resembles Larkin, pages 14–15. Reproduced with permission of Campus Folksong Club, University of Illinois.

10.22   My home's in Montana, I wear a bandanna,
My spurs are of silver, my pony is gray,
While riding the ranges my luck never changes,
With foot in the stirrup I gallop for aye.

10.23   When valleys are dusty my pony is trusty
He lopes through the blizzards, the snow in his ears,
The cattle may scatter but what does it matter
My rope is a halter for pig-headed steers.

10.24   When far from the ranches I chop the pine branches
To keep on my campfire as daylight grows pale,
When I have partaken of beans and of bacon
I whistle a merry old song on the trail.

XIII–J.   "THE WILD LUMBERJACK"
Korson, pages 352–53 = Shoemaker, *North,* pp. 196–97.
Sung in the Potter County logging camps, where it was collected
by John C. French. Reproduced with permission of University of
Pennsylvania Press.

1.4   One day I was out walking on the mountain,
          A wood robin was singing. I happened to spy
A handsome young lumberjack on the banks of the river,
          All dressed in white linen, and laid out to die.

Chorus

2.   So beat your drum lowly, and play your fife slowly,
          And play the dead march as you carry me along.
          Oh, take me to the mountain, and lay the sod o'er me,
          For I'm a wild lumberjack and I know I've done wrong.

10.01   Once out in the forest I used to go slashing;
          Once in the big timbers I used to be gay.
          I first took to drinking, and then to card playing,
          Was shot in the breast, and I'm dying today.

6.   Go, someone, write to my gray-haired mother,
          And also to my brothers and my sisters so dear;
          But there is another far dearer than mother,
          Who'd bitterly weep if she knew I was here.

13.   Go, someone, and bring me a cup of cold water—
          A cup of spring water, the poor woodsie said;
          But ere it had reached him his spirit had vanished—
          Gone to the Giver, the poor fellow was dead.

XIII–K.   GORDON 569, MRS. W. D. CHAPMAN. NO TITLE.[10]
          Reproduced with permission of Roberta Paul Gordon Nye.

Wrap me up in my old stable jacket
And say a poor buffer lies low
And get six stalwart lancers to carry me
With steps mournful, solemn and slow.

And get you six brandys and sodas
And get them all out in a row
And get you six jolly good fellows
To drink to the buffer below.

---

[10] The first and third stanzas are usual in "Old Rosin the Beau;" stanza 4 in
"The Prisoner's Love Song."

And then in the dusk of the twilight
When soft winds are whispering low
And darkening shadows are falling
Sometimes think of the buffer below.

Oh had I the wings of a little dove
So far, far away would I fly
Right back to the arms of my true love
And there would I lay me and die.

XIII–L.   "HIGHWAY BOY"
Reproduced with permission of the collector, Professor Herbert Halpert of Memorial University of Newfoundland.

Halpert Collection, from Mrs. Lafe Odell, Peaksville, New York,
1938 (FAC II 456). She had heard it many years before, frag-
mentary. After they captured him and got him into the prison he
told them:

When I'm dead and a-goin' to my grave
One pleasant funeral let me have
Let six highwaymen my bearers be
Give them broad swords and sweet liberty.

Let six pretty maidens attend my call
Give them white gloves, pink ribbons all
That they may say and tell the truth
Here goes a braver to a wicked youth.

Dig my grave both long, wide, and deep
Place a bottle of brandy at my head and feet
That every traveler that pass by
May drink a health to the highway boy.

XIII–M.   "JACK COMBS' MURDER"
Lomax d. 5620, from Bristol Taylor, Berea, Kentucky (JL 20).

As I passed by where Jack Combs was murdered,
    As I passed by so early one morn
I spied a cold corpse wrappen up in white linen
    Wrapped up in white linen as cold as the day.

"Go pick up your drums, play them as if I were with you,
  Go beat your Dead Marches whilest carrying me along
Go take me to the graveyard and throw the dirt over me
  For I have been murdered, you know they've done wrong.

"So cruel was the man that committed this murder,
  So cruel was he that held my arm
I might have applied to some friends that were near me
  To save my life before it was gone.

"I want my dear friends to bury my dead body
  And all that can sing, to sing my song
Each one of them have a bunch of red roses
  To keep me from smelling whilest carrying me along.

"Come then my dear brother and sit you down near me,
  Come then my dear mother and pity my wounds,
My head is aching and my poor heart is breaking
  With sad lamentations I surely must die."

XIII–N. "OLD TIME GAMBLER'S SONG"
Gordon 1720, from Terrell McKay: "Widely known here among
the old timers." Reproduced with permission of Roberta Paul
Gordon Nye.

I dreamed I went down to St James Infirmary
Thought I saw my baby lying there;
Laid out on a clean white table,
So pale and yet so fair.

If she's gone, let her go, God bless her,
For she's mine where ever she may be;
You may search this wide world over
You'll never find another pal such as she.

I may die out on the ocean
Be shot down in a gambling house brawl;
But if you follow me to the end of my story
You'l find a blonde was the cause of it all.

When I die, just bury me in a box back suit,
Blue shirt, roller hat, pair of shoes with toes so tall;
Put whiskey in my coffin, deck of cards in my hands
Don't let them weep and wail, don't let 'em moan at all.

Put marihuana in my coffin,
Smoke it as you carry me along;
Take even rolling dice shooters for pall bearers,
Coke sniffers to sing my funeral song.

Put a twenty dollar gold piece on my watch charm
So the boys'll all know I'm standing pat,
Put ice on my feet, for in the place where I'm going
I won't even be cool with that.

Just carve it on my tombstone
In letters bold and black,
"Here lies an old time gambler,
Pray God won't you please bring him back!"

XIII–O.   "I Once Was a Carman in the Big Mountain Con"
Hand, *Butte,* pages 30–32: recorded in 1945, "sung in the mines
of Butte . . . about 1905." Reproduced with permission of the editors of *Western Folklore Quarterly.*

'Twas once in the saddle I used to go dashing,
'Twas once as a cowboy I used to be brave;
But ain't it a pity, I came to Butte City
To work for Jim Brennan and now to my grave.

Oh beat your drums loudly; sound your fifes merrily;
Play the bagpipe as ye carry me on,
Lay a square pointed fan on the lid of my coffin
So I'll be known as I go along.

Get six jolly ladies to come and dance o'er me;
Get six husky carmen to carry me on;
Take me to The Flat boys, and throw the soil o'er me,
For I once was a carman in the Big Mountain Con.

There's Big Jack O'Neill; we call him The Rimmer;
To a hard-working miner he never was mean;
If you h'aint a Big Wheeler, when first you come over,
You'll have to go muckin' behind a machine.

There's Big Tim O'Malley, just over from Kerry;
The greenest young chaw that a man ever seen;
It was his ambition to gain a position,
So he had to go muckin' behind a machine.

Come all ye Corkonians, Fardowns, and Kerryonians,
Come all ye good people, from the land of the Green.
Come all ye Big Wheelers who ain't got your papers,
You'll have to go muckin' behind a machine.

Then hurrah for Old Ireland, the land of good miners,
The dear little isle that I see in my dreams;
I'll go back to Old Ireland to the girl who waits for me,
To hell with your mines and your mining machines.

XIII–O. Music

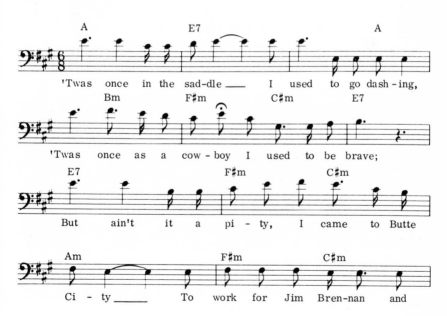

'Twas once in the sad-dle ___ I used to go dash-ing,
'Twas once as a cow-boy I used to be brave;
But ain't it a pi - ty, I came to Butte
Ci - ty ___ To work for Jim Bren-nan and

now   to my grave.   Oh   beat   your drums loud - ly;___

Sound   your fifes mer - ri - ly; Play   the bag - pipe ___

as ye   car - ry   me on,   Lay   a square point - ed

fan   on   the lid   of   my   cof - fin,

So   I'll   be known   as   I   go   a - long.

Get   six jol - ly   la - dies   to come and dance

o'er   me;   Get   six hus - ky

car - men   to   car - ry   me   on;   Take   me   to The

Flat   boys, and   throw the   soil o'er   me,___   For   I

once   was   a   car - man   in the Big Moun - tain Con.

XIII–P. "A Sun Valley Song"
WFQ XVIII (1959), page 38.
Collected by Jan Brunvand of Southern Illinois University. Reproduced with permission of the editors of *Western Folklore Quarterly*.

When I was a-skiing the hills of Sun Valley,
As I was a-skiing old Baldy one day,
I spied a young skier all wrapped in alpaca,
All wrapped in alpaca, and cold as *der Schnee*.

"I see by your suntan that you are a skier,"
These words he did say as I boldly *schussed* by;
"Come fall down beside me, and hear my sad story,
I caught a right edge and I'm dying today.

"It was once upon Baldy, I used to ski gaily,
It was once upon Baldy I used to ski by;
It was first down the canyon, and then through the narrows,
I caught a right edge and I know I must die.

"Get six from the ski school to carry my coffin,
Get six little bunnies to sing me a song;
Oh lower me gently and sprinkle *Schnee* o'er me,
For I was a skier, my life was not long."

XIII–Q. "Streets of Laredo" ("The Book-Worm's Lament")
Lomax d. 5638, a New York newspaper clipping (JL 62).

As I walked out in the streets of Laredo
As I walked out in Laredo one day
I spied a cowboy wrapped up in a story
Immersed in a novel by Mr. Zane Gray.

"Oh, beat the drum slowly and play the fife lowly
And play the Dead March as you give a look,
Take me to the green valley and pile the sod o'er
For I'm a young cowboy, was reading a book.

"'Twas once in the saddle I used to go dashing
It was once in the saddle I used to go gay

First to book reading and then to book buying
   Let the cattle go hang for I'm reading today.

"Let sixteen authors come handle my coffin,
   Let sixteen poets come sing me a song
Take me to the graveyard and lay the sod o'er me
   For I'm a poor cowboy and I know I've done wrong."

VIII–R. "Old Chape: The Troubadour of Red Fork Ranch"
       Coldiron, pages 43–44 (FAC III 241). Reproduced with permission
       of Kara Lee Eikelberry.

He rode up to the Ranch House door
   On the old Chisholm Trail;
The Ranchman said, "'Light, Stranger,
   And turn your horse in the horse corral."

The stranger 'lighted gracefully,
   A gentleman to the manner born;
He had a fiddle on his back
   And a banjo on his saddle horn.

"My name is John G. Chapin,
   Late of the U.S. Army;
Ain't goin' no place, partic'lar,
   As lief stay here as any."

He made the supper biscuits
   And to this day they tell
How he beat them with an iron spoon—
   He beat them to a fare you well!

And now he takes his violin
   And over it he bends;
He tunes it and he makes it sing
   For the Ranchman and his friends.

When night creeps up from the Cimarron,
   And swooping bats are on the wing,
He takes his banjo on his knee,
   He strums it and begins to sing.

He sways and nods and stamps his foot,
　　He lives the spirit of the part—
The troubadour of Red Fork Ranch—
　　He sang his way to every heart.

A cow boy he saw in Laredo
　　All wrapped in white linen one day,
(He shakes his head right solemnly)
　　"Wrapped in white linen cold as clay."

He wails out the final refrain,
　　He hears the dead march in his song,
He walks the streets of Laredo,
　　While they carry the cow boy along.

"Oh beat the drum slowly and play the fife lowly
　　And play the dead march as you carry me along,
Take me to the green prairie and there lay the sod o'er me,
　　For I'm a wild cowboy and I know I've done wrong."

Old Chape, the homeless drifter,
　　He had no kith or kin,
But for the gold of honest worth
　　Ralph Collins took him in.

Ralph made him cook at Red Fork Ranch;
　　He saw the Cattlemen's Empire
Swept away when the settlers came
　　Like grass before a prairie fire.

"Last night as I lay on the prairie
　　And looked up to the stars in the sky
I wondered if ever a cow boy
　　Would drift to that sweet bye and bye."

He saw the Old West pass away;
　　Red Fork became the town of Dover,
Old Chape—he found the last long Trail
　　And followed it when all was over.

XIII--S. "Cowboy's Lament"
Sung by Harry McClintock, Victor 21761 (FAC III 1035).

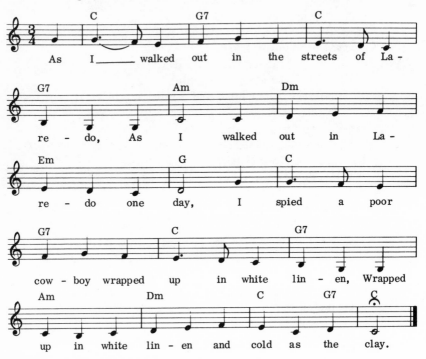

As I____ walked out in the streets of La-
re-do, As I walked out in La-
re-do one day, I spied a poor
cow-boy wrapped up in white lin-en, Wrapped
up in white lin-en and cold as the clay.

XIII–T. "Streets of Laredo"
LC 658B2, sung by L. Henson, Texas, recorded by Lomax (FAC
I 292).

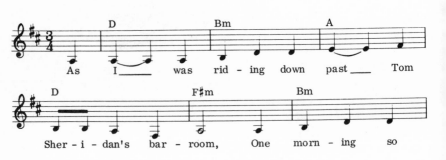

As I____ was rid-ing down past____ Tom
Sher-i-dan's bar-room, One morn-ing so

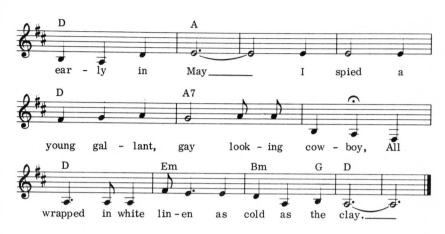

ear - ly in May_____ I spied a

young gal - lant, gay look - ing cow - boy, All

wrapped in white lin - en as cold as the clay._____

XIII–U. "Streets of Laredo"
LC 936B2, Texas, 1937, recorded by Lomax (FAC I 293).

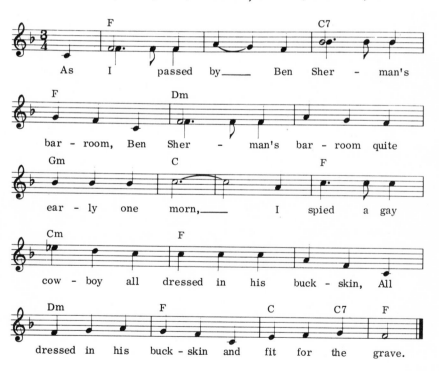

As I passed by_____ Ben Sher - man's

bar - room, Ben Sher - man's bar - room quite

ear - ly one morn,_____ I spied a gay

cow - boy all dressed in his buck - skin, All

dressed in his buck - skin and fit for the grave.

XIII–V.   "COWBOY'S LAMENT"
Hull, page 50. Reproduced with permission of Kansas State Historical Society.

BIBLIOGRAPHY

Significant texts, printed:

1872?   *Dodge City Journal,* December 8, 1948 (FAC III 117).
1886   Thorp (1921) pp. 41–44, Nebraska = Lomax (1910), pp.
              74–76; Thorp (1908) pp. 29–30.
1887   Wehman No. 952, New York.
late 1880's   Hull, p. 49, A, Kansas.
c. 1890   Hull, pp. 49–50, B, Kansas.
c. 1891   Belden, p. 397, H.
c. 1892   Hand, *Strassen,* p. 159, Michigan.
c. 1893   Gardner, p. 252, Michigan.
1898   Wister, p. 274 (FAC III 591).

1899	Eddy, p. 283, A, Ohio.
pre-1906	Belden, pp. 393–94, A, Missouri.
1906	Belden, p. 394, B, Missouri.
1908	Barry, p. 154, C, West Virginia.
1908	Hall, p. 217 (FAC III 79).
1909	Will, pp. 258–59 (FAC III 161).
1909	Barry, pp. 153–54, A and B, Mississippi.
pre-1910	Lomax (1910) pp. 74–76.
1913	Pound, *Nebraska,* p. 358, Nebraska.
(1880) 1913	*Bulletin, Northeast* VII, pp. 16–17, Kansas.
c. 1913	Flanders, pp. 250–52, Vermont.
1914	Pound, *American,* pp. 170–71, Wyoming (FAC III 778).
c. 1915	Parker, p. 1.
1916	Pound, *Syllabus,* p. 26.
1933	Allen, *Cowboy Lore,* pp. 118–20, Texas.
?	Larkin, pp. 14–15, Montana.
?	Sandburg, p. 263.

Significant texts, manuscripts, and field recordings:

Browne, *Alabama:* Florence Bailey (FAC II 233). Unknown: FAC I 577.

Fife. *Kansas:* Charles Oldfather, 1959 (FAC I 229). *Texas:* Slim Briggs, 1950 (FMR 526B).

Goldstein, *Scotland:* Lucy Stewart, 1960 (FAC I 475). Goldstein, *Texas.*

Gordon. Unknown: No. 2620, Lloyd McWold, *c.* 1900; No. 1125, Mrs. Ida Wells, *c.* 1890; No. 929, A. S. White; No. 569, Mrs. W. D. Chapman.

LC. *Virginia:* LC 1372B1, Mrs. C. Ward and Field Ward, 1937.

Lomax. *California:* d. 5654, Slim Critchlow, 1940 (JL 262). *Missouri* (?): d. 5634, Mrs. Lydia Jones, sent by Belden, 1906 (JL 29). *Oklahoma:* cylinder 24 in LC, Tom Hight. *Texas:* d. 5634, L. M. Hargus (1909), (JL 29); d. 5653, . P. Arnold, *c.* 1910 (JL 215); d. 5656, Ironhead Baker (JL 342); LC 545A, 1935 (FAC I 291). Unknown: d. 5634, from Sharlot Hall, *Out West,* March, 1908 (JL 29).

Piper. *Minnesota:* in Swedish (PC-F 124, 125).

UAFA. *Arizona:* R58B2, Desmond Powell.

WKFA. *Kentucky:* Mrs. N. A. Tobin, *c.* 1902 (FAC II 138); J. Combs (FAC II 188).

Other printed texts:

Ames, pp. 219–20.
Arkansas, pp. 15–16.

Autry, p. 30 (FAC III 487).
Baber, p. 77 (FAC III 273).
Barnes, *Cowboy*, p. 125.
Barry, p. 277.
Belden, pp. 393–97.
Binns, pp. 64–65.
Boni, p. 212.
Botkin, *American*, pp. 859–60 = Lomax (1938) pp. 417–20; *Western*, pp. 766–67.
Botsford, pp. 9–10.
Brown, *North Carolina*, II, pp. 615–18.
Callison, p. 158 (FAC III 315).
Clark, *Cowboy*, pp. 10–11 = Lomax (1910) pp. 74–76.
Clifton, p. 39.
Colorado I, No. 3, p. 20.
Combs, pp. 209–10.
Combs and Shearin, p. 15.
Coolidge, *Texas*, pp. 130–32.
Cowboy Songs, p. 17.
Cox, pp. 242–46.
Cox, *West Virginia*, pp. 24–26.
Cromwell, pp. 232–33.
Davis, *Songs*, pp. 287–88.
Dudgeon, p. 21.
Eddy, p. 284.
Farm Life, May, 1927 (FAC III 796, from Browne).
Flanders, pp. 250–52.
Fowke, *American*, p. 248.
Frey, p. 55.
Friedman, pp. 424–27, 465–66.
Frothingham, *Adventure Magazine*, March 10, 1922 (FAC III 392).
Gardner, p. 252.
Gray, Oklahoma, p. 23.
Hand, *Strassen*, pp. 144–46 = Lomax (1910) pp. 74–76.
Henry, p. 360.
Hobo News, fol. 24.
Howard, pp. 303–4.
Hubbard, p. 310.
Ives, pp. 260–61.
Jones, p. 4.
Kentucky Girls, pp. 34–35.

Keynote II (January, 1947).
Kincaid No. 1, p. 40; No. 3, pp. 28–29.
Klickman and Sherwin, pp. 27–28.
Larkin, pp. 13–15.
Lee, *Range,* p. 43.
Lindroth, pp. 11–12.
Literary Digest, September 16, 1916, p. 701 (FAC III 463).
Lomax (1938) pp. 417–22; *Best Loved,* pp. 206–7; *USA,* pp. 206–7.
Lone Ranger, pp. 22–23.
Luther, pp. 206–8.
MacKensie, p. 302.
Mammoth, No. 11, p. 205.
Moore, pp. 309–10.
Morris, pp. 41–43.
Nebraska I, pp. 3–4.
Neely and Spargo, pp. 181–84.
Pack, p. 63.
Pack, *Song Book,* pp. 91–92.
Patterson and Dexter, pp. 10–11.
Pie Plant Pete, p. 6.
Pittsburg (Kansas) *Headlight,* June 27, 1910 (JL 255).
Randolph II, pp. 180–81.
Rhinehart, 3d ed., p. 6.
Ridings, pp. 293–95 (FAC III 71).
Robinson, p. 35 (FAC III 135). Appears from same plates in *KFBI Songs of the Plains; Blue Grass Roy; Green Valley Boys from WKBF; Tiny Texas Cowboy and Mountain Ballads; Jimmy and His Hamlins Saddle Pals; Play and Sing: America's Greatest Collection of Old Time Songs and Mountain Ballads.*
Rogers' Favorite, p. 39.
Roundup Rangers, pp. 10–11.
Scarborough, pp. 354–58.
Shay, *Pious,* pp. 159–61.
Sires, pp. 4–5.
Sizemore, *Hearth,* p. 28; *Home,* p. 29; *Hymns,* p. 26; *Old Fashioned,* p. 26.
Stout, pp. 103–5 (3 versions).
Texas Centennial I, p. 11 (FAC III 488).
TFSB No. 7, p. 4.
Unidentified newspaper clippings: PC-F 122; "By Edward Geer," FAC III 797, from Browne; Gordon 932.
Wright, p. 166.

Unpublished thesis:

Pollan, pp. 53–54.

Commercial recordings:

A. W. Binder: Elkan-Vogel.
Al Bernard: Grey Gull 4173 = Buddy Moore: Van D. 74173.
Arkansas Woodchopper: Columbia 15463-D (FAC III 1066).
Bradley Kincaid: Supertone 9404; Gennett 6970.
Buddy Moore: Van D. 74173 (FAC III 1062) = Al Bernard: Grey Gull 4173.
Burl Ives: Okeh K-3, 6315; Decca A431, 8082; Columbia A, C103-A.
Captain Appleblossom: Okeh 45373 (FAC III 1067).
Charlie Herald: Canadian Bluebird 4964.
Dick Devall: Timely Tunes C-1563.
Dude Martin: Mc. Trans. 435.
Ed McCurdy: Elektra EKL-108.
Ewen Hall: Brunswick 141; Supertone S-2043 (FAC III 1071).
Gould String Orchestra: Decca 18706.
Harry McClintock: Victor 21761 (FAC III 1035).
Harvey Watson (Kincaid alias): Champion 15428.
Hillbillies, The: Regal-Zonophone (Australian) 1923.
Joe Werner: Bluebird 2076.
John Charles Thomas: Victor 1525.
Jules Allen: Victor 40178, Montgomery Ward 4099 (FAC III 1065).
Ken Maynard: Columbia 2301-D (FAC III 1063); unknown (FAC III 1072).
Luther Trio: Decca 1427.
Martin and Roberts: Conqueror 8011B (FAC III 1068); Romeo 5154 (FAC III 1073); Banner 32522; Melotone 12497; Oriole 8154; Perfect 12831.
Newton Gaines: Victor V40253-A.
Ranch Boys: Decca 65, 2645, 5061 (FAC III 1021).
Renan and Mason: Columbia 36134.
Rodeo Trio: Victor 40186.
Si Puckett: Supertone 9253 (FAC III 1070): Silvertone 8152 = Holland Puckett, Silvertone 5065, 25065.
Thomas and Novak: Musicraft 301-A.
Vernon Dalhart: Conqueror 7467, 7724; Oreole 1783; Perfect 12361; Romeo 599; Velvet Tone 7045 (FAC III 1069).

Kenneth Goldstein, "The Unfortunate Rake": Folkways FS 3805. "The Cowboy's Lament" sung by Bruce Buckley (A9), and Harry Jackson (A10).

Manuscripts and field recordings:

Abrahams. *Nevis, British West Indies:* 1962 (FAC II 535). Abrahams, p. 172.
Browne. *Alabama:* May Bailey (FAC II 233); Della Hall (FAC II 645); Mrs. Aldrich (FAC II 649); Della Collins (FAC II 650); N. Coleman (FAC II 651); Ed Geer (FAC II 679). Unknown: (FAC I 16).
Cheney. *Idaho:* W. E. Allred, pre-1936 (FAC II 499).
Dorson. *Michigan:* Marion Hatfield, 1948 (1934) (FAC II 567); Warren Hofstra, 1948 (FAC II 566); Mrs. Wm. Bowssmaren, 1940 (FAC II 398). *Missouri:* Jack Johnson, 1951 (FAC II 565). *Montana:* Mrs. Alfred Tennant, 1955 (c. 1915) (FAC II 568). *Ohio:* Pat Coe, 1953 (FAC II 564).
Duncan. *Oklahoma:* Guy Chambers (c. 1895) (FAC I 394).
Fife. *Maryland:* Frank Goodwyn, 1959 (FAC I 249). *Texas:* Slim Briggs, 1950 (FMR 526A2). *Utah:* G. Holyoke, 1945 (FMC II 426); D. Holyoke, 1953 (FMC I 861). *Kansas:* Kathy Dagel, 1959 (FAC I 104).
Fowke. *Canada:* Gordon Howard (FAC I 482); unknown (FAC I 600).
Gordon. Unknown: Wm. E. Underwood (No. 139); James Boyd, 1923 (No. 188); Lawrence Boucher (No. 1082); Elmer Sloan (No. 1209); F. E. Wade (No. 1417); Orval Harden (No. 1466A); J. R. C. Honeyman (No. 1659); Edith Spaulding (No. 2626); Edmund Aldrich (No. 12).
Guthrie. Unknown: LC (FAC II 286).
Halpert. *Kentucky:* Mrs. Lucille Tarry, 1948 (FAC II 142); Irene B. Ferren, 1952 (FAC II 140). *Mississippi:* LC 3028B2, 1939 (FAC I 282). *Texas:* Hoppy Cray, 1936 (FAC II 139). *Virginia:* LC 2816B3 and LC 2832B1, 1939 (FAC I 279, 281).
Hendren 320. Unknown.
IU-AFPM 359.4. Unknown: Gaspare Balvor (FAC III 980).
LC. Two unidentified texts (FAC I 331, II 148).
Lomax. *Kentucky:* d. 5634, Professor Shearin (JL 29); LC 6720B1, Mrs. A. Palmore (FAC I 322). *Missouri:* d. 5634, C. H. Williams (from Belden) (JL 29) and Elwood Adams (JL 29). *New York:* d. 5563, Mrs. F. L. Botsford (JL 3). *Texas:* LC 658B2, L. Henson, 1936 (FAC I 466); LC 5653A2, H. Stephens, 1942; LC 6508B2, J. Prude (FAC I 323); unidentified: LC 936B2 (FAC I 293), LC 2637A2 (FAC I 295), LC 3806A2; d. 5634, three texts: J. P. Arnold, D. L. Browning, E. Sevier (JL 29). *Virginia:* LC 1372B1, 1937 (FAC I 294); d. 5654, Nonnie Peters (JL 310).

West Virginia: d. 5634, D. E. McQuilkin (JL 29). Unknown: LC 545A
(FAC II 608); LC 4458B1, 1941 (FAC I 297); nine unidentified texts:
d. 5638 (JL 111), d. 5634 (JL 29), d. 5652 (JL 152); d. 5653.

Oklahoma. *Oklahoma:* Barney Wolverton, 1950 (FAC II 444).

Piper. *Oklahoma:* PC-F 47. Unknown: PC-F 123.

PNFQ. *Oregon:* C. W. Anders (No. 125); Dorotha Bristow (No. 82).
Washington: Mrs. M. L. Thompson (No. 129); E. Loppe (No. 122).
Unknown: three texts, Nos. 124, 126, 127.

Randolph. *Arkansas:* LC 5420B2, Mrs. O. Trail, 1942 (FAC I 299).
Missouri: Charles Ingenthron, 1941 (FAC I 298, II 269).

Robb, *New Mexico:* No. 775, R. Reed, 1951 (FAC I 177); No. 631, J.
Farris, 1951 (FAC I 184).

Sackett. *Kansas:* Mrs. E. D. Brennan (FAC I 543); Nancy Ellen Muller
FAC I 545); unidentified (FAC I 544).

Sorrels. *Idaho:* Dick and Jean Person (FAC I 62).

UAFA. *Arizona:* R50B1, Pauline Beals; R75, Paul Bailey.

WKFA. *Kentucky.* 21 texts: S. W. Butler, 1958 (FAC II 136); Lester
Wilson, Jr. 1948 (FAC II 141); Mrs. Will Clines, 1956 (FAC II 194);
Irene B. Ferren, 1952 (FAC II 195); mother of Martha Maddox, 1948
(FAC II 196); Purdy Tillman, 1948 (FAC II 197); Mrs. Birdie Creasey,
1952 (FAC II 198); Jerry Johnson, 1958 (FAC II 199); H. Wright, 1948
(FAC II 216); Mrs. Boyce Jones; Verona Smith, 1948; Mrs. Grace Grim-
stead, 1952; Mrs. Henry Grimes, 1956; Burie Stewart, 1958; Sarah
Maloney, 1935; Mary T. Blakey; Mrs. John Lampkins, 1949; from Knott
County, 1959 (FAC II 137); 1935 (FAC II 217); two texts, unidentified,
1949 and 1958. *Texas:* Milton Brown.

WPA. *New Mexico:* LC W1012, 1936 (FAC II 74). *North Carolina:* (FAC
II 455). *Wyoming:* LC 12273, three texts, 1930's (FAC II 223).

Discussion:

Abbott and Smith, pp. 260–61.
Ames, pp. 219–23.
Angell, pp. 76–87.
Barrett, Chapter 7.
Barry, pp. 277–80.
Belden, *Song-Ballads,* #68.
Brown, *North Carolina* II, pp. 614–15.
Callison, pp. 155–58 (FAC III 315).
Clark, N. M., letter to A. E. Fife, September 6, 1964 (FAC II 699).
Clifford, p. 592.

Combs and Shearin, p. 15.
Dobie, *Longhorns,* p. 216.
Dodge City Journal, December 9, 1948 (FAC III 117).
Eddy, p. 184.
Emrich, pp. 227–30.
Flanders, p. 252.
Fowke and Johnston, p. 161.
Frothingham, *Adventure Magazine,* March 10, 1922, pp. 179–80 (FAC III 825).
Goldstein, tape made in Scotland, March 1, 1960, and letter from him dated October 22, 1960 (FAC II 325); Goldstein, *Texas.* Folkways record FS 3805.
Gordon 1572, from E. D. Baker.
Hand, *Butte,* pp. 30–31; *Strassen,* pp. 144–61.
Hull, p. 48.
Hunter, pp. 457–58.
Jeffers-Johnson, p. 286.
Laws, pp. 57, 131.
Lomax, *Best Loved,* pp. 194–95; *USA,* pp. 194–95; d. 5558, W. D. Totten, Seattle, Wash., 1912 (FAC II 757); d. 5566, Paul Hutchinson, California, 1924 (FAC II 756); d. 5634, a series of texts (JL 29); d. 5638, three texts from H. M. Belden, 1910 (JL 95); d. 5641, letter from Oscar Fox giving date of joint publication of this item as 1923 (JL 122); d. 5656, galley proof with many additions and changes.
Moore, *Oklahoma,* p. 57.
Olney, Marguerite, letter, January 12, 1959 (FAC II 122).
Pollan, pp. 12–35, 50–66.
Pound, *American,* p. 273; *Origins,* p. 119.
Randolph II, p. 179.
Ridings, p. 292, n. 2.
Rios, pp. 4–6 (FAC III 610).
Scarborough, pp. 353–59.
Sires, p. 4.
Steckert, interview with Jesse Wight, Wyoming, 1956 (FAC I 570).
Thorp and Clark, p. 160.
WFQ XVII (1958) pp. 200–5; XVIII (1959), pp. 35–39.
WPA, Wyoming, LC 12273 (FAC II 223).

"Ballad of Bloody Thursday." Goldstein, FS 3805B7, sung by John Greenway.
"Ballad of Sherman Wu." Goldstein, FS 3805B9, sung by Pete Seeger.

"Bloody Thursday." Greenway, pp. 237–38.

"The Book-Worm's Lament." Lomax d. 5638: clipping from New York newspaper (JL 62).

"The Co-Pilot's Lament." Wallerich, pp. 14–15.

"Dugway Lament." WFQ XVIII (1959), p. 172.

"The Dying Lineman" ("The Lineman's Hymn"). Goldstein, FS 3805B4, sung by Rosalie Sorrels; FAC I 37; WFQ, XVII (July, 1958), pp. 203–4.

"The Dying Ranger." *Colorado* I, No. 3, pp. 20–21.

"Feathery Passage." Chambers, unpaged.

"Git Along Little Dogies." Gaines, pp. 148–49 (FAC III 27). Lomax d. 5654, Newton Gaines (JL 311).

"I Once Was a Carman." Goldstein, FS 3805B3, sung by Guthrie Meade. Hand, *Butte*, pp. 31–33; *Strassen*, pp. 160–61.

"Jack Combs" ("Jack Combs' Death Song," "Jack Combs' Murder," "The Dying Cowboy"). Bradley, p. 903 (FAC III 358). Combs, pp. 209–10. Combs and Shearin, p. 17. Lomax, d. 5620, Bristol Taylor (JL 20).

"Professor's Lament." Goldstein, FS 3805B10, sung by Roger Abrahams. WFQ XVII (1958), pp. 204–5.

"The Streets of Hamtramck." Goldstein, FS 3805B8, sung by Bill Friedland. WFQ XIX (1960), p. 59.

"A Sun Valley Song." Goldstein, FS 3805B6, sung by Jan Brunvand. WFQ XVIII (1959), p. 38.

"The Teacher's Lament." *Sing Out*, VII, No. 1 (1958), p. 24.

"Too Old to Work." Greenway, p. 306.

"Troubadour of Red Fork Ranch." Coldiron, pp. 43–44 (FAC III 241).

"The Wild Lumberjack." Goldstein, FS 3805B5, sung by Kenneth Goldstein. Hand, *Strassen*, pp. 159–60. Korson, pp. 352–53. Shoemaker, *North*, pp. 196–97.

No title: "I want no fenced in graveyard . . ." Lomax d. 5634, *Frontier Stories* (JL 29).

XIV

Chopo

*T*HE WEST WAS WON BY MEN on horse-
back: explorers, trappers, miners, buffalo hunters, outlaws, cowboys, and
even sod busters all depended so mightily on their mounts or dray horses
that, without them, the West could not possibly have been conquered,
at least not at the moment in history that it was. Railroads and auto-
mobiles have of course made their contribution, but only after the image
of civilization had been engraved upon the western landscape by the
clatter of horses' hooves.

Dozens of popular songs pay homage to horses of the West,[1] both
to the mustangs—wild progeny of the Spanish breed left behind by the
conquistadores—and to the domestic varieties that gave heart and sinews
to the civilizing dreams of Anglo-Americans.

Thorp speaks at some length of several horses he owned, but to
none did he give such high praise as he did to Chopo, the coal-black
offspring of a Morgan sire shipped out of the East and of a mustang
Arabian mare descended from a *caballada* abandoned by the Spanish.[2]

Chopo first proved himself on the trail drive that saw the demise of
"Little Joe the Wrangler."[3] During a night of terror just west of the

---

[1] See, for example, Robert Frothingham, *Songs of Horses* (Boston: Houghton
Mifflin Co., 1920).

[2] Thorp and Clark, pp. 51–53.

[3] *Supra,* Song I.

191

Pecos, hail, lightning, and sheets of rain had set the cattle on razor edge. A thunderbolt struck near, sending twenty-five-hundred steers into a mad stampede. On Chopo, Thorp kept stride with the leading steers, waving his slicker and shooting across the front of the cattle, hoping to get them running in a circle. One false step by Chopo would have meant instant death beneath the hooves of the crazy herd. After several miles of running, Thorp was able to perceive through the darkness that he was now riding lead, not on the entire herd, but upon a half-dozen strays who had broken off from the main band. Lost, he simply gave Chopo free rein, and after several hours he saw in the distance a spark of light that was indeed his own outfit's camp. Chopo had kept his footing in an hour of crisis and led his master back to camp "on a night black enough to render human senses absolutely useless."[4]

We have encountered the music only twice:[5] It is set here from the singing of "The Tune Wranglers."

XIV–A.   THORP (1908) pages 30–31

1.   Through rocky arroyas so dark and so deep
      Down the sides of the mountains so slippery and steep
      You've good judgment, sure footed, wherever you go
      You're a safety conveyance my little Chopo

2.   Whether single or double or in the lead of a team
      Over highways or byways or crossing a stream
      You're always in fix and willing to go
      Whenever you're called on, my chico Chopo.

3.   You're a good roping horse, you were never jerked down
      When tied to a steer, you will circle him round
      Let him once cross the string, and over he'll go
      You sabe the business, my cow horse Chopo.

4.   One day on the Llano, a hail storm began
      The herds were stampeded, the horses all ran
      The lightning it glittered, a cyclone did blow
      But you faced the sweet music my little Chopo.

---

[4] Thorp and Clark, pp. 52–53.
[5] Lee, *Cowboy*, p. 64, and sung by The Tune Wranglers on Bluebird B7612-A (FAC III 965).

5. Chopo my pony, Chopo my pride
    Chopo my amigo, Chopo I will ride
    From Mexico's borders 'cross Texas Llanos
    To the salt Pecos river I ride you Chopo.

XIV–B. LEE, *Cowboy*, page 65, has one additional stanza:

6. The thunder and lightning for you had no fears,
    You carried me safe with the stampedin' steers,
    You're jest a cow pony, but maybe you know
    How much you are to me—my little Chopo.

XIV–C. "CHOPO"
Sung by The Tune Wranglers: Bluebird B7612-A (FAC III 965).

Through rock-y ar-ro-yos so dark and so deep, Down the
sides of a moun-tain so slip-pery and steep. You've good

Stems up for verse-Stems down for chorus

judg-ment, Sure foot-ed where-ev-er you go. You're a
safe-ty con-vey-ance, My lit-tle Chop-o.

BIBLIOGRAPHY

Printed texts:

Lee, *Cowboy,* pp. 64–65; *Range,* pp. 44–45.
Lomax (1916), pp. 371–72 = Thorp (1921) pp. 23–24.
Thorp (1921) pp. 23–24.

Commercial recordings:

The Tune Wranglers: Bluebird B7612-A (FAC III 965).

Manuscript texts:

PNFQ 66. *Oregon:* Flora Dey.

Discussion:

Lomax d. 5639 (JL 501).
Thorp and Clark, pp. 51–53.

XV

Buffalo Range

CARL SANDBURG SPEAKS OF THE HOMERIC quali-
ties in "The Buffalo Range."[1] Life on the western frontier, like life
among Greek soldiers at the siege of Troy, was fraught with violence.
Men matched wits and sinews against raw nature and other men. Verbal
agreements were the best legal tender, and, while the exploitation of
frontier resources was the first order of business, the exploitation of men
by their peers met instantaneous and violent resistance.

"The Buffalo Range" tells the laconic story of a frontier entrepreneur
who beguiled a rugged group of cowboys into going west to hunt buffalo.
Working conditions were far worse than the cowboys had been given to
believe. At the end of the hunt the boss refused to pay the wages promised. So the cowboys killed him and returned home somewhat the wiser,
having vindicated their frontiersmen's dignity upon a man by whom
they had been willfully beguiled and degraded. The preservation of
honor among westerners required occasional "bone bleachings," just as
it had at the siege of Troy.

The sixty-some-odd stanzas and significant variants noted in the
numerous texts that we have studied do not constitute an epic poem.
But this is only a small part of the story: "Buffalo Range," like the heroic
literature of ancient times, has generated its analogues and parodies.

First there is "The Trail to Mexico," otherwise known as "The

---

[1] Sandburg, p. 270.

195

Hills of Mexico," "My Trip to Mexico," "Boggy (Boggus) Creek," "The Noted Cowboy." It is a fairly servile parody. A high-powered trail boss engages a group of cowboys to drive a herd of longhorns from Texas to (New) Mexico. The job proves more dangerous and uncomfortable than was to be expected. The boss refuses to pay off, so the punchers are constrained to send him "across lots to hell" and then return broke to their homes. The song dates, we think, from the early 1880's, perhaps ten years after "Buffalo Range."

There is also "The Crooked Trail to Holbrook," which, according to one of our sources, was composed by Charlie Cunningham while driving a herd from the Gila River to Holbrook in Arizona. Here the conflict between the trail boss and the cowboys is lost entirely. But we are rewarded with a sequence of realistic and vivid descriptions of the rugged terrain, the storms, the hardships of the trail, and especially with insights into the rugged and virile temperaments of the men themselves.

We aren't yet ready to pontificate on the precise relationship between two favorite railroad songs and "Buffalo Range." "Way Out in Idaho" and "In the State of Arkansas" ("Sanford Barnes," "Bill Safford"), nevertheless, treat a similar topic and with similar style and language. An unemployed man signs up to go to Arkansas or Idaho to work. In the Idaho song the exploiter even gets his victims drunk, putting them on the train for Pocatello after they have passed out. At the destination they meet nothing but hardship, poverty, inhumanity. Both songs, however, have jovial overtones, showing that the exploitation may contain more dramatic pose than fact (". . . I'll marry a girl I know/And we'll buy us a horse and buggy/And we'll go back to Idaho.") Both songs seems to date from the 1880's. "John Garner's Trail Herd"[2] is similar and was no doubt also influenced by "Buffalo Range." D. K. Wilgus cites "Muskoka" as another song that is tied into this group.[3]

Robert W. Gordon, founder and first curator of the Archive of Folk Music, Library of Congress, received copies of a "Buffalo Song" that is certainly related to "Buffalo Range."[4] Gordon got it from Joseph W.

---

[2] Thorp (1921) pp. 84–86.
[3] Sung by Tom Brandon on Folk-Legacy FSC-10 (12" LP).
[4] Gordon 685, 3782. *Adventure Magazine* (April 20, 1925) p. 191 (FAC III 349). We have also encountered it in *The Cattleman* (July, 1928), p. 22 (FAC III 230) and in a manuscript of the Arkansas WPA project, LC W2652 (FAC II 48).

Fapp, a notorious faro dealer who had it from the presumed author, "Whiskey" Parker, said to have composed it in 1872. Parker was a college graduate and of wealthy parents. A "youthful indiscretion" had made him a wanderer. With $150 and a gold watch (a maternal keepsake) he came to the Black Hills (1875–76) accompanied by a "Fallen Angel" picked up in Cheyenne. They took up adjoining lands, prospered, married, and reared a family, now loved and respected by all.[5] The song, though smelling somewhat of the lamp, gives images of frontier life in the decade of buffalo hunting not encountered elsewhere.

So much for the parodies and analogues. The antecedents of "Buffalo Range" are equally interesting, though here we shall trace it only to the eastern seaboard, leaving it to other scholars to take it on back across the Atlantic to the British Isles whence so much of the substance of the American folk song quite understandably comes. Mrs. Eckstrom cites an English sea song, "Canada-I-O" of the early 1800's, and an older love song "Caledonia," published in 1800.[6] Kittredge cites a British "Canada-I-O," a song of the love of a gallant lady and a sailor.[7]

In 1853 Ephriam Bailey, living in Hudson, Maine, hired out to Fields, Phillips, and Norcross to cut timber at Three Rivers, Provence of Quebec. The following spring, upon his return home, he wrote "Canada-I-O" in commemoration of his experience. There is no mistaking—the subject and the mood are the same as in "Buffalo Range." It is a "preacher of the gospel" who exploits the would-be lumberjacks. He even has them "sign papers" that they will stay on the job. Hardship and deception befall, but the lumbermen do collect wages before returning home and there is no retribution against their exploiter. This same song with essential changes of locale appears as "Michigan-I-O," "Collie's Run-I-O," "The Jolly Lumberman," and "The City of Winnepeg."[8] "The Teamster's Marseillaise" is also dependent on "Canada-I-O" for its subject and for most of its basic ideas.[9]

"Buffalo Range" is certainly dependent upon "Canada-I-O" and the degree of dependency is evident if you choose to compare them stanza

---

5 See text D.
6 *Bulletin, Northeast,* VI (1933), p. 11. Eckstrom and Smyth, pp. 21–32. Leach, pp. 773–75.
7 Cited in Gray, p. 37.
8 Rickaby, pp. 113–15.
9 JAFL XXVI (1913), p. 187.

by stanza in accordance with the numbers we have inserted between parentheses in the "Canada-I-O" which appears as Text E. But in our view, "Buffalo Range" has gained significantly. The boss–cowboy conflict, not contained in "Canada-I-O," culminating in unabashed murder, adds dramatic intensity. "Canada-I-O" prolongs the conditions of agreement between the preacher and the lumbermen and exposes in oratorical and bland style the adversities encountered. "Buffalo Range," on the contrary, moves boldly and precisely into the painful facts and the inevitable tragedy.

We are not sure that it will ever be possible to establish authorship. Mrs. Eckstrom says it must have been written by "a Maine man who carried 'Canada-I-O' west with him and altered it himself in the West."[10] But she reaches this conclusion on the basis of one double stanza, numbers 15 and 15.1 of the texts, which is absent from most texts of the "Buffalo Range" as traditionally sung. J. E. McCauley of Seymour, Texas, says it was written by a hunter called Buffalo Jack.[11] Gard reports that Lomax had received a letter from an old hunter who claimed to have been a member of the group that killed Crego: "On the way back to Jacksboro one of the beguiled skinners started a song about the trip and the hard times and old Crego and we all set in to help him. Before we got back to Jacksboro we had shaped it, and the whole crowd could sing it."[12]

J. Frank Dobie gives a different story. In August, 1941, he received a visit from James B. Freeman, then eighty-four years old. Freeman recorded "The Buffalo Hunt" for Dobie as he claimed to have composed it. Born in Tennessee in 1857, Freeman had come to Texas in 1872. In '77 he hired out to James Ennis, a Jacksborough buffalo hunter. Ennis was, unlike Crego, a generous and honorable man. Accompanied by a cook and two skinners, he loaded up with food, ammunition, and other supplies, crossed Pease River, moving first northeast and then to the south. In what is now Runnels County, Texas, they saw a ten-mile stretch between the Concho and Colorado rivers blackened by buffaloes "as close together as cattle in a trail herd." Ennis killed up to ninety head in a single day. The skinners, working as a pair, got "two bits" each per carcass, averaging month in and month out five dollars per day, food and

---

[10] *Bulletin, Northeast,* VI (1933), p. 12.
[11] Gard, *Buffalo,* p. 290.
[12] *Ibid,* pp. 290–91; also in Lomax, *Ballad,* pp. 55–56.

skinning knives furnished by Ennis. They worked late into the ꞁ
pegging out the hides, and still later capping and reloading cartriꞔ
for the next day's hunt. "The cook made plenty of sour dough bread a.ᴧ
knew how to turn buffalo hump with its alternate layers of fat and
lean. . . ."

Freeman said he made up his song little by little while at work on
the buffalo range, "not writing it down but keeping it in my head." 18<u>73</u>
was chosen to rhyme with "me." He doubts there were buffalo hunts as
early as '73 because the Indians were too bad. But by '77 the Comanches
and the Kiowas had been rounded up, so Freeman said he put the line
about their being "ready to pick us off" in memory of the old days. "In
the song I made out that Ennis was trying to beat us out of our pay just
as a joke on him. He was fair and square, and we all liked him. He
would laugh when I sung that part of the song."[13]

Dobie accepted Freeman's story and we find it plausible, though it
poses some questions. Why didn't Freeman say anything about "Canada-
I-O," which he would have had to know in order to come up with
"Buffalo Range"? How did "James Ennis" get replaced by "Crego" and
his pseudonyms?

Just in case James Ennis is the original "Crego," the story of one
of his escapades while on a buffalo hunt will be of interest. In February
of 1877 he was camped on Sweetwater Creek in Scurry County, Texas.
Going out alone on a foggy morning, he shot two bulls, skinned them,
and left the hides staked out beside the carcasses. The same afternoon
he wounded a bull, which turned and charged him. Ennis dropped his
gun and climbed the nearest mesquite tree with record speed. The bull
kept charging the tree until it snapped in two and Ennis landed astraddle
the buffalo, which, happily for Jim, was so terrified that it tore off across
the prairie letting Ennis slide to the ground unharmed.

Ennis recovered his gun, and as night fell he at last found the two
carcasses of his morning hunt. He built a fire, grilled some buffalo hump,
and then rolled up inside one of the hides to sleep the cold night out.
Warm and weary, he dozed off, only to be awakened by a wild jostling
that turned out to be a pack of hungry wolves gnawing at the bits of
flesh left on the hide, frozen by this time into a steel-like tube. At dawn
the wolves withdrew, but Ennis remained trapped in the frozen hide until

---

[13] Dobie, *Buffalo*, pp. 1–6.

at last a warm mid-morning sun had thawed it and he was able to crawl out. Back in camp, his fellow hunters scarcely recognized him because during that wild night of the wolves his hair had turned gray.[14]

Dobie's setting of the melody, as sung by James B. Freeman,[15] is typical of most renderings of the song, though sometimes it is treated in $\frac{4}{4}$ time, as is the case with Kathy Dagel, who injects a quick humor very appropriate for a serio-humorous treatment of the song.[16] Enthusiasts for early and authentic western singing styles are urged to hear four of the Library of Congress field recordings of this song which, though sung with differing texts, have interpretive techniques difficult to set in musical notation.[17] Abandonment of rhythm and form is typical, so that it resembles a monotonous chant hovering around one tonal center with little harmonic or melodic variation and expressing a kind of resignation, a matter-of-fact acceptance of a grim situation with little or no display of emotion: vibratoless tonal cries that make simple statements of fact and nothing more.

XV–A.   THORP (1908) pages 31–33

1.	Come all you Buffalo hunters and listen to my song
	You needn't get uneasy, for it isn't very long
2.	It's concerning some Buffalo hunters who all agreed to go
	And spend a summer working, among the buffalo.

3.1	'Twas in the spring of seventy three, that I came to Jacksborough
	There I met Bailey Griego,[18] who asked how I'd like to go
4.1	And spend the summer west of Pease River hunting
	On the range of the Buffalo.

---

[14] Gard, *Buffalo,* pp. 284–85.

[15] Text F.

[16] Text G.

[17] Numbers 57A1, 2075A10in., 78A4 from unidentified singers recorded in Texas by the Lomaxes (FAC I 307, 308, 326); number 2781B1 recorded in Kentucky by Halpert (FAC I 310).

[18] Although "Crego" is predominant, we have also encountered "Trege," "Gregor," "Crager," "Crigor," "Kehoe," "Crago," "Craig," and "Ennis." Thorp's "Bailey Griego" (Spanish for "Greek") offers the possibility of an epithet chosen to deprecate the central figure of the song. Note that in cowboy language the name "Greaser" is used to identify a low-caste Mexican.

5.1 Now being out of employment to Griego I n
When I could join his outfit if suited with th\
6.1 I agreed if he'd pay good wages and transporta
To go and spend the summer among the buffal\

7.1 Of course I'll pay good wages and transportation \
But if you should grow homesick and return to Jacksborough
8.1 Before the huntings over I want you now to know
That I'll not pay you back wages from the range of the
Buffalo.

9.2 Through promises and flattery he enlisted quite a train
Some ten or twelve in number all able bodied men
10. Our journey it was pleanant on the road we had to go
Until we crossed Pease River among the buffalo.

11. 'Twas here our pleasure ended, our troubles had begun
The very first beast I tried to skin Oh how I cut my thumb
12. When skinning off those buffalo hides for our lives we'd
little show
As the Indians tried to pick us off on the range of the
buffalo.

13. Salt meat and Buffalo hump to eat and hard old sour dough
bread
Strong coffee and alkali water to drink add a raw-hide for
a bed
14. The way the mosquitos chewed on us you bet it wasn't slow
Lord grant there's no place on earth like the range of the
buffalo.

17. When the summer at last ended old Griego began to say
My boys you've been extravagant, so I'm in debt to day
18.4 But among the buffalo hunters bankrupt law didn't go
So we left old Griegos bones to bleach among the buffalo.

19. Now we're back across Peace River and homeward we are
bound
In that forsaken country may I never more be found
20.1 If you see anyone bound out there pray warn them not to go
To that forsaken country, the land of the buffalo.

XV–C<small>OMPOSITE</small> <small>TEXT</small>

1.   Texts A, F.

2.   Texts A, F.

3.   'Twas in the town of Jacksboro in the spring of seventy-three
A man by the name of Crego came stepping up to me.

3.1   Text A.

3.11   'Twas in the spring of eighty-three, I happened in Jacksboro;
There I met with a fellow called Ira Crego by name.

3.2   Text B.

3.3   Text F.

4.   Text F.

4.1   Text A.

4.2   Text B.

5.   It's me being out of employment, this to Crego I did say,
"This going out on the buffalo range depends upon the pay.

5.1   Text F.

6.   Text F.

6.1   Text A.

6.2   I'll forsake my home and sweetheart and from old Texas go
And spend one trip so pleasantly on the trail to Mexico.

7.   Texts B, F.

7.1   Text A.

7.2   I'll pay to you good wages, fine transportation, too,
And I have six jolly fellows; I'm sure that they will go.

8.   Text F.

8.1   Text A.

8.2   And if you should get homesick and back to old Texas go
        I'll furnish you no horse to ride from the city of Mexico.

9.   It's now our outfit was complete—seven able-bodied men,
        With navy six and needle gun—our troubles did begin.

9.1   And now the outfit was complete, nine able-bodied men
        With leather chaps and Stetson, and Crego he made ten.

9.2   Text A.

9.3   With all this flattering talk he enlisted quite a few
        Some ten good able-bodied men to stay the season through.

9.4   By such talk and flatteration he enlisted twenty-one
        And when we got to Peace River our troubles they begun

9.5   This being said and ended, we started with our band
        Some twenty-five or thirty able-bodied men.

10.   Our trip it was a pleasant one, the trail we had to go,
        Until we reached Old Boggy creek in the hills of Mexico.

10.1   Some eight or ten in number who up the trail did go
        To spend a pleasant summer life in the hills of Mexico.

11.1   Text F.

11.2   Now boys we've crossed old Boggy Creek, our troubles have
            begun
        If first hail storms fell on us, Lord, how those yearlin's run.

11.3   It's now our pleasures are over, our troubles have begun;
        But with many six and buffalo guns, we thought our troubles
            fun.

12.   When skinning off those buffalo hides for our lives we'd
            little show

As the Indians tried to pick us off on the range of the
buffalo.

12.1   They run through the brush and the stickers, we stood but
little show
And the Indians watched to pick us up in the hills of
Mexico.

12.2   The water was salty as hell fire, the beef I could not go
And the Indians waited to pick us off while skinning the
buffalo.

12.3   Pease River's as salty as hell fire, the water I could never go—
O God! I wished I had never come to the range of the buffalo.

13.   Texts A, F.

13.01   Our water was salty as damnation, both gypsum and alkali,
Our meat it was old buffalo hump, our bread it was a sight.

13.1   Our meat it was buffalo hump and iron wedge bread,
And all we had to sleep on was a buffalo robe for a bed.

13.2   Our daily fare was buffalo and lots of sourdough bread
We got so very sick of it we wished we all were dead.

13.3   Our daily fare was buffalo with lots of sour-dough bread
The bunk we had to sleep in you'd never call a bed.

13.4   He fed us on such sorry chuck I wished myself most dead,
It was old jerked beef, croton coffee, and sour bread.

14.   Texts A, F.

14.01   And mosquitos by the millions; the Indians I'd rather fight
For they sucked the blood from every pore, on the range of
the buffalo.

14.1   The fleas and graybacks worked on us, O boys, it was not
slow,
I'll tell you there's no worse hell on earth than the range of
the buffalo.

14.2   We slept in prairie-dog towns, rattlesnakes and vinegarroons,
Our beds were made of buffalo hides, I'll have you all to
know.

15.   Text F.

15.1   Our hearts were cased with buffalo hocks, our souls were
cased with steel,
And the hardships of that summer would nearly make us reel.

16.   The boss he used to haze us though none of us were slow
Until we wished we'd never seen the range of the buffalo.

17.   Texts A, B, F.

17.1   The first snow fell, Old Crego fumed, and this to us did say
The boys had been outrageous, were in debt to him to stay.

17.2   Well now our summer's work is done, boys, the boss to us
did say
"I'm so deep in debt, boys, I see no show to pay."

17.3   The summer season being over, our leader refused to pay
The boys all being extravagant, they took his life that day.

18.   We coaxed him and we begged him and still it was no go—
We left old Crego's bones to bleach on the range of the
buffalo.

18.1   We tripped him and we kicked him to make the money flow
We left his pesky hide to bleach with the bones of the
buffalo.

18.2   With pistols and with rifles, I want you all to know
We left the driver's bones to bleach in the hills of Mexico.

18.3   But the skinners clubbed together and said that did not go
So we left old Trego's bones to bleach with the bones of the
buffalo.

18.4   Texts A, B.

18.5   Text F.

19.   Texts A, B, F.

20.   Go home to our wives and sweethearts, tell others not to go,
            For God's forsaken the buffalo range and the damned old
                buffalo.

20.1   Text A.

20.2   So back to our wives and sweethearts and tell others not to go
            No matter if they pay your fare to the range of the buffalo.

20.3   Text F.

XV–B.   "The Hills of Mexico"
        Haley, pages 201–2. Reproduced with permission of the Texas
        Folklore Society.

        3.2   I found myself in Griffin in the spring of eighty-three
                When a noted cow driver one morning came to me,
        4.2   Says: "How do you do, young fellow, say how'd you like to go
                And spend one summer pleasantly out in New Mexico?"

        5.1   I being out of employment to the driver thus did say:
                "A going out in New Mexico depends upon the pay.
        6.01   If you pay me good wages, transportation to and fro,
                I believe I'll go along with you out in New Mexico."

        7.   "Of course I'll pay good wages and transportation too
                Provided that you stay with me the summer season through.
        8.21   But if you do get homesick and want to Griffin go
                I will even loan you a horse to ride from the hills of Mexico."

        9.31   With all this flattering talk he enlisted quite a train,
                Some ten or twelve in number, strong able bodied men.
        10.01   Our trip was quite a pleasant one over the road we had to go
                Until we reached old Boggy Creek out in New Mexico.

11.21   Right there our pleasures ended, our troubles they begun.
         The first hail storm that came on us, Christ, how those
         cattle run.
12.11   In running through thorns and stickers we had but little show
         And the Indians watched to pick us off the hills of Mexico.

17.   The summer season ended, the driver could not pay,
         The outfit was so extravagant he was in debt today.
18.4   That's bankrupt law among the cowboys, Christ, this will
         never do.
         That's why we left his bones to bleach out in New Mexico.

19.   So now we'll cross old Boggy Creek and homeward we are
         bound,
         No more in this cursed country will ever we be found.
20.   Go home to our wives and sweethearts, tell others not to go
         To that God-forsaken country they call New Mexico.

XV–C.   "The Crooked Trail to Holbrook"
         Thorp (1921) pages 53–54: "Mailed me from Douglas, Arizona,
         by an old friend named Cotton."

         Come, all you jolly cowboys that follow the bronco steer,
         I'll sing to you a verse or two your spirits for to cheer;
         It's all about a trip that I did undergo
         On that crooked trail to Holbrook, in Arizona, oh.

         It was on the seventeenth of February our herd it started out,
         It would have made your hearts jump to hear them bawl and shout,
         As wild as any buffalo that ever swam the Platte,
         Those cattle we were driving and every one was fat.

         We crossed the Mescal Mountains on the way to Hidalgo,
         And when we got to Gilson Flats, Lord, how the wind did blow!
         But our spirits never failed us as onward we did go,—
         On that crooked trail to Holbrook, in Arizona, oh.

         That night we had a stampede; Lord, how the cattle run!
         We made it to our horses; I tell you, we had fun;
         Over the prickly pear and catclaw brush we quickly made our way;
         We thought of our long journey and the girls we'd left one day.

It's long by Sombserva we slowly punched along,
While each and every puncher would sing a hearty song
To cheer up his comrade as onward we did go,—
On that crooked trail to Holbrook, in Arizona, oh.

We crossed the Mogollon Mountains where the tall pines grow,
Grass in abundance and rippling streams do flow;
Our packs were always turning, of course our gait was slow,—
On that crooked trail to Holbrook, in Arizona, oh.

At last we got to Holbrook—a little gale did blow;
It blew up sand and pebble stones, and it didn't blow them slow,
We had to drink the water from that muddy little stream,
And swallowed a peck of dirt when we tried to eat a bean.

But the cattle now are shipped and homeward we are bound
With a lot of as tired horses as ever could be found,
Across the reservation no danger did we fear,
But thoughts of wives and sweethearts and the ones we love so dear.

Now we are back in Globe City, our friendship there to share;
Here's luck to every puncher that follows the broncho steer.[19]

XV–D.   "BUFFALO SONG"
          Gordon, *Adventure Magazine* (April 20, 1925), page 191 (FAC
          III 349). Reprinted with permission of Popular Publications, Inc.

Come all you pretty fair maids, these lines to you I write,
We're going on the range, in which we take delight,
We're going on the range as we poor hunters do,
While those tender-footed fellows do stay at home with you.

Our game it is the antelope, the buf'lo, elk, and deer;
They roam these broad prairies without the least of fear,
We rob them of their robes, in which we think no harm,
To buy us chuck and clothing to keep our bodies warm.

The buf'lo is the largest and the noblest of the van,
He sometimes refuses to throw us up his hands,

---

[19] This stanza from Lomax (1910) p. 123. Reproduced with permission of
Alan Lomax.

With shaggy mane uplifted and face toward the sky,
As if to say, "I'm coming; so, hunter, mind your eye."

While armed with the Sharps rifle and needle gun so true
We cause them soon to bite the dust, for they send their bullets
       through,
With nerves that never falter, and belt with forty rounds
We send them up Salt River to the Happy Hunting Grounds.

All the day long we go tramping around
In search of the buf'lo that we may shoot them down
And when we come upon them, if our guns have no defect,
We cause them to throw up their hands, and pass us in their checks.

Our house is made of buf'lo hides, we build them tall and round,
Our fire is made of buf'lo chips, our beds are on the ground.
Our furniture is the camp kettle, the coffee pot, and pan,
Our chuck is buf'lo beef and bread intermingled well with sand.

Our neighbors are the Cheyennes, the Arapohes, and Sioux,
Their mode of navigation is the buf'lo hide canoe;
And if they all should emigrate I'm sure we wouldn't care,
For a peculiar way they have of raising hunters' hair.

The hunters are jolly fellows, they like their lager beer,
The hunters are jolly fellows, they drink their whisky clear,
And now you've heard my song you mustn't think it queer
If I take a drink of whisky or a glass of lager beer!

XV–E.   "CANADAY I O"
       Bulletin, Northwest VI (1933) pages 10–11.

    (1) Come all ye jolly lumbermen, and listen to my song,
         But do not get discouraged, the length it is not long,
    (2) Concerning of some lumbermen, who did agree to go
         To spend one pleasant winter up in Canada I O.

    (3) It happened late one season in the fall of fifty-three,
         A preacher of the gospel one morning came to me;
    (4) Said he, "My jolly fellow, how would like to go
         To spend one pleasant winter up in Canada I O?"

(5) To him I quickly made reply, and unto him did say:
    "In going out to Canada depends upon the pay.
(6) If you will pay good wages, my passage to and fro,
    I think I'll go along with you to Canada I O."

(7) "Yes, we will pay good wages, and will pay your passage out,
    Provided you sign papers that you will stay the route;
(8) But if you do get homesick and swear that home you'll go,
    We never can your passage pay from Canada I O."

(8) "And if you get dissatisfied and do not wish to stay,
    We do not wish to bind you, no, not one single day;
(8) You just refund the money we had to pay, you know,
    Then you can leave that bonny place called Canada I O."

(9) It was by his gift of flattery he enlisted quite a train,
    Some twenty-five or thirty, both well and able men;
(10) We had a pleasant journey o'er the road we had to go,
    Till we landed at Three Rivers, up in Canada I O.

(11) But there our joys were ended, and our sorrow did begin;
    Fields, Phillips and Norcross they then came marching in;
    They sent us all directions, some where I do not know,
    Among those jabbering Frenchmen up in Canada I O.

    After we had suffered there some eight or ten long weeks
    We arrived at headquarters, up among the lakes;
    We thought we'd find a paradise, at least they told us so,
    God grant there may be no worse hell than Canada I O!

    To describe what we have suffered is past the art of man,
    But to give a fair description I will do the best I can;
(13) Our food the dogs would snarl at, our beds were on the snow,
    We suffered worse than murderers up in Canada I O.

(15) Our hearts were made of iron and our souls were cased with
            steel,
    The hardships of that winter could never make us yield;
(16) Fields, Phillips and Norcross they found their match, I know,
    Among the boys that went from Maine to Canada I O.

(20) But now our lumbering is over and we are returning home,
　　　To greet our wives and sweethearts and never more to roam,
(20) To greet our friends and neighbors; we'll tell them not to go
　　　To that forsaken G— D—— place called Canada I O.

XV–F.　"THE BUFFALO-SKINNERS"
　　　　Dobie, *Buffalo,* pages 5–6. Reproduced with permission of the Texas
　　　　Folklore Society.

1.　　　Come all you jolly buffalo-hunters and listen to my song,
　　　　And do not grow outrageous, for the length it is not long.
2.　　　It was concerning some buffalo-skinners who did agree to go
　　　　And spend one winter pleasantly amongst the buffalo.

3.3　　I happened into Fort Griffin early in the fall of '73
　　　　When James Ennis by name one morning came to me,
4.　　　Said, "My jolly young fellow, how would you like to go,
　　　　And spend one winter pleasantly amongst the buffalo?"

5.1　　I being out of employment, I to James Ennis did say,
　　　　"This going out on the buffalo range depends upon the pay.
6.　　　If you will pay good wages, find transportation to and fro,
　　　　I think I will go with you out amongst the buffalo."

7.　　　"Oh, yes, I will pay good wages, find transportation too,
　　　　Provided you will stay with me the winter season through.
8.　　　But if you do grow homesick and back to Griffin go,
　　　　I'll not pay you transportation from the range of the buffalo."

9.31　 With all such flatterations we enlisted quite a train,
　　　　Some four or five in number of good able-bodied men.
10.01　Our ride it was a pleasant one o'er the road we had to go,
　　　　Until we came to Pease River amongst the buffalo.

11.1　　There all of our pleasures ended, our sorrow did begin,
　　　　And the first darn tail I tried to split,—Christ, how a cut
　　　　　　my hand!
12.31　Pease River's as salty as hell-fire, with gyp and alkali too;
　　　　Oh God! I wisht I never had come out amongst the buffalo.

13.   We lived on buffalo hump and salty water bread,
        Strong coffee and alkali water to drink, and a buffalo hide
        for a bed.

14.   The way the mosquitos and gray-backs worked upon us was
        not slow.
        God grant there's no worse hell on earth than amongst the
        buffalo.

15.   Our souls were cased with iron, our hearts were cased with
        steel,
        The hardships of one winter's work could never make us
        yield.

12.01   While skinning them darned ol' stinkers our lives they had
        no show,
        For the Indians watched to take our scalps while skinning
        them buffalo.

17.   And after the winter was over Ennis swore he could not pay,
        For the outfit had been so extravagant that he was in debt
        that day.

18.5   But we showed him amongst the skinners that the bankrupt
        did not go,
        And we took poor Ennis' hides to pay for skinning them
        buffalo.

19.   Oh, now we've crossed the Brazos River and homeward we
        are bound,
        No more in that God-forsaken country will ever we be
        found.

20.3   We'll go home to our wives and sweethearts, tell others not
        to go
        To that God-forsaken buffalo range to skin them buffalo.

XV–F.   Music

Come all you jol - ly buf - fa - lo hunt - ers and lis - ten to my song, And do not grow out- rag - eous,— For the length it is not long. It was con- cern - ing some buf - fa - lo skin - ners___ who did a - gree to go, And spend one win - ter pleas - ant - ly a - mongst the buf - fa - lo.

XV–G.   "Buffalo Skinners"
Sung by Kathy Dagel, Kansas, 1959 (FAC I 107).

Come all you jol - ly skin - ners and lis - ten to my song, There are not man - y ver - ses, It - 'll not de - tain you long, It's con - cern - ing some young fel - lows who did a - gree to go, And spend one sum - mer pleas - ant - ly on the range of the buf - fa - lo.

BIBLIOGRAPHY

Significant texts:

(1887)   Dobie, *Buffalo*, pp. 5–6 (FAC III 792).
early 1880's Gordon 685 = *Adventure Magazine* (October 20, 1924), p. 191
             (FAC III 393).
1910   Lomax (1910) pp. 158–63.
1910   Lomax d. 5662, Joe Harris, Westwater, Utah (JL 390).
?   Hoffman, from Shoemaker MS, Pennsylvania (FAC II 671).
?   Sandburg, pp. 270–73.

Printed texts:

Abrahams, pp. 172–73.
Allen *Cowboy Lore*, pp. 109–11.
Arkansas, p. 23.
Beck, pp. 21–23.
Big Round-Up, pp. 66–67.
Boatright, p. 5.
Botkin, *American*, p. 568 (= Callison, pp. 115–18), pp. 854–55.
Callison, pp. 117–18 (FAC III 314).
Carmer, p. 172.
Clark, *Cowboy*, p. 9.
Cowboy Songs, p. 11.
Davis, *Tip-Top*, p. 38.
Frey, pp. 70–71.
Friedman, pp. 429–30.
Frontier Times, November 1925, p. 39.
Gard, *Buffalo*, pp. 291–93.
Haley, pp. 201–2 (FAC III 157).
Hendren 541: unidentified newspaper clipping.
Larkin, pp. 83–86 = Lomax (1938) pp. 335–38.
Lindroth, pp. 11–12.
Lomax (1938) pp. 335–38; *American*, pp. 390–92; *Ballad*, pp. 55–56; *Best
   Loved*, pp. 174–75; *USA*, pp. 174–75.
Lone Ranger, p. 38.
Mammoth No. 11, p. 204.
Moore, pp. 289–91.
Pound, *American*, pp. 181–83 = Lomax (1910) p. 158.
Reinbach, p. 22.

Robinson, p. 54. Appears from same plates in *KFBI Songs of the Plains;*
   Blue Grass Roy, No. 4, p. 17.
Seeger, No. 7.
Sing 'em Cowboy, pp. 52–53.
Sires, pp. 34–35.
Treasure Chest, pp. 36–37.

Commercial recordings:

Bill Bender: Asch 410-3B, Stinson 410-3A, Varsity 5144 (FAC III 1077).

Manuscripts and field recordings:

Dorson. *Michigan:* Joan Schwartz, 1947 (FAC II 545).
Fife. *Kansas:* Kathy Dagel, 1959 (FAC I 107).
Halpert. *Kentucky:* LC 2781B1, 1939 (FAC I 310).
LC. Unknown: LC 2075A10, 2088B10.
Lomax. *Arkansas:* d. 5662, Tom Hight (JL 426). *Illinois:* Mary Meers,
   American School of Air MS (FAC II 262). *New York:* LC 2075A10,
   1939 (FAC I 308). *Texas:* d. 5653, H. Summers, 1907 (JL 186); d. 5662,
   Mrs. M. P. Elder, 1909 (JL 408); LC 78A4, 1934 (FAC I 326); d. 5662,
   J. E. McCauley, (JL 419), T. A. Pilgrim (JL 415), J. W. Light (JL 399),
   unsigned MS sent to *Dallas News* and unpublished (JL 409). Unknown:
   d. 5662, J. P. Nunn (JL 425), F. F. Simmons (JL 390), unknown (JL
   414).
PNFQ 43, 387. Unknown.
Seeger. Washington, D.C.: LC 2088B1, 1936 (FAC I 309).
WPA. *New Mexico:* LC W1021, 1936–37 (FAC II 80). *Wyoming:* LC
   W12271, 1930's (FAC II 231).

Discussion:

Allen, *Cowboy Lore,* p. 39.
Angell, pp. 40–49.
Barrett, Chapter 7.
Beck, p. 21.
Botkin, *American,* p. 854.
Bulletin, Northeast, VI (1933), pp. 10–13.
Dobie, *Buffalo,* pp. 1–6 (FAC III 792).
Fowke, *American,* p. 251.
Fowke and Johnston, pp. 68–69.
Gard, *Buffalo,* pp. 276–94 (plus entire book).
Garretson (entire book).
Gordon 685.

Gordon, *Adventure Magazine*, April 20, 1925, p. 191 (FAC III 349).
Gray, pp. 37–39.
Laws, pp. 17, 18, 31, 81, 136–37.
Lomax (1938), p. 335, note; *Ballad*, pp. 55–56; *Best Loved*, pp. 159–60; *USA*, pp. 159–60; LC numerical text 200A1 (FAC II 146); d. 5662; listed in letter to Carnegie Foundation, 1908.
Sandburg, p. 270.
Sandoz (entire book).
Wilgus, pp. 161, 255.

"Hills of Mexico" ("Boggy Creek")

Printed texts:

Haley, pp. 201–2 (FAC III 157).
Lomax, d. 5659, from Tom Hight's Scrapbook, Arkansas; d. 5685, *Dallas News*, n.d., two texts.
Lomax (Lilly), pp. 24–29 (FAC III 742).
McConathy, pp. 80–81.
PTFLS II (1923), p. 45 (FAC III 172).

Manuscripts and field recordings:

Fife. *Arizona:* Bye Hutchins, 1959 (FAC I 51).
Lomax. *Texas:* d. 5653, H. Knight (JL 200); d. 5654, from Uvalde; d. 5656, F. A. Pilgrim (JL 335); d. 5662, Mrs. M. P. Elder, 1909, and J. W. Light; d. 5685, unsigned MS sent to *Dallas News*, unpublished (JL 467); LC 57A1 (FAC I 307 = UTFA 39A1, FAC I 439). Unknown: d. 5656, J. Blankinship (two texts); d. 5662, Biddle.
Oklahoma. *Oklahoma:* Mrs. R. O. Brannon, 1950 (FAC II 446).
WPA. *Arkansas:* LC W2652, 1936 (FAC II 53).

Discussion:

Barrett, Chapter 7.
Bulletin, Northeast, VI (1933), p. 12.
Laws, pp. 136–37.

"Crooked Trail to Holbrook"

Printed texts:

Lomax (1910), pp. 121–23; (1938), pp. 27–28 (from Mrs. M. B. Wight).
Thorp (1921) pp. 53–54.

Manuscripts and field recordings:

Lomax. *Arizona:* d. 5638, 5656, Mrs. M. B. Wight (JL 349) = Lomax
(1910) pp. 121–23, and (1938) pp. 27–28, as corrected there. Unknown:
d. 5634, 5656.
PNFQ 94. Unknown.

Discussion:

Bulletin, Northeast, VI (1933), p. 12.
Laws, p. 247.
Literary Digest (February 21, 1914), p. 379 (FAC III 464).
Lomax d. 5672, Mrs. M. B. Wight, Arizona, 1907 (JL 433).

"WAY OUT IN IDAHO"

Printed texts:

Botkin, *Sampler,* pp. 554–55.
Botkin and Harlow, pp. 440–41.
Gordon, *Adventure Magazine* (October 20, 1923) = Gray, pp. 37–39.
Gray, pp. 37–39.
Jordan and Kessler, pp. 298–300.
Lomax, *Singing,* pp. 269–70 = LC 1634B1, Blaine Stubblefield, 1938 (FAC
II 179).

Manuscripts and field recordings:

Gordon 419. *Washington:* Ben A. Ranger, 1926 (1887).
LC. *Idaho:* LC 1634B1, Blaine Stubblefield, 1938 (FAC II 179).
Lomax. *Texas:* d. 5654, J. M. Grigsby, 1912 (JL 260).
Sorrels. *Idaho:* Blaine Stubblefield (FAC I 32).

Discussion:

Bulletin, Northeast, VI (1933), pp. 10–13.
Gordon 419, Ben A. Ranger, 1926.
Gray, pp. 37–39.
Literary Digest (February 21, 1914), p. 379 (FAC III 464).

XVI

The Cowboys Christmas Ball

*T*HORP GOT HIS TEXT OF LARRY CHITTENDEN's memorable poem
from Miss Jessie Forbes at Eddy, New Mexico, in 1898.[1] Save for half a
dozen words, it is as printed in Chittenden's *Ranch Verses*.[2] The high
poetic artistry, the multiple and authentic imagery of life in Anson City,
Jones County seat, in western Texas in the 1890's, the Homeric stanzaic
form consisting of six double stanzas, where one or two are normal for
the Anglo-American folk ballad, make it difficult for this precious specimen of frontier balladry to be fully absorbed in the oral tradition of the
American West. Yet these very qualities set it apart as a masterpiece of
"western" verse. The poet first evokes the vast frontier environment with
its exotic animals, its vistas of prairie and emptiness. Then he brings in
the image of man and an emergent agrarian civilization. Next his poetic
eyes focus on Anson itself, and the scene is activated by the cowboys and
other pioneer characters who, driven by loneliness, converge upon the
Morning Star Hotel. Windy Bill, the caller, provokes them to "stake
their pens" and "stampede." The tempo quickens in a crescendo of
warmth and animation until T-Bar Dick falls exhausted. The dancers
have achieved near orgiastic release, which will permit them to abide
loneliness once more.

Chittenden has concentrated in this song a great many of the images
that shape the cowboy myth, and hence assisted in bringing into American English many of its western tags: prairie dogs, coyotes, badgers,

---

[1] Thorp (1921), p. 35.
[2] New York: G. P. Putnam's Sons, 1893. Pp. 12–17.

antelopes, and rattlesnakes; ranches, Spanish ponies, whiskered wheat, tenderfeet, and trail herds; Windy Bill, T-Bar Dick, Little Pitchfork, Big Boston, and Spur Treadwell; stampedes, spurs, high-heeled boots, waterfalls (a hair style), rustling, locking horns, heifers, and mavericks. If we are to judge a literary product by how well it does what it sets out to do, rather than by arbitrary notions concerning universal beauty, then Larry Chittenden's poem may gain respect among critics as it already has among ordinary mortals, especially westerners.

Anson City still has its annual Christmas Ball—in double memory, now, of the Yuletide and of Larry Chittenden's poem. "The Cowboys New Years Dance," by Mark Chisholm,[3] is an undisguised parody and, like the general run of parodies, not so fine as the original, though it does show that Roswell, New Mexico, has strived to vie with Anson City in its commitment to the cowboy heritage.

Our music comes from the singing of J. K. Plauche, Albuquerque, New Mexico, as recorded by J. D. Robb. Insertion within the song of a stanza of "Buffalo Gals," most beloved of the early play-party repertoire, adds color and atmosphere.

XVI–A.   THORP (1908) pages 33–36

1.   Way out in Western Texas where the Clear Forks waters
           flow
        Where the cattle are a brewin' and the Spanish ponies grew
        Where the Northers come a whistlin' from beyond the
           Neutral Strip
        And the prairie dogs are sneezin' as though they had the grip
        Where the coyotes come a-howlin' round the ranches after
           dark
        And the mocking-birds are singin' to the lovely Medder Lark
        Where the possum and the badger and the rattlesnakes
           abound
        And the monstrous stars are winkin' o'er a wilderness
           prefound
        Where lonesome tawney prairies melt into air'y streems
        While the Double Mountains slumber in heaven'ly kinds of
           dreams
        Where the Antelope is grazin' and the lonely plovers call
        It was there that I attended The Cowboys Christmas Ball.

---

[3] Song XXII of this work.

2.   The town was Anson City—old Jones' County Seat
Where they raised Poled Angus cattle and waving whiskered
    wheat
Where the air is soft and balmy and dry and full of health
And the prairies is exploding with Agricultural wealth
Where they print the "Texas Western" that Hue McCall
    supplies
With news and yarns and stories of most amazin' size
Where Frank Smith "pulls the badger" on knowin'
    tenderfeet
And Democracy's triumphant and mighty hard to beat
Where lives that good old hunter John Milsap from Lamar
Who used to be the sheriff "back east in Paris sah"
'Twas there I say at Ansen with the lovely widder Wall
That I went to that reception The Cowboys Christmas Ball.

3.   The boys had left the ranches and come to town in piles
The ladies kinder' scatterin' had gathered in for miles
And yet the place was crowded as I remember well
'Twas gave on this occasion at the Morning Star Hotel
The music was a fiddle and a lively tambeurine
And a "Viol" came imported by the stage from Abilene
The room was togged out gorgeous with Mistletoe and
    shawls
And the candles flickered festious around the airy walls
The women folks looked lovely the boys looks kinder treed
'Till the leader commenced yellin' "whoa fellers lets
    stampede"
And the music started sighin' and a wailin' through the hall
As a kind of introduction to "The Cowboys Christmas Ball."

4.   The leader was a feller that came from Tomsons ranch
They called him "Windy Billy" from little Deadmans
    branch
His rig was kinder keerless big spurs and high heeled boots
He had the reputation that comes when fellers shoots
His voice was like a bugle upon the Mountains height
His feet were animated and a mighty moving sight
When he commenced to holler "now fellers stake yer pen"
Lock horns ter all them heifers and russle them like men
Saloot yer lovely critters neow swing and let 'em go
Climb the grape vine round 'em all hands do-ce-do
You Mavericke jine the round-up jest skip the water fall
Auh hit was gettin' active "The Cowboys Christmas Ball.

5.   The boys were tolerable skittish the ladies powerful neat
That old bass Viols music just got there with both feet
That wailin' frisky fiddler I never shall forget
And Windy kept singin' I think I hear him yet
O'Yes Chase your Squirrels and cut 'em to our side
Spur Treadwell to the centre with Cress P Charlie's bride
Doc' Hollis down the middle and twice the ladies chain
Van Andrews pen the fillies in big T Diamonds train
All pull your freight together neow swallow fork an change
Big Boston lead the trail herd through little Pitchfork's range
Purr round yor gentle pussies neow rope 'em balance all
Huh hit was gettin' active "The Cowboys Christmas Ball.

6.   The dust riz fast and furious we all just galloped round
Till the scenery got so giddy that T Bar Dick was down'd
We buckled to our partners an' told 'em to hold on
Then shook our hoofs like lightning until the early dawn
Don't tell me 'bout Cotillions or Germans No Sir 'Ee
That whirl at Anson City just takes the cake with me
I'm sick of lazy shufflings of them I've had my fill
Give me a frontier break-down backed up by Windy Bill
McAllister aint nowhere when Windy leads the show
I've seen 'em both in harness and so I sorter know
Oh Bill I shant forget you I'll oftentimes recall
That lively gaited sworray "The Cowboys Christmas Ball.

XVI–B.   "The Cowboys' Christmas Ball."
        Sung by J. K. Plauche, New Mexico, 1950 (FAC I 603).
        Reproduced with permission of the collector, Dean Emeritus John
        Donald Robb of the University of New Mexico.

North come a - whist-lin' from be-yond the Neut-ral
Strip, And the prai - rie dogs are sneez - in' as
though they had the grip. Where the lone - some tawn - y
prai - ries melt in - to air - y dreams, And the
Dou - ble moun - tains slum - ber in the heav-en - ly kinds of
dreams. Where the an - te - lope is graz - in' and the
lone - ly plov - ers call, It was there that I at -
tend - ed the cow - boy's Christ - mas ball.
Oh buf - fa - lo gals won't you come out to - night,
Come out to-night, Come out to-night, Buf - fa - lo gals won't you
come out to-night and dance -by the light of the moon.

BIBLIOGRAPHY

Printed texts:

Barrett, pp. 208–11: from *The Galveston Daily News* and *The Dallas Morning News,* December 27, 1891.

Briegel, *Rodeo,* pp. 8–9; *Souvenir,* p. 8.

Cattleman (March, 1920) pp. 171, 173; (March, 1935) p. 98; (December, 1952) p. 11.

Chittenden (1893) pp. 12–17 (FAC III 782); (1925) pp. 12–17 (FAC III 458).

Clark, *Cowboy,* p. 70.

Coleman and Bregman, pp. 38–39.

Cowboy Tom, pp. 6–7.

Cox, *Historical,* p. 246.

Hendren 358, unidentified newspaper clipping.

Lee, *Cowboy,* pp. 20–21.

Lomax (1916) pp. 335–39; (1938) pp. 246–49; *Cattle,* pp. 112–16.

Oklahoma: unidentified newspaper clipping from Mrs. Lilian Ward (FAC III 732).

Sires, pp. 38–39.

Siringo, *Song,* pp. 27–31.

Thorp (1921) pp. 35–39.

Westermeier, pp. 279–80: from *Field and Farm* (December 25, 1897), p. 6.

Field recordings:

Robb. *New Mexico:* J. K. Plauche, 1950 (FAC I 603).

Discussion:

Barrett, pp. 208–11.

Cattleman (January, 1953), pp. 196–97.

Gillis, p. 101.

Lomax (1938) p. 246; *Cattle,* ix–x; d. 5558, J. B. Underwood, 1912.

XVII

Chase of the O. L. C. Steer

*A*BOOK IS YET TO BE WRITTEN on frontier boasting. Man must have felt especially empty and insecure when faced with so much raw nature. Is this why thousands of songs, tales, and anecdotes of frontier life concern men who talked bigger than they acted? Like Anatole France's ebullient Tartarin, Rap (Ray), Bob, and Johnny talk themselves into a state where they must prove that a lowly longhorn steer is not too much for them. But the steer runs them to a frazzle and when last seen is still grinning about his triumph. Rhyme and rhythm are so rich and so flawless that we have suspected authorship by someone with more than a mite of culture. Corroboration of this view has just arrived at the writing of the final draft of this book in the discovery of a letter from Agnes Morley Cleaveland to Neil M. Clark.[1] Mrs. Cleaveland, author of a work that gives a poignant feminine view of ranch life in the 1880's and '90's,[2] and sister of the famous athlete Ray Morley, claims she wrote "Chase of the O. L. C. Steer." The title, she says, should read "A. L. C.," and the first line should read, "Did you ever hear of the Alcy steer . . ." Ray in the song was, of course, her famous brother. Mrs. Cleaveland also claims authorship to "When Bob Got Throwed,"[3] another cowboy classic that Thorp published in his 1921 edition.[4]

---

[1] Dated November 7, 1945, Santa Fe, New Mexico (FAC II 699).
[2] *No Life for a Lady*. (Boston: Houghton Mifflin Co., 1941).
[3] Another letter to Mr. Clark dated August 7, 1945. (FAC II 746).
[4] Pp. 164–65.

Outside of Thorp we have encountered the "Chase of the O. L. C. Steer" only three times: in an unpaged and undated pamphlet that seems to have been printed about 1905 (it carries an article on Teddy Roosevelt's inauguration);[5] in a manuscript in the files of the Pacific Northwest Farm Quad supplied by Mrs. Cuba King;[6] and in a manuscript sent to Mrs. A. H. Griep of Cadillac, Michigan, from a friend at Ogallala, Wyoming,[7] the same city whence came the text for Thorp's 1921 edition.[8] Variations in these texts are not significant: Rap's (Ray's) horse is variously a "Gray Black," "Gray Buck," or "Dudley": Johnny's brag is that he will rope a locomotive in one text, in the others, a coyote. In one text the triumphant steer carries an XXX brand (read "3-X") rather than the O. L. C.

We have not been able to locate a melody.

XVII–A. THORP (1908) pages 36–38

1.   Did you ever hear of the O L C Steer
            With widely flaring horns
        He smashes the trees as he splits the breeze
            And the Cow-boys ropes he scorns

2.   That O L C's fame it soon became
            Of camp fire yarns the pet
        I'll stake my rocks that I get that ox
            Quoth Rap Who'll take my bet?

3.   Why of course my Gray Black horse
            Will run on him he said
        Show me his track I'll bring him back
            I'll bet alive or dead.

4.   Up Johnny spoke "No brags I make"
            Straight goods I give you now
        I'll put my string on anything
            From a coyote to a cow.

---

[5] FAC III 68, pp. 8–9.
[6] PNFQ 60.
[7] Dorson Collection (FAC II 388).
[8] P. 21.

5.   Then up spoke Bob with this here job
         You bet I'm going to cope
      Just you watch me if you want to see
         How Texas punchers rope.

6.   These cow-boys three for modesty
         Have always been well known
      For don't you know unless they blow
         Their horns they'd not be blown.

7.   Meanwhile the steer devoid of fear
         Was trailing o'er the Mesa
      He sniffed the air what did he care
         He knew he was a racer.

8.   With firm intent on business bent
         Three youths rode up the trail
      The steer he saw dropped his jaw
         And then he whisked his tail.

9.   The other day I chanced that way
         That steer was grinning yet
      Six weeks have passed not yet the last
         Of why that steer they didn't get.

10.   If they once begin for yours [hours?] they'll chin
         And tell although they hit him
      And ran all day how he got away
         And why they didn't get im"

BIBLIOGRAPHY

Printed texts:

Stanley, p. 36 (FAC III 68, pp. 8–9).
Thorp (1921) pp. 21–23.

Manuscripts:

Dorson. *Wyoming*: Mrs. A. H. Griep (FAC II 388).
PNFQ 60. Unknown: Mrs. Cuba King.

XVIII

The Pecos Stream

THE FIVE STANZAS OF "The Pecos Stream" printed
by Thorp in 1908 belong to a loosely knit cluster of verses that had floated
about the frontier since the 1870's, and which probably derive from an
earlier woodsman's song that Fowke and Johnston date from the 1850's
or earlier.[1] The cowboy stanzas constitute a serio-comic complaint about
hardships encountered by the punchers in the course of a typical day's
work. Lomax, in preparing his own first two editions, was perplexed by
the significant variation shown in the fifteen to twenty separate texts he
had assembled. In fact, he made two separate songs—"The Kansas Line"[2]
and "The Dreary, Dreary Life"[3]—apparently by combining stanzas from
his various sources in a more or less random manner. In the edition of
1938[4] he retains only one of the songs, "The Kansas Line."

In 1908 Thorp gave five of the most usual stanzas. In 1921 he
offered eight by combining some of Lomax's texts with his own. Thorp's
1908 text is the earliest we have found in print, though we believe the
song goes back at least to the early 1880's: that, as with "Buffalo Range,"
it is a cowboy adaptation of a Maine lumberman's song, in this case "The
Shantyman's Life."

The poetic form of "The Pecos Stream" demands attention. Typi-

---

[1] "The Shantyman's Life." See Fowke and Johnston, pp. 67, 195.
[2] (1910) pp. 22–23.
[3] (1911) pp. 233–36.
[4] Pp. 15–17.

cally, cowboy ballads are rhymed AA/BB when offered in the double
stanzaic form, or A/B/C/B if written singly:

double stanza

Come all you melancholy folks wherever you may *be*
I'll sing you about the cowboy whose life is light and *free.*

single stanza

Come all you melancholy folks
    Wherever you may *be*
I'll sing you about the cowboy
    Whose life is light and *free.*

True rhyme (i.e., identity of the last stressed vowel and all that follows
it—"cold"/"hold") often gives way to assonance (identity of the last
stressed vowel but not of what follows it—"advice"/"wife"). Even assonance is not obligatory.

In "The Pecos Stream" there is an inconsistent but real tendency
toward a much richer rhyme, as illustrated by Thorp's second stanza.
This is readily perceptible if we rewrite it in six lines rather than four:

When the spring work comes *in*	A
Then our troubles *begin*	A
The weather being fierce and *cold*	B
We get almost *froze*	C
With the water in our *clothes*	C
And the cattle we can scarcely *hold*	B

The same tendency is noted in "The Shantyman's Life" and in several
other cowboy songs influenced by or influencing "The Pecos Stream."[5]

Two musical settings are offered. Dobie's tune is notable for its $\frac{6}{8}$
rhythm: All verses are sung to the same melody, whereas Larkin offers
both a verse and chorus.

---

[5] See "The Cowboy's Life," Thorp (1921) pp. 44–45; Lomax (1910) pp.
20–21; Lomax (1938) pp. 281–82; "A Song of the Range," Thorp (1921), pp.
140–42; "Border Ballad," in *Cattleman,* July, 1915, p. 42. The last item, attributed to Douglas Johnson, is reproduced here since it does not appear in easily
accessible texts.

XVIII–A.   THORP (1908) pages 38–39

    1.   A cowboys life is a weary dreary life
                  Some people think it free from all care
            Its rounding up cattle from morning to night
                  On the lone prairie so drear.

    2.01   When the spring work comes in then our troubles begin
                  The weather being fierce and cold
            We get almose froze with the water on our clothes
                  And the cattle we can scarcely hold.

    4.   Just about four o'clock the cook will holler out
                  "Roll out boys its almost day"
            Through his broken slumbers the puncher he will ask
                  Has the short summer night passed away.

    5.   "Saddle up" "Saddle Up" the boss will holler out
                  When we're camped by the Pecos stream
            Where the wolves and the owls with their terrifying howls
                  Disturb us in our midnight dreams.

    6.5   Once I loved to roam but now I stay at home
                  All you punchers take my advice
            Sell your briddle and your saddle quit your roaming and
                  travels
                  And tie on to a cross eyed wife.

XVIII–OTHER STANZAS

    1.   Texts A, B.

    1.1   Some folks say that we are free from care
                  Free from all other harm;
            But we round up the cattle from morning till night
                  Way over on the prairie so dry.

    1.2   Now it's way over on the Pecos Line
                  In the hands of all mankind
            But we round up the cattle from morning until night
                  Over on the Pecos Line.

1.3 The cowboy's life is a dreary, dreary life
   He's driven through heat and cold
 I'm almost froze with the water on my clothes
   A riding through the heat and the cold.

1.4 The cowboy's life is a dreary, dreary life
   All out in the Midnight rain
 I'm almost froze with the water on my clothes
   Way up on the Kansas Line.

1.5 Text B.

1.6 Text B.

1.7 The cowboy's life is a dreary old life
   All out in the sleet and the snow
 When winter time comes he begins to think
   Where his summer wages go.

1.8 Come all you jolly cowmen, don't you want to go
   Way up on the Kansas line
 Where you whoop the cattle from morn till night
   All out in the midnight rain.

2. Springtime sets in, double trouble will begin
   The weather is so fierce and cold
 Clothes are wet and frozen to our necks
   The cattle we can scarcely hold.

2.1 I want all brave-hearted men
   Who ain't afraid to die
 To whoop up the cattle from morning till night
   Way up on the Kansas line.

3. You are speaking of your farms, you are speaking of your
   charms
   You are speaking of your silver and gold;
 But a cowboy's life is a dreary, dreary life
   He's driven through the heat and the cold.

3.1 You talk about your farms and your chantain[6] charms
     Your chantain silver and gold
    Though the wolves and the owls in their very towering
     howls
    May disturb us in our midnight dreams.

3.2 Talk about your farms and your city charms
     Talk about your silver and your gold
    Take a cowman's advice, get a rich and lovely wife
     And always, always stay at home.

4. Texts A, B.

4.1 Think I heard my boss man say
     I want all brave-hearted men who ain't afraid to die
    To whoop up the cattle from morning till night
     Way up on the Kansas Line.

4.2 Half past four the noisy cook will roar
     "Whoop – a – whoop – a – hey!"
    Slowly you'll rise with sleepy-feeling eyes
     The sweet dreamy night passed away.

4.3 "Sing, who-o, who-o, whoop, cows away;
     He works all night and he works all day.
    Whoop-i-wo; whoop-i-way;
     For very poor chuck and darned poor pay;
    Sing, whoop-i-whoa who-ay."

5. Text A.

5.1 Transported we are by the harness of man
     On the banks of the Brasso stream
    Though the wolves and owls in their very towering howls
     May disturb us in our midnight dreams.

5.2 The wolves and owls with their terrifying howls
     Will disturb us in our midnight dream
    As we lie on our slickers on a cold wintery night
     Way over on the Pecos stream.

---

[6] "Chinaman" frequently in lieu of "chantain."

6.   I used to run about, now I stay at home
            And take care of my pretty little wife
        I've been almost froze with the water in my clothes
            In the middle of the prairie so dry.

6.1   I used to run about, now I stay at home
            Take care of my wife and child
        Nevermore to roam, always stay at home
            Take care of my wife and child.

6.2   The cowboy call is the "early I rise
            Take care of my little wife,
        The cowboy call is the "early I rise
            Take care of my little wife.

6.3   Its whooping and hollowing from morning till night
            Take care of my wife and child
        Its whooping and hollowing from morning till night
            Take care of my wife and child.

6.4   Oh, the cowboy is called "the early I rise"
            Take care of my dear little wife
        Some whoop and some hollow from morning till night
            Till the middle of the prairie is gone dry.

6.5   Texts A, B.

7.   The greener lad he thinks its play
            He'll soon peter out on a cold rainy day
        With his big bell spurs and his Spanish hoss
            He'll swear to you he was once a boss.

XVIII–B.   "THE DREARY, DREARY LIFE"
            MS from Mrs. Phillip Bliss, Yakima, Washington (PNFQ 116).

1.   A cowboy's life is a dreary, dreary life;
            Some say it's free of care.
        Rounding up the cattle from morning till night,
            On the bald prairie so bare.

4.   Just about four o'clock old cook will holler out:
          "Roll out, boys; it's almost day."
       Through his broken slumbers the puncher he will ask:
          "Has the short summer night passed away?"

1.6   The cowboy's life is a dreary, dreary life;
          He's driven through the heat and cold,
       While the rich man's a-sleeping on his velvet couch,
          Dreaming of his silver and his gold.

2.01   When the spring work sets in, then our troubles will begin,
          The weather being fierce and cold.
       We're almost froze, with the water on our clothes,
          And the cattle we can scarcely hold.

1.5   The cowboy's life is a dreary, weary one;
          He works all day to the setting of the sun,
       And then his day's work is not done,
          For there's his night guard to go on.

5.   "Saddle up! Saddle up!" the boss will holler out,
          When camped down by the Pecos stream,
       Where the wolves and owls with their terrifying howls
          Will disturb us in our midnight dream.

3.2/1.3 You are speaking of your farms; you are speaking of your
            charms;
          You are speaking of your silver and gold;
       But a cowboy's life is a dreary, weary life;
          He's driven through the heat and cold.

6.5   Once I loved to roam, but now I stay at home.
          All you punchers take my advice;
       Sell your bridle and your saddle, quit your roaming and
          your travel,
          And tie onto a cross-eyed wife.

XVIII–C. "The Cowboy's Life"
MS from Mrs. A. H. Griep, collected by Patricia Goetz, Michigan, 1950, Dorson Collection (FAC II 389).

The bawl of a steer to a cowboy's ear
   Is music of sweetest strain
And the whelping notes of the gray coyotes
   To him are a glad refrain.
And his jolly songs speed him along
   As he thinks of the little gal
With golden hair who is waiting there
   At the bars of the home corral.

For a kingly crown in the noisy town
   His saddle he wouldn't change,
No life so free as the life we see
   Way out on the Yaso Range.
His eyes are bright and his heart's as light
   As the smoke of his cigarette
There's never a care for his soul to bear,
   No trouble to make him fret.

The rapid beat of his bronco's feet
   On the sod as he speeds along
Keeps living time to the ringing rhyme
   Of his rollicking cowboy song.
Hike it, cowboys, for the range away
   On the back of a bronc of steel
With a careless flirt of the rawhide quirt
   And the dig of a rolled heel.

The winds may blow and the thunder growl
   Or the breeze may safely moan
A cowboy's life is a royal life,
   His saddle his kingly throne.
Saddle up, boys, for the work is play
   When love's in the cowboy's eyes
When his heart is light as the clouds of white
   That swim in the summer sky.

XVIII–D. "Border Ballad"
Cattleman (July, 1915) page 42. Reproduced from the University of Texas Magazine, n.d. (FAC III 727).

> Oh, the cowboy's life is the life of the wind
>   As he clatters across the plains
> With a laugh and a yell and a hearty word
>   And a smile at the driving rain.

> Oh, the cowboy's life is a life of flame
>   As he clatters across the plain
> While the coyotes howl in the gathering night
>   But the dreams he sees are vain.

> Oh, the cowboy's life is a life of dust
>   Though the cowboy laughs at fear
> But when he travels the last, long trail
>   Is there no one to drop him a tear?

XVIII–E. "The Cowboy's Life"
Dobie, More Ballads, pages 173–74 (FAC III 64). Reproduced
with permission of the Texas Folklore Society.

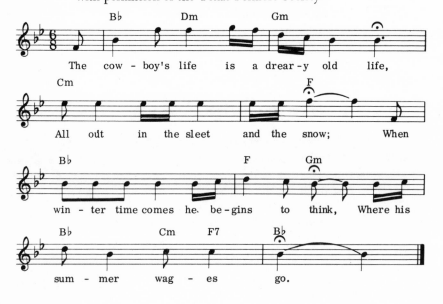

The cow-boy's life is a drear-y old life,
All out in the sleet and the snow; When
win-ter time comes he. be-gins to think, Where his
sum-mer wag-es go.

XVIII–F. "THE DREARY LIFE"

Larkin, pages 40–42. Reproduced with permission of Margaret Larkin and Oak Publications.

Rather fast

Come all you jol - ly cow - boys, don't you want to go, 'Way out on the Tex - as line, Where we punch up cat - tle from morn - ing till night, All out in the mid-night rain.

Chorus

The cow - boy's life is a drea-ry, drea-ry life, He's driv - en through heat and cold. I'm al - most froze with the wa - ter on my clothes, A - rid - ing through the heat and cold.

2, 3, 4 stanzas

The wolves and the owls with their

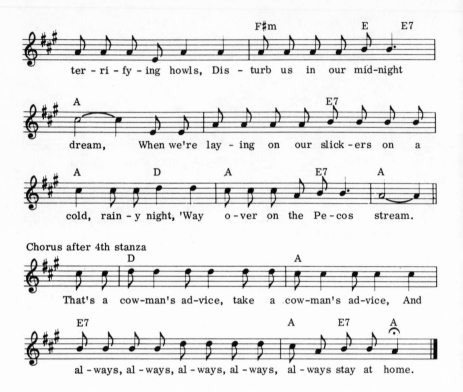

ter - ri - fy - ing howls, Dis - turb us in our mid-night

dream,   When we're lay - ing on our slick - ers on a

cold, rain - y night, 'Way o - ver on the Pe - cos stream.

Chorus after 4th stanza

That's a cow-man's ad-vice, take a cow-man's ad-vice, And

al - ways, al - ways, al - ways, al - ways, al - ways stay at home.

BIBLIOGRAPHY

Printed texts:

Arkansas, pp. 44–45.

Big Round-Up, p. 31.

Carlson, p. 61.

Cattleman (July, 1915), p. 42 (reproduced by the *University of Texas Magazine,* n.d. (FAC III 727).

Clark, *Cowboy,* p. 25 = Lomax (1911) pp. 233–36.

Dobie, *More Ballads,* pp. 173–74 (FAC III 64). (This is a wholly different text except for stanza 1, which is our 1.7.)

Felton, p. 36.

Frey, p. 54.

Gaviani, unpaged.
Grinnell, pp. 40–41 (FAC III 254).
Larkin, pp. 39–43.
Lomax (1910) pp. 22–23; (1911) pp. 233–36; (1938) pp. 15–17; d. 5652, unidentified newspaper clipping (JL 130).
Lomax (Lilly), pp. 24–29 (FAC III 742).
Lone Ranger, p. 30.
Luther, p. 202.
Patterson and Dexter, pp. 42–43.
Reinbach, p. 21.
Sing 'em Cowboy, pp. 63–64.
Thorp (1921) pp. 61–62.
Treasure Chest, p. 31.

Manuscripts and field recordings:

Fife. *California:* Ben Allen, 1954 (FMR 545B3).
Hendren 287. Unknown.
ISUHM. *Idaho:* Addie Haws (FAC II 688).
Lomax. *Arizona:* d. 5653, 5652, King Sloan (JL 195, 130). *Oklahoma* or *Texas:* LC cylinder 15, William Davey, 1908–1910. *Texas:* d. 5638: "1887, Doorkey Ranch on the Concho, 47 miles from Angelo, given me by Tom Pickett, Fort Worth, livery stable boy" (JL 91); d. 5652, E. H. Walker, 1910 (JL 129); LC 5679B1, S. Matthews, 1942; d. 5652, Marcus Morrow (JL 130), William Wilson (JL 130). Unknown: d. 5634 (JL 43); d. 5638; d. 5652, Blanche L. House (JL 130), three texts (JL 130); d. 5653 (JL 196, 212); d. 5654.
PNFQ. *Idaho:* Kathrene Hall, No. 235. *Washington:* Mrs. P. Bliss, No. 116.

Discussion:

Barrett, Chapter 7.
Clark, N. M., letter to A. E. Fife, September 6, 1964 (FAC II 699).
Fowke and Johnston, pp. 67, 195.
Lomax d. 5652 (JL 130).
Rickaby, p. 200.
Thorp, *Banjo,* p. 196 (*supra* p. 14).
Thorp and Clark, p. 23.
Wilgus, p. 160.

XIX

Old Time Cowboy

"OLD TIME COWBOY" (also "Melancholy Cowboy") combines a bit of frontier realism with a small dose of self-adulation. Ruggedly individualistic, the cowboy bases society not upon law but upon personal integrity and honor among men. He loves the West not for its bounteous gifts, but for the challenge it offers. He is charitable to all save those who ask the wrong questions, and proud to the point of unabashed showmanship—all of which takes us right back to the glorious moments of the gallant knights of King Arthur's Court.

"Old Time Cowboy" will probably not survive as a *chef d'oeuvre* of cowboy poetry. Its diction and style are rough, like the men of the era it represents. Thorp got it from Tom Beasley of Hueco, Texas, and said it was written by an old cow puncher by the name of Rogers who claimed he was dragging his rope along and someone else's calf got tangled up in it, so he landed in the Huntsville Pen.[1] The only music we have found is from the hillbilly era.

XIX–A. THORP (1908) pages 40–41

1. Come all you melancholy folks wherever you may be
I'll sing you about the cowboy whose life is light and free
2. He roams about the prairie and at night when he lies down
His heart is as gay as the flowers in May in his bed upon the ground.

---

[1] Thorp (1921) p. 121.

240

3. They're a little bit rough I must confess the most of them at
    least
    But if you do not hunt a quarrel you can live with them in
    peace
4. For if you do your sure to rue the day you joined their band
    They will follow you up and shoot it out with you just man
    to man.

5. Did you ever go to any cowboy whenever hungry or dry
    Asking for a dollar and have him you deny
6. He'll just pull out his pocket book and hand you a note
    They are the fellows to help you out whenever you are
    broke.

7. Go to their ranches and stay awhile they never ask a cent
    And when they go to town their money is freely spent
8. They walk straight up and take a drink paying for everyone
    And they never ask your pardon for anything they have done.

9. When they go to their dances some dance while others pat
    They ride their bucking bronchos and wear their broad
    brimmed hats
10. With their California saddles and their pants inside their
    boots
    You can hear their spurs a-jingling and perhaps some of
    them shoot.

11. Come all softhearted tenderfeet if you want to have some fun
    Go live among the cowboys they show you how it's done
12. They'll treat you like a prince my boys about them there's
    nothing mean
    But dont try to give them too much advice for all of 'em
    aint so green.

XIX–B. "MELANCHOLY COWBOY"
    Lomax d. 5653, unidentified (JL 197).
    Variant lines as follows:

5.1 You can go to a cowboy hungry, wet, or dry
    And ask him for a few dollars in change and he will not
    deny.

9.1   They go to the ball room, they swing the pretty girls round
       They ride their bucking broncos and wear their broad
           brimmed hats.

12.1   But take the kind advice of me as I gave it to you before
       For if you don't, they'll order you off with an old Colt's 44.

XIX–C. "The Melancholy Cowboy."
        Arkansas, pp. 33–34.

BIBLIOGRAPHY

Printed texts:

Arkansas, pp. 33–34.
Branch, pp. 166–69.
Buck Jones, p. 28.
Hendren 539, unidentified newspaper clipping.
Lee, *Cowboy,* p. 11; *Range,* p. 8.
Lomax (1911) pp. 263–64; (1938) pp. 220–21.
Thorp (1921) pp. 121–22.

Manuscripts:

Hendren 426. Unknown.
Lomax. D. 5653 (JL 197).

Discussion:

Clark, N. M., letter to A. E. Fife, September 6, 1964 (FAC II 699).

XX

Pecos River Queen

THORP WROTE "THE PECOS RIVER QUEEN" from a story told him by the one and only Roy Bean, otherwise known as "the law west of the Pecos." Near Langtry, Texas, the Comstock railroad trestle had been built, said to have been at one time the highest in the West. According to Bean, a girl named Patty Moorhead, "as pretty and full of fire as they come, even in Texas," had ridden her horse across the trestle. In the song, Thorp gives Bean's anecdote legendary components: he makes her the "Pecos River Queen"; a suitor has been added whom the dauntless beauty will marry if he will but follow her on horseback across the trestle; but he fails to pass the test so Patty remains unwed.[1] The subject follows a central theme of the ancient and universal suitors' test stories.

Patty Moorhead is only one of a score of frontier women whom Thorp admires. The pages of his autobiography are filled with anecdotes about them: Calamity Jane, Belle Starr, Battle Axe, Pearl Hart, and Jean Beaumondy, to name but a few. They were a special breed especially dear to frontiersmen because they kept alive leitmotifs of feminine generosity and individuality in a world of violence and action. Yet his idealization of these notorious frontier women is not without a sense of moderation. Upon reading numerous anecdotes about them in his virile autobiography, one gets the notion that the ideal of womanhood for

---

[1] Thorp and Clark, p. 40.

244

Thorp, as for many frontier men, was to be found somewhere between those who toted a stiletto and a waterfall, and those who carried a bustle and a Bible.

The whole story reminds the editors of their vain attempt to locate the stone statue of Belle Starr erected at Ponca City, Oklahoma, in the 1880's. We arrived in a nearly empty town on a Sunday morning and inquired at police headquarters for the notorious female outlaw's monument. The clerk's face, bewildered at first, gave way to a sudden illumination: "Oh," exclaimed the officer, "you mean the statue of the pioneer woman!" Following his directions, we arrived at a park surrounding the lovely statue of an idealized pioneer woman, narrow-waisted, long skirts flowing in the breeze, *sans décolleté*. Under one arm she gripped a Bible, trailing with the other hand a small boy, all spick and span in his starched shirt and knee britches. The image of the Queen of the Desperadoes had been removed and replaced by a more civilized female breed. So our search for the bust of Belle Starr had met with failure. A bit like Sir Lancelot in his quest for the Grail, or Don Quixote for Dulcinea, we feel that with the loss of Belle Starr's bust a treasure of our western heritage has also vanished.

No music is available.

XX–A.   THORP (1908), pages 39–40

1.   Where the Pecos river winds and turns in its journey to the sea
     From its white walls of sand and rock striving ever to be free

2.   Near the highest railroad bridge that all these modern times have seen
     Dwells fair young Patty Moorhead the Pecos River Queen

3.   She's known by all the cowboys on the Pecos river wide
     They know full well that she can shoot that she can rope and ride

4.   She goes to every roundup every cow work without fail
     Looking out for all Her Cattle branded "walking hog oh rail."

5.   She made her start in cattle, yes, made it with her rope
     Can tie down ev'ry maverick fore it can strike a lope

6.   She can rope and tie and brand it as quick as any man
        She's voted by all cowboys as A 1 top cow hand.

7.   Across the Comstock Railroad bridge the highest in the west
        Patty rode her horse one day a lovers heart to test
8.   For he told her he would gladly risk all dangers for her sake
        But the puncher wouldn't follow so she's still without a
        mate.

BIBLIOGRAPHY

Printed texts:

Clark, *Cowboy.*
German, unpaged (FAC III 708).
Lomax (1916) pp. 369–70 = Thorp (1908) pp. 39–40.
Thorp (1921) pp. 126–27.

Manuscripts:

PNFQ 358. Unknown.

Discussion:

Clark, N. M., letter to A. E. Fife, September 6, 1964 (FAC II 699).
Lomax d. 5639 (JL 501).
Thorp and Clark, p. 40.
Wilgus, pp. 164–65.

XXI

Who's Old Cow?

"*W*HOSE OLD COW?" is a song about the roundup. Punchers representing all the brands on a given range establish a round-up camp. Cattle in the area are driven to it and the different brands and earmarks are "read" so that ownership is clearly established. Unbranded calves or "dogies" are given the same brand that is carried by the cows they are suckling. Earmarks are often used in addition to brands, as further proof of ownership.

The job of "calling" the brands was given to the puncher who best knew all the markings of a particular range. As the "cutters" pushed each animal past the caller he shouted out the brand, thus letting the punchers know to which bunch each critter was to be driven.

Nigger Add of the LFD outfit was, as Thorp puts it, "a dictionary on earmarks and brands." That he was well known and respected in his area, witness the story of his marriage. Punchers on the ranges where Add worked all sent wedding gifts. There being no telephones it was, of course, hard to know what other friends were sending. On the wedding day Add and his bride drove to the Roswell, New Mexico, freight depot to claim gifts he had been advised were there. Much to his amazement, there were nineteen cookstoves![1]

"Whose Old Cow?," written by Thorp, has not been widely dis-

---

[1] Thorp and Clark, p. 285.

247

seminated. Apart from Thorp's two books and several editions of Lomax's work on cowboy songs we have rarely encountered it. Notwithstanding, the song does give authentic insights about roundups and brands, and is worthy of preservation. Its limited popularity may result from its encumbrance by technical terms accessible only to learned men like Nigger Add himself. Yet who knows? Save for Thorp's poem and a few other esoteric cowboy texts the art of reading and calling cattle brands might even perish from the earth!

XXI–A. THORP (1908) pages 42–44

1. Twas the end of roundup the last day of June
        Or maybe July I dont just remember
    Or it might have been August 'twas some time ago
        Or perhaps 'twas the first of September.

2. Anyhow 'twas the roundup we had at Mayou
        On the lightning rod's range near Cayo
    There was some twenty wagons "more or less" camped about
        On the temporal in the Cañon.

3. First night we'd no cattle so we only stood guard
        On the horses somewhere 'bout two hundred head
    So we side-lined and hoppled we belled and we staked
        Loose'd our hot rolls and fell into bed.

4. Next morning 'bout daybreak we started our work
        Our horses like possums felt fine
    Each "one 'tending' knitten!" none trying to shirk
        So the roundup got on in good time.

5. Well we worked for a week 'till the country was clear
    And the boss said "now boys we'll stay here
    We'll carve and we'll trim 'em an' start out a herd
    Up the east trail from old Abilene.

6. Next morning' all on herd an' but two with the cut
    An' the boss on Piute carving fine
    'Till he rode down his horse and had to pull out
    An' a new man went in to clean up.

7.   Well after each outfit had worked on the band
        There was only three head of them left
        When Nig Add from L F D outfit road in
        A dictionary on earmarks an' brands.

8.   He cut the two head out told where they belonged
        But when the last cow stood there alone
        Add's eyes bulged so he did 'nt 'no just what to say
        'Ceptin boss der's sumpin' here monstrous wrong.

9.   White folks smarter'n Add an' maybe I'se wrong
        But here's six months wages dat I'll give
        If anyone'll tell me when I reads de mark
        To who dis long horned cow belongs.

10.   Overslope in right ear an' de underbill[2]
        Left ear swallerfork an de undercrop
        Hole punched in centre an' de jinglebob
        Under half crop an' de slash an split.

11.   She's got O block an' lightnin' rod
        Nine forty-six an' A bar eleven
        T terrapin an' ninety-seven
        Rafter cross an' de double prod.

12.   Half circle A an' diamond D
        Four cross L an' three P Z
        B W I bar X V V
        Bar N cross an' A L C

13.   So if no' o' you punchers claims dis cow
        Mr Stock 'Sociation need'nt get alarmed
        For one brand more or less wont do no harm
        So old nigger Add'l just brand her now

----

[2] We retreat from the nearly impossible task of describing all the marks and brands spieled off so rhythmically by Nigger Add here. Connoisseurs should consult their state brand books. For a popular but incomplete account we suggest Duncan Emrich, *It's An Old Wild West Custom* (New York: Vanguard Press, 1949), pp. 213–26.

XXI–B. "BRANDS"

From Margery McMichael, Oregon (PNFQ 30).

From Canada down to the Rio Grande, from Kansas to the coast,
Wherever you see a steer's big side,
You'll spot a big brand on his hide—
At least on the hides of most.

There's the Flyin' W and Circle B,
The Big Box X and the old Bar Z,
The Doodle Bug and the Flyin' V,
The IXL an' the Lazy P.

The W Bar and the Big Bar T,
The Circle J and the Rafter B,
Circle 6 and the Crooked Bar,
XIT, an' the big Lone Star.

Over the range where the cattle run, the men are branded, too,
Level eyes and stubborn jaws,
Legs that are bent to hold a hoss,
Skin tanned to a leather hue.

BIBLIOGRAPHY

Printed texts:

Branch, pp. 125–26.
Lomax (1938) pp. 117–18 = Thorp (1921) pp. 166–68.
Thorp (1921) pp. 166–68.

Discussion:

Arnold and Hale (entire book).
Barrett, Chapter 7.
Dobie: note of Thorp's authorship in his copy of Lomax, *Cowboy Songs.*
Emrich, pp. 213–26.
Lomax d. 5639 (JL 501).
PNFQ 30.
Thorp and Clark, pp. 22, 285.
Wilgus, pp. 164–65.

XXII

The Cowboys New Years Dance

THORP PRINTED THIS in his 1908 edition; we have never encountered a reference to it elsewhere. He listed Mark Chisholm as the author. It is an obvious parody of "The Cowboys Christmas Ball," song XVI of this collection, and may be sung to the same melody.

XXII–A. THORP (1908) pages 44–48

1.   We were sitting' round the ranch house some twenty hands
       or more
       Most of us Americans but a few from Arkansas
       One Dutchman from the fatherland one Johnny Bull from
       Leeds
       A Cornishman from Cornwall all men of different creeds.

2.   They were a sittin' an' a arguin' busy as a hill of ants
       How they'd get rid of the money they had buried in their
       pants
       That they'd made by hard cow punching working all the
       year around
       From sunup until sundown an' a sleepin' on the ground

3.   Where at night the polecat saunters round the chuck box
       after grub
       And in passing by your hot roll gives your head a friendly
       rub

251

Where the rattlesnake lays dormant his fangs are like a
lance
'Twas with them that I attended The Cowboys New Years
Dance.

4.   The town was Roswell City old Chaves' county seat
Where they raise fine shorthorn cattle that are mighty hard
to beat
Where they send the frail consumptive in search of instant
health
And the hills is just a bustin' with their pent up mineral
wealth

5.   Where the wells are all artesian and flow fish and water too
'Least so says the Roswell people so I sorter guess it's true
Where laughin' Joe the darky bust up Mulkey's show one day
By laughin' at prayer meetin' and old Abe he went away

6.   Charles Perry he was a sheriff and G Curry county clerk
Where they caught Bill Cook the outlaw and sent him off
to work
Where the moonbeams on the Pecos seem to glitter and to
glance
I received an invitation to the Cowboys New Years Dance.

7.   The boys had been invited and they just come in herds
The ladies more numerous had flocked to town like birds
Old Roswell was just crowded there was horses everywhere
Looked like some long procession headed for a county fair

8.   Where everything was orderly as I remember well
Invitations were extended to the Roswell Stone Hotel
The music was a fiddle a guitar and a banjo
And the way those three boys played em'
It was fully half the show the women folks set together

9.   All the boys stood in the door 'till the caller commenced
yellin'
For just one couple more
And the music started windin' an' a wailin' like some hants
That had come to cast their hoodo on the Cowboy New
Years Dance.

10.   The caller was a feller one of Atkinson's men
Who had the reputation of once being in the pen
His outfit sort of gaudy big spurs an' conchas bright
Fringed leggin's and gold buttons six feet about his height

11.   He was tall an' angular an, a broncho buster right
        An' at callin' out the dances he was simply out of sight
        Soon he commenced to beller now fellers all begin
        Grab your lovely partners an' every one jine in

12.   First bow to your partners now four hands cross an' change
        An' chase those pretty footies once around the range
        Join once again your partners around the circles prance
        It was getting interesting the Cowboys New Years Dance,

13.   Next dance will be the Lancers round up your ladies boys
        Cut them all to the centre and never mind the noise
        Chase your lovely critters all into the branding pen
        Everybody swing everybody else's girl and swing them once
          again

14.   Dash your line on the nearest filly and drag her from the
          herd
        Re-sume your former places and swing her like a bird
        Now Brownfield strike out in the lead all grand right and
          left
        Swing each one when half way round never mind their hat

15.   Now ladies to the centre all hands do se do
        Right hand in left hand out swing and let her go
        Trail block Jack to your settees for that winds up the lance
        My but it was getting furious the Cowboys New Years Dance.

16.   The refreshments came round often till all hands had their
          fill
        Past round uncerimonous like by Broncho Buster Bill
        Though his gait was quite uncertain he never lost his feet
        And at complementing ladies he was mighty hard to beat

17.   To close up the night proceedings we ragged "Turkey in the
          Straw"
        Till we wore out musicians and they could play no more
        We were served with soda water red eye and pilsner beer
        And the conversation never lagged 'twas most penetrating
          clear

18.   'En those who never danced before would dance with all
          their might
        'En the most peaceably inclined citizens went a hunting for
          a fight
        So we saddled up our horses drifted homeward to the ranch
        With a happy recollection of the Cowboys New Years Dance.

XXIII

Speckles

UNDERDOGS, WHETHER ANIMAL or human,
play an important role in the popular ballads of America. "Speckles" tells
the story of a no-'count horse who outruns a band of Apache Indians
with two passengers aboard—no mean feat, even for a thoroughbred.
The song is also spiced with genuine images of life on the open ranges:
the drifting horse trader, a grasshopper plague, cowboy hospitality, the
use of horses as a medium of exchange, encounters between Rangers and
Indians, and the value of a swift and steady mount when Indians are
on the warpath. It also evokes images of the deep arroyos and high mesas
that are the proper setting for the cowboy culture.

Thorp says he wrote "Speckles" at his ranch at Palma, New Mexico,
in 1906. Stanzas 11 to 19 were lost in the 1908 printing: they are added
here from Thorp's 1921 edition.[1] Lomax used the first ten stanzas in his
1916 edition of *Cowboy Songs*,[2] changing the title to "Freckles." Thorp's
typesetter must have slipped again since, despite "Speckles" in the title,
"Freckles" is used in the text.

---

[1] Pp. 144–45.
[2] Pp. 360–61.

254

XXIII–A. THORP (1908) pages 48–49

1. He was little 'en peaked 'en thin 'en Narr'y a no 'account horse
   Least that's the way you'd describe him in case that the beast had been lost.
2. But for single and double cussedness 'en double fired sin
   The horse never come out O' Texas that was half way knee-high to him

3. The first time that ever I saw him was nineteen year ago last spring
   'Twas the year we had grasshopper that come 'en 'et up everything
4. That a feller rode up here on evening 'en wanted to pen overnight
   A small bunch of horses he said 'en I told him I guessed 'twas all right,

5. Well the feller was busted the horses was thin 'en the grass around here kind of good
   'En he said if I'd let him hold here a few days He'd settle with me when he could
6. So I told him all right turn them loose down the draw
   That the latch string was always untied
   He was welcome to stop a few days if he liked 'En rest from his weary ride.

7. Well the cus stay'd around for two or three weeks till at last he decided to go
   And that horse away yonder being too poor to move He gimme, the cuss had no dough
8. Well at first the darn brute was as wild as a deer 'en would snort when he came to the branch
   'En it took two cowpunchers on good horses too to handle him here at the ranch.

9. Well winter came on and the range it got hard and my mustang commenced to get thin
   So I fed him along and rode him round some and found out old Freckles was game

For that was what the other cus called him just Freckles
   no more or no less
His color couldn't describe it something like a paintshop
   in distress.

XXIII–B.   THORP (1921) pages 144–45
    In addition to the ten stanzas of the 1908 edition:

11.   Them was Indian times, young feller, that I'm a-telling
          about,
         And oft's the time I've seen the red men fight and put the
          boys in blue to rout.

12.   A good horse in them days, young feller, would often save
          your life—
         One that in any race could hold the pace when the red-
          skin bands were rife.

13.   I was a-settin' one night at sunset, jest inside that hall
         En Mollie had gone to the milk-pen as she heard the milk
          cows bawl,

14.   When out o' brush en thicket, ridin' towards me out o' the
          west,
         Comes Antelope John, his horse on the run, en ridin' like
          one possessed.

15.   "Apaches are out!" he shouted; "for God's sake, hurry and
          go!
         They're close behind, comin' like the wind; catch your
          horse and come on, Joe!"

16.   Old Speckles was saddled, I grabbed my gun, picked
          Mollie up as I passed;
         With the grit of her kind she hung on behind and never
          a question asked.

17.   Down through canons deep, over mesas steep, Old Speckles
          never failed;
         In his heart of steel he seemed to feel the red-skins on our
          trail;

18.   On, ever onward, towards Fort Craig he sped the whole
        night through;
        Though handicapped by a double load, he out-stripped
        the red-skins too.

19.   Never will I forget that ride, en how at first day-break
        We galloped out of the chaparral en entered the old fort
        gate.

BIBLIOGRAPHY

Printed texts:

Lomax (1916) pp. 360–61.
Thorp (1921) pp. 142–45.

Discussion:

Gillis, p. 103.
Lomax d. 5639 (JL 501).
Thorp, *Banjo,* p. 202 (*supra,* p. 24).
Thorp and Clark, p. 42.
Wilgus, pp. 164–65.

SONGS OF THE COWBOYS

N. Howard Thorp

News Print Shop
ESTANCIA, NEW MEXICO

1st Book of Cowboy Songs
published in the U. S.
Songs marked + are by
the Author

N Howard Jack Thorp
Alameda N. M.

PREFACE

❦ ❦

To the Ranchmen of the West this little volume is dedicated as a reminder of the trail days and round-ups of the past. To the younger generation who know not of the trip from Texas to Dodge and the north, it will tend to keep alive the memories of an industry now past.

I have gathered these songs from the cow camps of different states and territories. They embrace most of the songs as sung by the oldtime cow punchers. I plead ignorant of the authorship of them but presume that most of the composers have, ere now, "Gone up the dim narrow trail."

I mount this little book on one of the best cow horses that ever lived, and start it on its journey; together may they meet all the old time cowboys and receive a welcome at their hands, is the earnest wish of

THE AUTHOR.

CONTENTS

Little Joe, the Wrangler

Little Joe, the wrangler, will never wrangle more;
  His days with the "Remuda"—they are done.
'Twas a year ago last April he joined the outfit here,
  A little "Texas Stray" and all alone.

'Twas long late in the evening he rode up to the herd
  On a little old brown pony he called Chaw;
With his brogan shoes and overalls a harder looking kid
  You never in your life had seen before.

His saddle 'twas a southern kack built many years ago,
  An O. K. spur on one foot idly hung,   [hind
While his "hot roll" in a cotton sack was loosely tied be-
  And a canteen from the saddle horn he'd slung.

He said he'd had to leave his home, his daddy'd married
    twice
  And his new ma beat him every day or two;
So he saddled up old Chaw one night and "Lit a shuck"
    this way
  Thought he'd try and paddle now his own canoe.

Said he'd try and do the best he could if we'd only give
    him work
  Though he didn't know "straight" up about a cow,
So the boss he cut him out a mount and kinder put him on
  For he sorter liked the little stray somehow.

Taught him how to herd the horses and to learn to know
    them all
To round'em up by daylight; if he could
To follow the chuck-wagon and to always hitch the team
    And help the "cosinero" rustle wood.

We'd driven to red river and the weather had been fine;
    We were camped down on the south side in a bend
When a norther commenced blowing and we doubled up
      our guards
    For it took all hands to hold the cattle then.

Little Joe the wrangler was called out with the rest
    And scarcely had the kid got to the herd
When the cattle they stampeded; like a hail storm, long
    they flew
    And all of us were riding for the lead.

'Tween the streaks of lightning we could see a horse far
    out ahead
    'Twas little Joe the wrangler in the lead;
He was riding "old Blue Rocket" with his slicker 'bove
    his head
    Trying to check the leaders in their speed.

At last we got them milling and kinder quieted down
    And the extra guard back to the camp did go
But one of them was missin' and we all knew at a glance
    'Twas our little Texas stray poor wrangler Joe.

Next morning just at sunup we found where Rocket fell
  Down in a washout twenty feet below
Beneath his horse mashed to a pulp his horse had rung
    the knell
  For our little Texas stray—poor wrangler Joe.

Windy Bill

Windy Bill was a Texas man
  And he could rope you bet,
Talk of the steer he could'nt tie down
  Had'nt sort'er been born yet;
The boys they knew of an old black steer
  A sort of an old outlaw,
Who ran down in the bottom
  Just at the foot of the draw.

This slim black steer had stood his ground
  With punchers from everywhere
The boys bet Bill two to one
  He couldn't quite get there
So Bill brought up his old cow horse
  His weathers and back were sore
Prepared to tackle this old black steer
  Who ran down in the draw.

With his grazin' bits and sand stacked tree,
  His chaps and taps to boot,
His old maguey tied hard and fast,
  Went out to tackle the brute.

Bill sorter sauntered around him first;
 The steer began to paw
Poked up his tail high in the air
 And lit down in the draw.
The old cow horse flew at him like
 He'd been eatin' corn
And Bill he landed his old maguey
 Around old blackies horns.
The old time cow horse he stopped dead still,
 The cinches broke like straw
Both the sand stacked tree and old maguey,
 Went driftin' down the draw.
Bill landed in a big rock pile
 His face and hands were scratched;
He 'lowed he always could tie a steer
 But guessed he'd found his match.
Paid up his bet like a little man
 Without a bit of jaw
And said old blackie was the boss
 Of all down in the draw.
There's a moral to my song, boys,
 Which I hope that you can see
Whenever you start to tackle a steer
 Never tie hard your maguey.
Put on your dalebueltas
 'Cordin' to California law
And you will never see your old rim-fires
 Driftin' down the draw.

"The Tenderfoot"

I thought one spring just for fun
I'd see how cow-punching was done
So before the roundup was begun
   I tackled a cattle king.

Said he "my boss is down in town
He's at the Palace, his name is Brown;
I think to the ranch he'll take you down."
   "That's what I want," says I

We started to the ranch next day
Brown augered me most all the way
Told me cow-punching was just child's play
   It was no work at all.

For all you have to do is ride
Its only drifting with the tide
Oh how that old cow puncher lied
   He surely had his gall.

He saddled me up an old gray hack
With three set-fasts upon his back
Then padded him up with gunny sacks
   And used my bedding all.

Put me in charge of the Caballada
And told me not to work too hard
For all I had to do was ride
   And keep the horses near.

I had one hundred and sixty head
Sometimes I wished that I were dead
Brown's head would often get bright red
  If any got away.

Straight to the bushes they would take
As if they were running for a stake
I've often wished their necks they'd break
  But they would never fall.

Sometimes I couldn't head them all
At other times my horse would fall
And I'd roll on like a cannon ball
  Till earth got in my way.

When I got on he gave a bound
Sprung in the air and turned around
Just then my head hit on the ground
  It was an awful fall.

He picked me up and carried me in
He bathed my head and commenced to grin
Says that's the way they all begin
  You're doing very well.

To-morrow morning if you don't croak
I'll give you another horse that's broke
You'll not need a saddle or even a rope
  "No, I'll quit right here," says I.

"California Trail."

❧ ❧ ❧

List all you Californ'y boys
   And open wide your ears
For now we start across the plains
   With a herd of mules and steers.
Now bear it in mind before you start
   That you'll eat jerked beef not ham
And antelope steak oh cuss the stuff
   It often proves a sham.

You cannot find a stick of wood
   On all this prairie wide
Whene'er you eat you've got to stand
   Or sit on some old bull hide.
It's fun to cook with Buffalo Chips
   Or Mesquite green as corn
If I'd once known what I know now
   I'd have gone around Cape Horn.

The women have the hardest time
   Who emigrate by land
For when they cook out in the wind
   They're sure to burn their hands.
Then they scold their husbands 'round
   Get mad and spill the tea
I'd have thanked my stars if they'd not come out
   Upon this bleak prairie.

Most every night we put out guards
  To keep the Indians off
When night comes round some heads will ache
  And some begin to cough.
To be deprived of help at night
  You know it's mighty hard
But every night there's someone sick
  To get rid of standing guard.

Then they're always talking of what they've got
  And what they're going to do
Some will say they are content
  For I've got as much as you.
Others will say I'll buy or sell
  And damned if I care which
Others will say boy's buy him out
  For he doesn't own a stitch.

Old rawhide shoes are Hell on corns
  While tramping through the sands
And driving a Jackass by the tail
  Damn the overland.
I would as lief be on a raft at sea
  And there at once be lost
John let's leave this poor old mule
  We'll never get him across.

"Top Hand"

While you're all so frisky I'll sing a little song
Think a horn of whiskey will help the thing along
It's all about the Top Hand when he's busted flat
Bumming round town, in his Mexican hat
He'd laid up all winter and his pocket book is flat
His clothes are all tatters but he don't mind that.

See him in town with a crowd that he knows
Rolling cigarettes an' a smoking through his nose.
First thing he tells you, he owns a certain brand
Leads you to think he is a daisy hand
Next thing he tells you 'bout his trip up the trail
All the way to Kansas to finish out his tale.

Put him on a horse, he's a handy hand to work
Put him on the branding pen he's dead sure to shirk.
With his natural leaf tobacco in the pockets of his vest
He'll tell you his Californy pants are the best.
He's handled lots of cattle, has'nt any fears
Can draw his sixty dollars, for the balance of his years.

Put him on herd, he's a cussin all day
Anything tries, its sure to get away.
When you have a round up he tells it all about
He's going to do the cuttin' and you can't keep him out.
If anything goes wrong he lays it on the screws
Say's the lazy devils were trying to take a snooze.

When he meets a greener he aint afraid to rig
Stands him on a chuck box and makes him dance a jig.
Waives a loaded cutter, makes him sing and shout,
He's a regular Ben Thompson, when the boss aint about.
When the boss aint about he leaves his leggins in camp.
He swears a man who wears them is worse than a tramp.

Say's he's not caring for the wages that he earns
For Dad's rich in Texas 'n got wagon loads to burn
But when he goes to town he's sure to take it in
He's always been dreaded, wherever he has been.
He rides a fancy horse, he is a favorite man
Can get more credit than a common waddie can.

When you ship the cattle he's bound to go along
To keep the boss from drinking and to see that nothing's
Wherever he goes, catch on to his game   [wrong
He likes to be called with a handle to his name.
He's always primping with a pocket looking glass
From the top to the bottom he's a bold Jackass.
          Waddie Cow boy.

Grand Round-up."

🌿 🌿 🌿

(Repeat last two lines of each stanza.)
Air Bonnie Lies Over the Ocean

I hear there's to be a grand round up
  Where cow-boys with others must stand
To be cut out by the riders of judgment
  Who are posted and know all the brands.

The trail to that great mystic region
  Is narrow and dim so they say
While the one that leads down to perdition
  Is posted and blazed all the way.

Whose fault is it then that so many
  Go astray on this wild range and fail
Who might have been rich and had plenty
  Had they known of the dim narrow trail.

I wonder if at the last day some cow-boy
  Un-branded and un-claimed should stand
Would he be mavericked by those riders of judgment
  Who are posted and know all the brands?

My wish for all cow-boys is this
  That we may meet at that grand final sale
Be cut out by the riders of judgment
  And shoved up the dim narrow trail.

"Little Adobe Casa"

❧ ❧ ❧

Just one year ago to-day,
  I left my eastern home
Hunting for a fortune and for fame,
  Little did I think that now,
  I'd be in Mexico
In this little adóbe casa on the plains.
                 Chorus.
  The roof is ocateo,
  The coyotes far and near
The Greaser roams about the place all day
  Centipedes and Tarantulas
  Crawl o'er me while I sleep
In my little adóbe casa on the plains.
  Alacranies on the ceiling,
  Cockroaches on the wall.
My bill-of-fare is always just the same
  Frijoles and tortillas
  Stirred up in chili sauce
In my little adóbe casa on the plains.
  But if some dark eyed mujer
  Would consent to be my wife
I would try to be contented and remain
  'Till fate should show a better place
  To settle down for life
Than this little adóbe casa on the plains.

The Texas Cow-boy.

Come all you Texas cow-boys
  And warning take of me
Don't go out in Montana
  For wealth or liberty
But stay home here in Texas
  Where they work the year around
And where you'll not get consumption
  From sleeping on the ground.

Montana is too cold for me,
  And the winters are too long
Before the round-ups have begun,
  Your money is all gone
For in Montana the boys get work
  But six months in the year
And they charge for things three prices
  In that land so bleak and drear.

This thin old hen-skin bedding
  'Twas not enough to shield my form
For I almost freeze to death,
  Whene'er there comes a storm.
I've an outfit on the Mussleshell
  Which I expect I'll never see
Unless by chance I'm sent
  To represent this A R and P T.

All along these bad lands,
  And down upon the dry
Where the cañons have no bottoms
  And the mountains reach the sky
Your chuck is bread and bacon
  And coffee black as ink
And hard old alkali water
  Thats scarcely fit to drink.

They'll wake you in the morning
  Before the break of day
And send you out on circle,
  Full twenty miles away.
With a ''Tenderfoot'' to lead you
  Who never knows the way
You're pegging in the best of luck
  If you get two meals a day.

I've been over in Colorado
  And down upon the Platte
Where the cow-boys work in pastures
  And the cattle all are fat
Where they ride silver mounted saddles
  And spurs and leggin's too
And their horses are all Normans
  And only fit to plow.

Yes I've traveled lots of country,
   Arizona's hills of sand
Down through the Indian Nation
   Plum to the Rio Grande
Montana is the bad-land
   The worst I've ever seen
Where the cow-boys are all tenderfeet
And the dogies are all lean.

"Mustang Gray."

There was a brave old Texan
   They called him Mustang Gray
He left his home when quite a boy
   And went roaming far away.

Chorus.

He'll go no more a-rangering
   Those savages to affright
He has heard his last war-whoop
   He fought his last fight.

When our country was invaded
   By the Indian warriors train's
He used to mount his noble charger
   And scout the hills and plains.

He would not sleep within a tent
No pleasures did he know
But like a brave old frontiersman
A-scouting he would go.

Once he was taken prisoner
And carried far away
Had to wear the yoke of bondage
Through the streets of Monterey.

A señorita loved him
And with a brave woman's pride
She opened the gates and gave him
Her father's horse to ride.

And when this gallant life was spent
This was his last command
Pray bury me in old Texas soil
On the banks of the Rio Grande.

And when the weary treveller
Is passing by his grave
He may sometimes shed a farewell tear
O'er the bravest of the brave.

Sam Bass

Sam Bass was born in Indiana, it was his native home
And at the age of seventeen, young Sam began to roan
He first went down to Texas, a cow-boy bold to be
A kinder hearted fellow, you'd scarcely ever see.

Sam used to deal in race stock, had one called the Den-
ton mare
He watched her in scrub races,   took her to the County
Fair.
She always won the money, wherever she might be
He always drank good liquor, and spent his money free.

Sam left the Collins ranch in the merry month of May
With a herd of Texas cattle the B'ack Hills to see
Sold out in Custer City and all got on a spree
A harder lot of cow-boys you'd scarcely ever see.

On the way back to Texas, they robbed the U. P. train
All split up in couples and started out again
Joe Collins and his partner were overtaken soon
With all their hard earned money they had to meet their
doom.
Sam made it back to Texas all right side up with care
Rode into the town of Denton his gold with friends to
share
Sam's life was short in Texas 'count of robberies he'd do
He'd rob the passengers coaches the mail and express too

Sam had four bold companions, four bold and daring lads
Underwood and Joe Jackson, Bill Collins and Old Dad
They were four of the hardest cow-boys that Texas ever
knew
They whipped the Texas Rangers and ran the hoys in
blue.

Jonis borrowed of Sam's money and didn't want to pay
The only way he saw to win was to give poor Sam away
He turned traitor to his comrades they were caught one
    early morn
Oh what a scorching Jonis will get whem Gabriel blows
    his horn.

Sam met his fate in Round Rock July the twenty-first
They pierced poor Sam with rifle balls and emptied out
    his purse
So Sam is a corpse in Round Rock, Jonis is under the clay
And Joe Jackson in the bushes trying to get away.

Bucking Broncho

My love is a rider, wild bronchos he breaks
Though he's promised to quit it, just for my sake
He ties up one foot, the saddle puts on
With a swing and a jump he is mounted and gone.

The first time I met him, 'twas early one spring
Riding a broncho a high headed thing
He tipped me a wink as he gaily did go
For he wished me to look at his bucking broncho.

The next time I saw him, 'twas late in the fall
Swinging the girls at Tomlinson's ball
He laughed and he talked, as we danced to and fro
Promised never to ride on another broncho.

He made me some presents, among them a ring
The return that I made him was a far better thing
'Twas a young maiden's heart, I'd have you all know
He'd won it by riding his bucking broncho.

Now all you young maidens, where'er you reside
Beware of the cow-boy who swings the rawhide
He'll court you and pet you and leave you and go
In the spring up the trail on his bucking broncho.

Educated Feller

We were camped upon the plains near the Cimmaron
When along came a stranger and stopped to argue some
He was a well educated feller his talk just come in herds
And astonished all the punchers with his jaw breaking
     words.

He had a well worn saddle and we thought it kind'er
     strange
That he didn't know much about working on the range
He'd been at work he said, up near the Santa Fe
And was cutting cross country to strike the 7 D.

Had to quit an outfit up near Santa Fe
Had some trouble with the boss, just what he didn't say
Said his horse was 'bout give out would like to get
     another
If the punchers wouldn't mind and it wasn't too much
     bother.

Yes we'll give you a horse, he's just as sound as a bun
They quickly grabbed a lariat and roped the Zebra Dun.
Turned him over to the stranger
Then they waited to see the fun.

Old Dunny stands right still not seeming to know
Until the strangers' ready and a fixing up to go
When he goes into the saddle old Dunny leaves the earth
He travels right straight up for all he was worth.

But he sits up in his saddle just pullin his mustach
Just like some summer boarder a waitin for his hash
Old Dunny pitched and bauled and had wall eyed fits
His hind feet perpendicular his front ones in his bits.

With one foot in the stirupp, he just thought it fun
The other leg around the saddle horn the way he rode
        old Dun.
He spurred him in the shoulder and hit him as he whirled
Just to show these flunky punchers the best rider in the
        world.

The boss says to him, you needn't go on
If you can use the rope like you rode old Dun.
You've a job with me if you want to come
You're the man I've been looking for since the year one.

I can sling the rope, an' I'm not very slow
I can catch nine times out of ten for any kind of dough

Now there's one thing and a sure thing I've learned
    since I was born
That all these educated fellows are n t green horns.

Cow Boys Lament.

'Twas once in my saddle I used to be happy
    'Twas once in my saddle I used to ' e gay
But I first took to drinking, then to gambling
    A shot from a six-shooter took my life away.

My curse let it rest, let it rest on the fair one
    Who drove me from friends that I loved and from home
Who told me she loved me, just to deceive me
    My curse rest upon her, wherever she roam.

Oh she was fair, Oh she was lovely
    The belle of the Viliage the fairest of all
But her heart was as cold as the snow on the mountains
    She gave me up for the glitter of gold.

I arrived in Galveston in old Texas
    Drinking and gambling I went to give o'er
But, I met with a Greaser and my life he has finished
    Home and relations I ne'er shall see more.

Send for my father, Oh send for mother
    Send for the surgeon to look at my wounds
But I fear it is useless I feel I am dying
    I'm a young cow-boy cut down in my bloom.

Farewell my friends, farewell my relations
  My earthly career has cost me sore
The cow-boy ceased talking, they knew he was dying
  His trials on earth, forever were o'er.

Chor· Beat your drums lightly, play your fifes merrily
  Sing your dearth march as you bear me along
Take me to the grave yard, lay the sod o'er me
  I'm a young cow-boy and know I've done wrong.

Chopo.

Through rocky arroyas so dark and so deep
Down the sides of the mountains so slippery and steep
You've good judgment, sure footed, wherever you go
You're a safety conveyance my little Chopo

Whether single or double or in the lead of a team
Over highways or byways or crossing a stream
You're always in fix and willing to go
Whenever you're called on, my chico Chopo.

You're a good roping horse, you were never jerked down
When tied to a steer, you will circle him round
Let him once cross the string, and over he'll go
You sabe the business, my cow horse Chopo.

One day on the Llano, a hail storm began
The herds were stampeded, the horses all ran
The lightning it glittered, a cyclone did blow
But you faced the sweet music my little Chopo.

Chopo my pony, Chopo my pride
Chopo my amigo, Chopo I will ride
From Mexico's borders 'cross Texas Llanos
To the salt Pecos river I ride you Chopo.

Buffalo Range.

Come all you Buffalo hunters and listen to my song
You needn't get uneasy, for it isn't very long
It's concerning some Buffalo hunters who all agreed to go
And spend a summer working, among the buffalo.

'Twas in the spring of seventy three, that I came to
    Jacksborough
There I met Bailey Griego, who asked how I'd like to go
And spend the summer west of Pease River hunting
On the range of the Buffalo.

Now being out of employment to Griego I named the
    day
When I could join his outfit if suited with the pay
I agreed if he'd pay good wages and transportation to,
To go and spend the summer among the buffalo.

Of course I'll pay good wages and transportation to
But if you should grow homesick and return to Jacksbor-
    ough
Before the huntings over I want you now to know
That I'll not pay you back wages from the range of the
    Buffalo.

Through promises and flattery he enlisted quite a train
Some ten or twelve in number all able bodied men
Our journey it was pleanant on the road we had to go
Until we crossed Pease River among the buffalo.

'Twas here our pleasure ended, our troubles had begun
The very first beast I tried to skin Oh how I cut my
    thumb
When skinning off those buffalo hides for our lives we'd
    little show
As the Indians tried to pick us off on the range of the
    buffalo.

Salt meat and Buffalo hump to eat and hard old sour
    dough bread
Strong coffee and alkali water to drink add a raw-hide
    for a bed
The way the mosquitos chewed on us you bet it wasn't
    slow
Lord grant there's no place on earth like the range of
    the buffalo.

When the summer at last ended old Griego began to say
My boys you've been extravagant, so I'm in debt to day
But among the buffalo hunters bankrupt law didn't go
So we left old Griegos bones to bleach among the buffalo.

Now we're back across Peace River and homeward we
    are bound
In that forsaken country may I never more be found

If you see anyone bound out there pray warn them not
 to go
To that forsaken country, the land of the buffalo.

The Cowboys Christmas Ball

Way out in Western Texas where the Clear Forks wa-
 ters flow
Where the cattle are a brewin' and the Spanish ponies
 grew
Where the Northers come a whistlin' from beyond the
 Neutral Strip
And the prairie dogs are sneezin' as though they had
 the grip
Where the coyotes come a-howlin' round the ranches af-
 ter dark
And the mocking-birds are singin' to the lovely Medder
 Lark
Where the possum and the badger and the rattlesnakes
 abound
And the monstrous stars are winkin' o'er a wilderness
 prefound
Where lonesome tawney prairies melt into air'y streems
While the Double Mountains slumber in heaven'ly kinds
 of dreams
Where the Antelope is grazin' and the lonely plovers call
It was there that I attended The Cowboys Christmas
 Ball.

The town was Anson City—old Jones' County Seat
Where they raised Poled Angus cattle and waving
    whiskered wheat
Where the air is soft and balmy and dry and full of health
And the prairies is exploding with Agricultural wealth
Where they print the "Texas Western" that Hue Mc-
    Call supplies
With news and yarns and stories of most amazin' size
Where Frank Smith "pulls the badger" on knowin' ten-
    derfeet
And Democracy's triumphant and mighty hard to bea'
Where lives that good old hunter John Milsap from La
    mar
Who used to be the sheriff "back east in Paris sah"
'Twas there I say at Ansen with the lovely widder Wal
That I went to that reception The Cowboys Christmas
    Ball.
The boys had left the ranches and come to town in piles
The ladies kinder' scatterin' had gathered in for miles
And yet the place was crowded as I remember well
'Twas gave on this occasion at the Morning Star Hotel
The music was a fiddle and a lively tambeurine
And a "Viol" came imported by the stage from Abilene
The room was togged out gorgeous with Mistletoe and
    shawls
And the candles flickered festious around the airy walls
The women folks looked lovely the boys looks kinder
    treed

'Till the leader commenced yellin' "whoa   fellers   lets
     stampede"
And the music started sighin' and a wailin' through the
     hall
As a kind of introduction to ·"The Cowboys Christmas
     Ball".

The leader was a feller that came from Tomsons ranch
They called him "Windy Billy" from little Deadmans
     branch
His rig was kinder keerless big spurs and high heeled
     boots
He had the reputation that comes when fellers shoots
His voice was like a bugle upon the Mountains height
His feet were animated and a mighty moving sight
When he commenced to holler"'now fellers stake yer pen"
Lock horns ter all them heifers and russle them like men
Saloot yer lovely critters neow swing and let'em go
Climb the grape vine round'em all hands do-ce-do
You Mavericke jine the round-up jest skip the water fall
Auh hit was gettin' active"The Cowboys Christmas Ball.

The boys were tolerable skittish the ladies powerful neat
That old bass Viols music just got there with both feet
That wailin' frisky fiddler I never shall forget
And Windy kept singin' I think I hear him yet
O'Yes Chase your Squirrels and cut'em to our side
Spur Treadwell to the centre with Cress P Charlie's
     bride

Doc' Hollis down the middle and twice the ladies chain
Van Andrews pen the fillies in big T Diamonds train
All pull your freight together neow swallow fork an
    change
Big Boston lead the trail herd through little Pitchfork's
    range
Purr round yor gentle pussies neow rope'em balance all
Huh hit was gettin' active "The Cowboys Christmas Ball

The dust riz fast and furious we all just galloped round
Till the scenery got so giddy that T Bar Dick was down'd
We buckled to our partners an' told'em to hold on
Then shook our hoofs like lightning until the early dawn
Don't tell me 'bout Cotillions or Germans No Sir 'Ee
That whirl at Anson City just takes the cake with me
I'm sick of lazy shufflings of them I've had my fill
Give me a frontier break-down backed up by Windy Bill
McAllister aint nowhere when Windy leads the show
I've seen 'em both in harness and so I sorter know
Oh Bill I shant forget you I'll oftentimes recall
That lively gaited sworray "The Cowboys Christmas Ball

Chase of the O. L. C. Steer

Did you ever hear of the O L C Steer
    With widely flaring horns
He smashes the trees as he splits the breeze
    And the Cow-boys ropes he scorns

That O L C's fame it soon became
  Of camp fire yarns the pet
I'll stake my rocks that I get that ox
  Quoth Rap Who'll take my bet?

Why of course my Gray Black horse
  Will run on him he said
Show me his track I'll bring him back
  I'll bet alive or dead.

Up Johnny spoke "No brags I make"
  Straight goods I give you now
I'll put my string on anything
  From a coyote to a cow.

Then up spoke Bob with this here job
  You bet I'm going to cope
Just you watch me if you want to see
  How Texas punchers rope.

These cow-boys three for modesty
  Have always been well known
For don't you know unless they blow
  Their horns they'd not be blown.

Meanwhile the steer devoid of fear
  Was trailing o'er the Mesa
He sniffed the air what did he care
  He knew he was a racer.

With firm intent on business bent
  Three youths rode up the trail

The steer he saw droppped his jaw
  And then he whisked his tail.

The other day I chanced that way
  That steer was grinning yet
Six weeks have passed not yet the last
  Of why that steer they didn't get.

If they once began for yours they'll chin
  And tell although they hit him
And ran all day how he got away
  And why they didn't git im"

The Pecos Stream

A cowboys life is a weary dreary life
  Some people think it free from all care
Its rounding up cattle from morning to night
  On the lone prairie so drear.

When the spring work comes in then our troubles begin
  The weather being fierce and cold
We get almose froze with the water on our clothes
  And the cattle we can scarcely hold.

Just about four o'clock the cook will holler out
  "Roll out boys its almost day"
Through his broken slumbers the puncher he will ask
  Has the short summer night passed away.

"Saddle up" "Saddle Up" the boss will holler out
    When we're camped by the Pecos stream
Where the wolves and the owls with their terrifying
    howls
    Disturb us in our midnight dreams.

Once I loved to roam but now I stay at home
    All you punchers take my advice
Sell your briddle and your saddle quit your roaming and
    travels
    And tie on to a cross eyed wife.

The Pecos River Queen.

Where the Pecos river winds and turns in its journey to
    the sea
From its white walls of sand and rock striving ever to
    be free
Near the highest railroad bridge that all these modern
    times have
Dwells fair young Patty Moorhead the Pecos River Queen

She's known by all the cowboys on the Pecos river wide
They know full well that she can shoot that she can rope
    and ride
She goes to every roundup every cow work without fail
Looking out for all Her Cattle branded "walking hog oh
    rail."
She made her start in cattle, yes, made it with her rope
Can tie down ev'ry maverick fore it can strike a lope

She can rope and tie and brand it as quick as any man
She's voted by all cowboys an A 1 top cow hand.

Across the Comstock Railroad bridge the highest in the
  west
Patty rode her horse one day a lovers heart to test
For he told her he would gladly risk all dangers for her
  sake
But the puncher wouldn't follow so she's still without a
  mate.

Old Time Cowboy

Come all you melancholy folks wherever you may be
I'll sing you about the cowboy whose life is light and free
He roams about the prairie and at night when he lies
  down
His heart is as gay as the flowers in May in his bed upon
  the ground.

They're a little bit rough I must confess the most of them
  at least
But if you do not hunt a quarrel you can live with them
  in peace
For if you do your sure to rue the day you joined their
  band
They will follow you up and shoot it out with you just
  man to man.

Did you ever go to any cowboy whenever hungry or dry
Asking for a dollar and have him you deny
He'll just pull out his pocket book and hand you a note
They are the fellows to help you out whenever you are
broke.

Go to their ranches and stay awhile they never ask a cent
And when they go to town their money is freely spent
They walk straight up and take a drink paying for
everyone
And they never ask your pardon for anything they have
done

When they go to their dances some dance while others
pat
They ride their bucking broncos and wear their broad
brimmed hats
With their California saddles and their pants inside their
boots
You can hear their spurs a-jingling and perhaps some of
them shoot.

Come all softhearted tenderfeet if you want to have
some fun
Go live among the cowboys they show you how it's done
They'll treat you like a prince my boys about them there's
nothing mean
But dont try to give them too much advice for all of 'em
aint so green.

Who's Old Cow

Twas the end of roundup the last day of June
  Or maybe July I dont just remember
Or it might have been August 'twas some time ago
  Or perhaps 'twas the first of September.

Anyhow 'twas the roundup we had at Mayou
  On the lightning rod's range near Cayo
There was some twenty wagons "more or less" camped
    about
  On the temporal in the Cañon.

First night we'd no cattle so we only stood guard
  On the horses somewhere 'bout two hundred head
So we side-lined and hoppled we belled and we staked
  Loose'd our hot rolls and fell into bed.

Next morning 'bout daybreak we started our work
  Our horses like possums felt fine
Each "one 'tendin' knitten!" none trying to shirk
  So the roundup got on in good time.

Well we worked for a week 'till the country was clear
An' the boss said "now boys we'll stay here
We'll carve and we'll trim 'em an' start out a herd
Up the east trail from old Abilene.

Next morning' all on herd an' but two with the cut
An' the boss on Piute carving fine

'Till he rode down his horse and had to pull out
An' a new man went in to clean up.

Well after each outfit had worked on the band
There was only three head of them left
When Nig Add from L F D outfit road in
A dictionary on earmarks an' brands.

He cut the two head out told where they belonged
But when the last cow stood there alone
Add's eyes bulged so he did'nt 'no just what to say
'Ceptin boss der's sumpin' here monstrous wrong.

White folks smarter'n Add an' maybe I'se wrong
But here's six months wages dat I'll give
If anyone'll tell me when I reads de mark
To who dis long horned cow belongs.

Overslope in right ear an' de underbill
Left ear swallerfork an de undercrop
Hole punched in centre an' de jinglebob
Under half crop an' de slash an split.

She's got O block an' lightnin' rod
Nine forty-six an' A bar eleven
T terrapin an' ninety-seven
Rafter cross an' de double prod.

Half circle A an' diamond D
Four cross L an' three P Z
B W I bar X V V
Bar N cross an' A L C

So if no' o' you punchers claims dis cow
Mr Stock 'Sociation need'nt get alarmed
For one brand more or less wont ,do no harm
So old nigger Add'l just brand her now

The Cowboys New Years Dance.

BY MARK CHISHOLM

We were sitting' round the ranch house some twenty
    hands or more
Most of us Americans but a few from Arkansas
One Dutchman from the fatherland one Johnny Bull
    from Leeds
A Cornishman from Cornwall all men of different creeds
They were a sittin' an' a arguin' busy as a hill of ants
How they'd get rid of the money they had buried in their
    pants
That they'd made by hard cow punching working all
    the year around
From sunup until sundown an' a sleepin' on the ground
Where at night the polecat saunters round the chuck box
    after grub
And in passing by your hot roll gives your head a friend-
    ly rub
Where the rattlesnake lays dormant his fangs are like
    a lance
'Twas with them that I attended The Cowboys New
    Years Dance.

The town was Roswell City old Chaves' county seat

Where they raise fine shorthorn cattle that are mighty
    hard to beat

Where they send the frail consumptive in search of in-
    stant health

And the hills is just a bustin' with their pent up mineral
    wealth

Where the wells are all artesian and flow fish and water
    too

'Least so says the Roswell people so I sorter guess it's
    true

Where laughin' Joe the darky bust up Mulkey's show
    one day

By laughin' at prayer meetin' and old Abe he went away

Charles Perry he was a sheriff and G Curry county clerk

Where they caught Bill Cook the outlaw and sent him
    off to work

Where the moonbeams on the Pecos seem to glitter and
    to glance

I received an invitation to the Cowboys New Years
    Dance.

The boys had been invited and they just come in herds

The ladies more numerous had flocked to town like birds

Old Roswell was just crowded there was horses every-
    where

Looked like some long procession headed for a county fair
Where everything was orderly as I remember well
Invitations were extended to the Roswell Stone Hotel
The music was a fiddle a guitar and a banjo
And the way those three boys played em'
It was fully half the show the women folks set together
All the boys stood in the door 'tlll the caller commenced
      yellin'
For just one couple more
And the music started windin 'an' a wailin' like some
      hants
That had come to cast their hoodo on the Cowboy New
      Years Dance.

The caller was a feller one of Atkinson's men
Who had the reputation of once being in the pen
His outfit sort of gaudy big spurs an' conchas bright
Fringed leggin's and gold buttons six feet about his
      height
He was tall an' angular an, a broncho buster right
An' at callin' out the dances he was simply out of sight
Soon he commenced to beller now fellers all begin
Grab your lovely partners an' every one jine in
First bow to your partners now four hands cross an'
      change
An' chase those pretty footies once around the range
Join once again your partners around the circles prance
It was getting interesting the Cowboys New Years
      Dance,

Next dance will be the Lancers round up your ladies boys
Cut them all to the centre and never mind the noise
Chase your lovely critters all into the branding pen
Everybody swing everybody else's girl and swing them
    once again
Dash your line on the nearest filly and drag her from
    the herd
Re-sume your former places and swing her like a bird
Now Brownfield strike out in the lead all grand right
    and left
Swing each one when half way round never mind their
    hat
Now ladies to the centre all hands do se do
Right hand in left hand out swing and let her go
Trail block Jack to your settees for that winds up the
    lance
My but it was getting furious the Cowboys New Years
    Dance.

The refreshments came round often till all hands had
    their fill
Past round uncerimonous like by Broncho Buster Bill
Though his gait was quite uncertain he never lost his feet
And at complementing ladies he was mighty hard to beat
To close up the night proceedings we ragged "Turkey in
    the Straw"
Till we wore out musicians and they could play no more
We were served with soda water red eye and pilsner

beer
And the conversation never lagged 'twas most penetrat-
        ing clear
'En those who never danced before would dance with all
        their might
'En the most peaceably inclined citizens went a hunting
        for a fight
So we saddled up our horses drifted homeward to the
        ranch
With a happy recollection of the Cowboys New Years
        Dance.

Speckles

He was little 'en peaked 'en thin 'en Narr'y a no 'account
        horse
Least that's the way you'd describe him in case that the
        beast had been lost
But for single and double cussedness 'en double fired sin
The horse never come out O' Texas that was half way
        knee-high to him

The first time that ever I saw him was nineteen year ago
        last spring
'Twas the year we had grasshoppers that come 'en 'et
        up everything
That a feller rode up here one evening 'en wanted to pen
        overnight

A small bunch of horses he said 'en I told him I guessed
'twas all right,

Well the feller was busted the horses was thin 'en the
grass around here kind of good
'En he said if I'd let him hold here a few days He'd set-
tle with me when he could
So I told him all right turn them loose down the draw
That the latch string was always untied
He was welcome to stop a few days if he liked 'En rest
from his weary ride.

Well the cus stay'd around for two or three weeks till
at last he decided to go
And that horse away yonder being too poor to move He
gimme, the cuss had no dough
Well at first the darn brute was as wild as a deer 'en
would snort when he came to the branch
'En it took two cowpunchers on good horses too to handle him here at the ranch

Well winter came on and the range it got hard and my
mustang commenced to get thin
So I fed him along and rode him round some and found
out old Freckles was game
For that was what the other cus called him just Freckles
no more or no less
His color couldn't describe it something like a paintshop
in distress.

Them was Indian times young feller that I'm a tellin'
    about
And oft's the time I've seen the red men fight and put
    the boys in blue to route
A good horse in them days young feller would save your
    life
One that in any race could hold the pace when the red-
    skin bands were rife.

LEXICON

of Cowboy and Western Words

PIONEERING IN THE WEST imposed new vocabulary to match the new mode of life in a new environment. For many, the time may already have come when lexical aids are required for intelligent reading of cowboy literature, as it has for the reading of Chaucer. The lexicon that follows should help.

adobe. In Spanish, *adobe*—dried brick. Clay, mixed with water and straw, is placed in molds about 18 × 10 × 6 inches, then removed to dry and bake in the sun. It was a common building material in the Hispanic Southwest. Adobe gives excellent insulation but requires protection from moisture which causes rapid erosion.

alacrán, pl. *alacranes.* Spanish for scorpion.

alkali. The Great Basin and other regions of the Southwest present innumerable instances of small basins that accumulate alkaline wastes due to the nature of soils and lack of drainage. These range all the way from dry basins crusted with whitish soil and supporting a limited vegetation to such phenomena as the Great Salt Lake itself. As an adjective, alkalied means: "acclimated to the country; a person or animal ill from drinking alkali water; one who is drunk."

amigo. Spanish for friend. "Chopo my *amigo . . .*"

antelope. Also called "pronghorn" (*antilocapra americana*). Unique to North America, this svelte denizen of the sage is in no way related to species of

African ruminants bearing the same name. Unlike the deer family, male and female both have horns. Their range once extended from the northern reaches of Arizona and New Mexico through the Rocky Mountain area and on up into the prairie provinces of Canada.

arroyo. Spanish for small stream. In the Southwest it means a precipitous gully or channel cut in soft earth by the waters from sudden violent storms.

bad lands. Used to identify areas in the West where erosion has been so violent that little or no vegetation remains in a region of buttes, mesas, and other exotic and forbidding forms where man and beast find it hard to make their way.

badger. To "pull the badger" was a term applied to an extortion game involving the use of faked evidence; by extension, to play a practical joke. To "badger," i.e. harass or bait someone, may come from the practice of pitting a badger against a dog. *See* M. M. Mathews, *A Dictionary of Americanisms* (University of Chicago Press, 1951), I, 60–61; and *Grose's Classical Dictionary of the Vulgar Tongue* (London, 1823) p. 7, under "badgers."

belly, *v.* Though we have not found this term elsewhere, we feel sure that it is the equivalent of "flank-hobbling." With the typical hobbling of the front feet alone, some horses manage a clumsy gallop sufficient to go great distances; by attaching the hobbles to a flank strap with a short piece of rope this is impossible.

Ben Thompson. The allusion in all probability is to a noted Southwestern gunslinger who went with his parents, natives of Nova Scotia, to Texas in 1845. He was in the Texas Confederate forces and is said to have killed a sergeant and a lieutenant in a barracks-room brawl in July, 1861. He led a hard gun-filled life until he was shot down in the Vaudeville Theater, San Antonio, Texas, March 11, 1884, along with his friend John King Fisher. (*See* J. H. Plenn, *Texas Hellion, The True Story of Ben Thompson.* New York: New American Library, 1955.) There was also a notorious Kansas gunslinger by this name who fled into Texas following the murder of C. B. Whitney on August 15, 1873. Thompson's brother Billy was tried and acquitted of the crime on September 14, 1877. (*See* Nyle H. Miller and Joseph W. Snell, *Why the West Was Wild.* Kansas State Historical Society, 1963, pp. 635–40.)

Big T Diamond. A brand; by extension, the owner of that brand.

bit. Metal bar that traverses a horse's mouth. There are many types, ranging from a straight metal bar to variously curbed or articulated types. *See* GRAZIN BIT.

boys in blue. In the Civil War the Union troops were known as the "boys in blue." The same term is also sometimes applied to members of a city police force.

brand. *n.* Mark burned into the hides of cattle or other animals to identify ownership. *v.* To put such a mark on an animal. To assure that brands for each owner were distinctive, registration thereof by a state official came into being, and brand books were, and still are, issued periodically. Brands were inflicted with a "branding iron," "running iron," or simply an "iron." Under open-range conditions irons were heated in a small fire. Critters were roped, thrown, and tied, then branded and. released. "Reading" or "calling" brands was a necessity whenever cattle of different owners were to be separated. When cattle were sold, old brands were canceled (also with an iron) and the new brand burned on. The expert rustling of branded cattle necessitated careful modification of brands using appropriate irons. Often the brand also became the recognized name for the home ranch; the rancher might even be known by his brand in lieu of his family name and hands long employed there likewise. For specific brands in this study consult the index.

branding pen. Range corrals were built to make branding easier. They were designed to receive and confine a herd and to separate the critters into branding pens small enough to handle one animal at a time. Later, chutes made branding possible without the spectacular but inefficient process of roping, throwing, and tying.

brogan shoe. A coarse shoe of untanned leather.

bronco (bronc, broncho). In Spanish *bronco,* adjective meaning rough, coarse, harsh. An ungentled horse; a horse not yet sufficiently gentled to be reliable. Bronc buster: professional "breaker" of ungentled horses. The art is much more than the mere capacity to stay in the saddle: the bronc buster must also be able to instill the discipline and skills that will turn a wild animal into a reliable cow horse. A bronco steer (p. 207) is a critter so wild that he has antisocial tendencies even among his own kind.

buck, *v.* The efforts of an ungentled horse or wild steer to unseat its rider. Prior to being "broken" almost any range horse will make a most vigorous struggle to "throw" its rider. Adams (p. 22) lists a half column of names to identify the pitches and other movements that characterize bucking, this terminology being developed as systematically and as comprehensively as is the lingo of boxing or wrestling.

buffalo. Popular name for *bison americanus.* Vast herds roamed the plains of central and western United States into the 1880's. They were ruthlessly exploited for hides and for sport (so called!). The hump was considered a delicacy. Their droppings, dried, made satisfactory fuel for campfires.

bull hide, bull-hide canoe. The hides of cattle or of buffalo were commonly known as bull hides. The bull-hide canoe was a circular boat with a frame of bent willow covered with buffalo hide. It was used extensively on the Missouri River by Mandan and Hidatsa Indians.—A. H. Woodward, Patagonia, Arizona.

bulldog, *v. See* DOG.

bunkhouse. Building serving for sleeping quarters for the hired hands on a ranch.

caballada. Spanish for a band of horses. *Syn. remuda.*

cack. A disreputable horse.

California law. *See* DALLY.

California pants. A style of pants used on the range, usually of striped or checked heavy wool of excellent double weave. —Adams, p. 27.

California saddle. *See* RIM FIRE.

canyon (*cañon*). From the Spanish *cañon*—cannon, tube, pipe. In the Southwest it came to mean a gorge.

carve, *v. Syn.* cut (of cattle).

casa. Spanish for house.

catclaw. Species of *acacia greggii*. Widely spread in the arid regions of the West and Southwest.

caverango. Mexican hostler. *See* WRANGLER.

cavvy (cavyard, cavvy yard, covy-yard). From the Spanish *caballada*. *Syn. remuda*.

cayuse. A scrubby, undesirable horse said to be named from a Northwest Indian tribe that liked horses.

chantain. We have not encountered this word anywhere else.

chaparajos (*chaparejos*). Spanish for leather breeches or overalls. *See* CHAPS.

chaparral. Term applied to *Atriplex, adanostroma arctostaphilos,* and other genera of thorny evergreen shrubs of the Southwest. Usually more than stirrup high, they form thickets and areas of cover ideal for the protection of range cattle despite the annoyance to punchers constrained to ride therein.

chaps. Spanish, *chaparejos* or *chapareras*—leather trousers or overalls. Worn over the ordinary trousers to protect the horseman's legs from injuries caused by brush, fences, etc. *Syn.* leggings.

chico. Spanish for small, young, (*adj.*). *n.* a boy. A term of endearment.

chili. Sauce made from ground pods of the red (chili) pepper. By extension, a soup using beans, red pepper, and other ingredients.

chuck. Range name for food.

chuck box. The typical chuck wagon had a box extending all the way across the rear and bolted to the wagonbed itself. Its sturdy hinged door could be dropped down to form a table.

chuck wagon. A wagon equipped to serve as a mobile kitchen for cowboys on trail or roundup.

cinch. From the Spanish *cincha*—girth, cinch. Girth that passes around the horse's body to anchor the saddle. For heavy work there are generally two.

circle (herding). On roundup a crew of punchers fans out to gather all the cattle on a certain range. The circle riders are those who take the outer perimeter; a circle horse is one chosen with sufficient stamina ("bottom," in cowboy lingo) to endure the greater mileage.

cocinero. (Spanish for a male cook). At roundup or on trail herd, the role of the cook was extremely important. He didn't have to ride but he managed almost everything except the herd. He took charge of the teams and wagons hauling food, bedding, water, and supplies. He managed the *remuda,* assisted, of course, by the wrangler. Often the Anglo-American punchers reduced *cocinero* to the more manageable *coosie.*

Colt 44. In 1875 Colt produced a single action 45-calibre pistol known as the Peacemaker. Three years later it appeared in a model accommodating the same 44-40 cartridge used in the Winchester rifle, thus permitting a westerner to carry a single type of cartridge for both rifle and pistol. This new weapon acquired further utility in the West because its sturdy frame recommended it for the gruesome sport of pistol-whipping, a practice by local marshals of clubbing tough hombres over the head, or by outlaws to intimidate their victims. —Summarized from Larry Koller, *The Fireside Book of Guns* (New York: Simon and Schuster, 1959), pp. 131-32.

concha. Spanish—shell, case. In western lingo, a slightly convex metal disk, usually made of silver, used as an ornament on horses' or cowboys' gear.

coulies (couless). From the French *couler,* to flow. *Syn. arroyo.* The term still persists on Rocky Mountain and northern cattle ranges in preference to the Mexican term.

covy-yard. Cavy-yard. *See* REMUDA.

cow. Term used to designate cattle generally, regardless of sex or age. *Syn.* critter.

cowboy. Used to identify the cowboy by almost everyone except the cowboys themselves who prefer puncher, cow puncher, hand, cow hand, as general terms, and a list of other epithets so long that it takes Adams (p. 42) almost a full column to give the ones familiar to him. In Revolutionary days, and again in the early conflicts with Mexico, the term, as a proper name, was applied to certain mounted troops who marauded behind enemy lines. Now it comes near being universal, American movies having taken the cowboy's image and name to all parts of the world.

coyote. From the Mexican *coyotl*. *Canis latrans* is of the same genus as the dog and the wolf. His range extended from the Mississippi to the Pacific Coast and from well down in Old Mexico to Arctic regions. He has survived well against the inroads of civilized man: specimens have recently been seen in Los Angeles. Gregarious animal that he is, nights on the prairie he did close harmony with sundry companions scattered far and wide.

critters. Cattle. By extension, other domestic or wild animals, including women.

Cross-P Charlie. Not infrequently a puncher was known largely by his first name preceded by the brand of the ranch where he worked, as here: "Charlie of the Cross-P outfit."

croton coffee. Croton is a genus of *euphorbiaceous* plants, many of which have medicinal properties. Croton oil, from an East Indian species (*Croton tiglium*) is a violent cathartic. It is doubtful that Croton was ever used in the making of coffee, though through excessive boiling lumberjack or range coffee may have approached its flavor.

cut, *v., n.* At a roundup, the range cattle were assembled into smaller units for any number of purposes. It took an expert hand and a well-trained cutting horse to ride into the herd, locate and isolate the animals as desired. A *cut* (*n.*, p. 248) was used to identify an animal or a herd, separated from the main group for whatever purpose.

cutter. Slang for pistol.

dally. In Mexican, ¡*dale vueltas!* "give it some twists." Anglicized to "dally welters," then simply "dally." In roping cattle a full turn is taken around the horn of the saddle at the moment of making a catch. This is done in such a way that the rope can be released at once, or so that slack can be taken up. If the lasso is tied fast, saddle and rider may be torn from the horse. To "take your dally welters according to California law" meant to use a dally rather than to tie the lasso fast to the saddle horn, so that a "snake steer" could be released if rider and mount got into trouble.

deer. Two species are prevalent in the Rockies and the Southwest. The mule deer, *odocoileus hemeonus,* is a large deer whose range is from parts of Old Mexico to the Arctic Circle. It prefers coniferous surroundings. Its popular name, "mule," is substantiated by its prominent ears. The white-tail deer, *odocoileus virginianus,* prefers hardwood or second growth vegetation and is somewhat smaller than the mule deer.

dog, *v.* Rodeo sport in which a horseman rides alongside a critter, drops on its neck and throws the animal off its feet. Adams (p. 23) says a Negro puncher, Tom Pickett, was the first to practice the art, that it appeared first in rodeos as an exhibition only. Now it is a regular part of the rodeo repertoire.

dogie (dogy, dobie). Scrubby calf, orphan calf, unbranded calf, or calves generally. Derivation is uncertain: Spanish, *dogal, n.* slip or hangman's knot, i. e., a calf fit to be killed? English, dough-gut, a lean potbellied calf carrying the scars of malnutrition?

dough. Slang for money.

dude. Applied by genuine range folk to the city-bred man out in the wide-open spaces merely for kicks.

earmark, *n., v.* Earmarks as well as brands are used to assert ownership: both were frequently inflicted upon the animal at the same time. At roundup the brand caller shouted the name of earmark and brand. See Song XXI, "Whose Old Cow?" Adams (p. 56) lists the names of more than thirty earmarks.

elk. *Cervus canadensis.* A magnificent denizen of the virgin lands from coast to coast and from southern Arizona, New Mexico, and Texas to sub-Arctic tundra. It frequents forest areas that are interspersed with open meadows. Its range has been greatly reduced by the civilizing activities of man. It is also known by the name wapiti.

filly. Young female horse: By extension, an unmarried young woman.

forty-five. Gun of that calibre.

frijoles. Spanish for dried beans.

grapevine. Figure in a square dance.

graybacks. *Pediculus humanis corporis.* The common body louse, as popularly called in the mid-1850's and later.

grazin bit. Good general purpose lightweight bit with a small curb in the mouthpiece.

Greaser. The "gringo's" (Anglo-American's) name for the common run of Mexicans.

greener. *Syn.* tenderfoot, greenhorn.

greenhorn. *Syn.* tenderfoot.

grub. *Syn.* chuck.

hack. Probably derived from "hackney," meaning to the cowboy a beaten-down carriage horse.

harness. "in . . .": said of a dance caller in doing his job.

hen-skin bedding. Bed cover stuffed with feathers.

hobble. Leather cuffs connected with a chain to the forelegs of a horse, which, so restrained, can still move enough for a night's grazing. Yet he is sufficiently restricted to be easily located when needed a few hours later. *See also* BELLY, SIDE-LINE.

hot roll. Cowboy's bedroll.

iron. *See* BRAND.

iron-wedge bread. The reference is probably to what was commonly called hard tack or sea biscuit, commonly issued to soldiers or carried by frontiersmen. Pieces of the GI variety, used up to 1919, measured 3″ × 3¼″. *See* John D. Billings, *Hard Tack and Coffee* (Boston, 1887), pp. 113–19.

jerky, jerked beef. From the Mexican Indian *charqui*—dried buffalo or beef. The flesh was cut in strips and dried. When cooked it swelled to considerable proportions; it was sometimes ground into meal.

jimpson (jumpson) weed. *Datura stramonium;* also known as thorn apple.

kack (Southern/Texas). A variant of the California tree, having a small pummel but double cinch. In "Little Joe's" case it may simply have been an old pack saddle, frequently called kack, kyack, or kyax. —Arthur Woodward of Patagonia, Arizona (FAC II 696).

lariat. From the Spanish *la reata,* a rope used to tie pack animals in single file. Later extended to mean any rope used in working cattle.

lasso. Portuguese *laco,* noose. n. A long rope, usually made of hide, with a running eyelet or *honda* at one end for making a loop. Also used as a verb. *Syn.* rope.

leggin's. In Texas the term leggin's was preferred to chaps.

llano. Flat, treeless, open prairie.

loco, n. Spanish—mad, crazy. Species of *astragalus* producing a drug which affects animals, especially horses. Several species are spread widely in the mountain West. The effect is cumulative. Used also as an adjective.

maguey. Rope made from the fibers of various species of the century plant (especially *agave americana*); used now only by trick ropers.

maverick, *n., v.* An unbranded calf of uncertain ownership. As a verb it is the act of placing one's own brand on such an animal. Adams (p. 97) derives it from the name of Samuel E. Maverick who sold a range herd to a neighbor. Since many of the Maverick cattle were unbranded the purchaser of the Maverick brand claimed and branded every animal he encountered, including some that did not belong to Maverick: hence to "maverick" came to mean to steal and brand unbranded cattle. A proper name.

mesa. Spanish for table, table land, etc. Usual term applied to the flat-top mountains or elevated plateaus characteristic of many regions of the Southwest.

mesquite. In Spanish, *mezquite.* A spiney shrub of the pea family growing in the Southwest and Mexico.

mujer. Spanish for woman.

mustang. In Spanish, *mesteno,* derived from *mesta*—a group of horse breeders. It originally referred to the bands of wild horses in the Southwest. Here it means simply a fiery and treacherous cow horse.

Nation, (the). The Indian Nations. In 1838 the "Five Civilized Nations" of Indians were moved to the Indian Territory (Oklahoma). The Oklahoma Territory was opened to the whites for settlement in 1889, but the area was still known to many as "the Nation" or "the Indian Nations."

Navy six. The Colt model 1851 percussion six-shot revolver, .36 caliber, was officially called the "Navy" size, and other makes of similar size were also often called "Navys." This Colt was common in the West until the Colt model 1873 cartridge revolver—the "Peacemaker"—became common in the late 1870's. —H. J. Swinney, Director, Idaho Historical Society.

Needle gun. A long-disused western slang term for any of the breechloading Springfield military rifles of the models of 1865 through 1884, so called from their long slim firing pin. Not to be confused with the Prussian "Needle Gun" of 1848, which was probably entirely unknown in the American West. —H. J. Swinney, Director, Idaho Historical Society.

night horse. The night horse was selected for being sure-footed, keen of sight, with an unfaltering sense of direction and an even temper. He was picketed at night for instant use and typically not ridden at any other time. Night herd, *v.*: take charge of cattle on the bed ground during roundup or trail drive.

Norman (horses). A stock breed of dray horses, not suitable for the speed and quick reactions required of a cow horse.

ocateo (*ocatillo*). *Fouquireria splendens:* also called slimwood or coachwhip. A beautiful desert cactus whose whiplike stems flare out from its central base like a vase.

outfit. All the hands engaged in a given cattle operation, as a roundup, a trail drive, etc.: the supplies, wagons, gear, equipment, and mounts of such a group; a ranch together with its herds, buildings, and equipment; wearing apparel.

outlaw. Vicious, untamable horse; a wild cow or steer; man of similar character. *Syn.* snake.

poled Angus. One of the species of beef cattle that have replaced the long-horns throughout the Southwest.

prickly pear. General term applied to cacti of the genus *opuntia* characterized by flattened stems: widely spread from Montana south.

puncher/cow puncher. Usual name for a man who worked with cattle; it derived from the necessity of prodding cattle which lie down in a railroad car: they must be kept on their feet to avoid being trampled by the other cattle. Appears also as a verb, "to punch cows."

pussies. Women.

quirt. In Spanish, *cuerda*—cord; becomes Mexican *cuarta*, meaning whip. It consists of a wooden or leaded stock braided over with rawhide tapered into three or four loose rawhide thongs. The stock may serve as a blackjack or to pacify horses that tend to rear. A loop in the butt of the stock serves to anchor it on the rider's wrist or the saddle.

ranch. From the Spanish *rancho*. A farm, especially one devoted to the breeding and raising of livestock. Note also: rancher, ranchman, ranch hand, etc.

range. Unfenced country where cattle graze.

rawhide. Many frontier crafts depended upon use of the tanned hides of cattle; ropes, chaps, saddles, horsegear, chair seats, clothing, and other items too numerous to mention were contrived by the use of rawhide.

red eye. Slang for whiskey.

remonta/remontha. See REMUDA.

remuda. From the Spanish *remudar*, to exchange. The herd of extra saddle horses not under saddle, used by the cow hands on roundup or trail drive. *Syn. caballada, remontha, remonta,* cavvy, cavyard, or simply the hosses or string (of horses).

rig, *v.* To "rig" has been used to designate the action of harnessing and hooking up horses; also to contrive or manipulate fraudulently. Here the meaning seems to be to play the leading role in hazing a newcomer.

rim fire. Single cinch saddle, also called a "California rig" or "rimmy." —Adams, p. 128.

road brand. During trail driving days, Texas law required that all cattle being driven beyond the northern borders of the state were to be branded with "a large and plain mark . . . on the left side of the stock behind the shoulder." This road brand served to distinguish trail-drive cattle from critters belonging to the ranges through which the trails passed. A similar brand is used today by the Forestry Service on cattle authorized to graze in the national forests.

rope, *n.* The cow hand's rope was the very sustenance of life itself, weapon and slave. With it he captured animals, both domestic and wild; he dragged firewood to camp, staked his horses; duelled; tied his packs. As a verb it meant to do almost anything you can do with a rope, especially to rope cattle. *Syn. lasso.* In a square dance it meant to join hands for a new figure.

roping horse. Roping and cutting place more demands upon the horse than any other range skill: speed, sudden and violent maneuver, a calm temperament under maximum pressure. The roping horse requires the further skill of keeping a taut rope in the second following a catch so that the puncher can dismount and throw and tie the critter. The well-trained roping horse will face the caught animal and keep backing off just enough to avoid the hazards of a slack rope.

roundup. Probably derived by translation from the Spanish *rodeo,* action of surrounding. This represented the cattleman's annual harvest: used transcendentally as a symbol of death (see Song VI, "Grand Round-up"); as the image of a gathering of folks for a cowboy dance (see Song XVI, "The Cowboys Christmas Ball").

rustle. To herd the *remuda;* to steal cattle; by extension, to choose partners at a dance.

rusty, *n.* Cattle culled out of a herd because they were not in good condition.

sabe/savy, *v.* In Spanish, *sabe,* know. In cowboy lingo it survives as a verb and also as a noun meaning to know, skill, know-how.

sand-stacked tree. Probably a willful corruption of "Sam Stack," well-known saddle maker.

screws. We have not encountered the term elsewhere. From the context it must mean the "hold men" at a branding, i.e., riders whose job it was to hold a cut or small herd from which single critters were isolated, lassoed, thrown, and tied by the cutter. In Song V-B the "Top Screw" seems to be used as a pejorative for the boss of a branding crew.

señorita (senoretta). Spanish for unmarried young woman.

set-fast (also setfasts). Saddlesore.

seven up. A card game played widely in the West since the days of the trappers, then commonly known as "All Fours." *See* J. R. Bartlett, *Dictionary of Americanisms* (Boston, 1860).

shack. Small, crudely built frontier home. Webster derived it from the Aztec *xacalli*, which gave in Mexican-Spanish *jacal*, the latter being influenced possibly by ramshack or ramshackle.

Sharps rifle. Any of the single-shot breechloading rifles on the system invented by Christian Sharps, popular in percussion form in the 1850's and 1860's, and modified into cartridge rifles in the late 1860's. The most-used powerful western rifle, particularly by buffalo hunters, until the advent of repeaters and the end of the hide trade put the Sharps company out of business in 1881. —H. J. Swinney, Director, Idaho Historical Society.

shorthorn cattle. One of the breeds of beef cattle that has supplanted the traditional longhorns of the Southwest.

side-line, *v.* To hobble a horse, front and hind leg on the same side of the animal; animals hobbled on the front feet sometimes learn to travel quite fast.

sleeper, *n.* A calf earmarked by a cattle thief who intends to come back and steal it later. —Adams, p. 146.

slick, *n.* Name for an unbranded animal; also a man who has smooth but dishonest ways, especially an outsider.

slicker. Cow hands had to work outdoors in any kind of weather. The slicker, a raincoat resembling an oilskin, was carried tied in the cantle drop of the saddle, ready to be worn when needed.

snake. A wild and dangerous steer.

sombrero. The Spanish *sombra* (shade) gave rise to *sombrero,* a hat, especially one that casts plenty of shade. Such hats became a "tag" of the cowboy's gear. Though movie and TV specimens exaggerate both crown and brim, a cow hand found a good hat extremely useful—as a barrier to sun and rain, as protection against twigs and leaves, even as a temporary basin for water.

sourdough bread. On roundup or trail drive the cook kept a sourdough keg ever fermenting. It contained a batter of flour, water, and salt, kept in a state of constant readiness by exposure to the sun during the day and by wrapping in blankets at night. Whenever the cook withdrew dough for baking, he added sufficient flour and water to replace it.

Spanish (horse, pony). The term "Spanish" was typically used to distinguish horses native to the Southwest and descending from animals left in the Americas by the *conquistadores* as opposed to various breeds brought into North America by the colonists or imported since the era of colonization. —Arthur H. Woodward, Patagonia, Arizona.

spurs. Metal instrument worn on cowboys' boots to assist in controlling the mount. They became an essential piece of cowboy equipment seldom removed from his boots. They may have been more useful as a status symbol than for controlling one's mount. One of the simplest and most commonly used was the "OK" spur.

stake. On trail herd or roundup, corrals for cow horses were rarely available. For the *remuda,* a makeshift corral was constructed by planting stakes and stretching a single strand of rope around them. Night horses, or other horses under saddle, were picketed with a rope tied to a stake pin. "Stake your pen" (see Song XVI, "The Cowboys Christmas Ball") was the caller's way to direct the formation of squares for a dance.

stampede. From the Spanish *estampida,* the running of cattle. Cattle raised on the open ranges were wild animals. Any sudden noise or other unusual occurrence might set them in a mad run dangerous alike to man and beast. Many western songs and stories tell of the drama, excitement, and tragedy of cattle (or buffalo) stampedes.

stock saddle. General term for any saddle sufficiently rugged and with characteristics suitable for working cattle. Names for each type usually derive from the shape of the "tree," the frame on which they are built.

stray, *n.* Name given to cattle which arrive on a range not open to that particular brand.

string, *n. Syn.* rope, lasso; also *remuda.*

T-Bar Dick. I.e., Dick who works for, or owns, the T-Bar spread.

tailings, *n.* Stragglers; cattle that stray or lag during a roundup or trail drive. One or more hands might be assigned to gather and hustle them on.

tally book. At spring roundup one hand kept a ledger or tally book in which he recorded the number of animals branded—the only device whereby an owner could know the size of his increase. The term is used transcendentally to designate God's record of souls saved by His divine grace.

taps. From the Spanish *tapaderas* (*tapar,* to close or shield). Toe guards that prevent the foot from passing all the way through the stirrups and that shield the cowboy's feet from brush. It also regulated the exact position of the foot on the stirrup floor.

tarantula. Applied to several species of large spiders of the southwestern United States. Their superficial resemblance to a European spider of the same name caused our Anglo- and Hispanic-American forebears to carry over the name. Their bite is mildly toxic. Genus *eurypelma.*

tarp (tarpaulin, tarpoleon). Canvas used for protecting the hot roll, or for sundry other purposes.

temporal. We have not encountered the word elsewhere. From context it should mean a ground cover, but botanical indices of southwestern plants do not list it. Could the Spanish *temporal,* an adjective meaning "temporary," have come to be used as a noun meaning "campsite"?

tend knitten, *v.* A horse "tending knitten" (knitting) is attentive, alert, ready to respond to the cowboy's every wish.

tenderfoot, *n.* *Syn.* greenhorn, greener, dude. According to Adams (p. 164) it was first applied to cattle imported to the Southwest, later to men new in the region.

top screw. *See* SCREWS.

tortilla. "A large, round, thin unleavened cake prepared from a paste made of corn, baked on a heated iron plate or stone slab; used in lieu of bread in Mexico." —Webster.

trail boss. Man in charge of a trail drive: song and legend have made of him the consummate hero among westerners. Of him Adams says (p. 168), "the world will never see his likes again."

trail drives. Perhaps the most dramatic of all cowboy activity. Drives over great distances began in the 1830's and continued up into the 1880's. Driven hard during the first day or so in order to get them off the home range, they were subsequently trailed easily along so that they could graze and put on fat en route. The work of trail driving was highly organized, with riders cooperating as skillfully as the members of a professional athletic team.

tree. The frame of wood or pressed rawhide over which the saddle is constructed. Saddles are commonly named from the shape of the tree on which they are built.

trim, *v.* Of cattle, to cut, to carve, i.e., to separate animals from the main herd for any given reason.

vaquero. Spanish for cowboy. The term gives rise in cowboy lingo to buckaroo, admitting contamination from the verb buck. (Recall that an initial *v* in Spanish is pronounced like a *b*.) It in all probability served to fix the term cowboy, which is a faithful translation of *vaca* (cow), and *ero*, a suffix meaning a person who deals with something.

vinegarroon. Large scorpion found in the Southwest and Mexico.

waddie. Name for an ordinary cowboy, usually one who floated from ranch to ranch, being engaged for seasonal work only. Adams (p. 173) thinks it may be derived from wad, *i.e.*, something you use to temporarily stop a leak until you can do the job up good and proper.

waterfall. Chignon or roll of hair worn low on the neck, popular in the 1860's. Also a hat of the same period, usually one with a long, drooping feather in back. Here it may designate a figure in a square dance, or may refer to a woman wearing a waterfall. *See* M. M. Mathews, *A Dictionary of Americanisms* (University of Chicago Press, 1951), II, 1840–1841.

wheat, whiskered. Bearded wheat (*Iriticum aestivum*) was nearly abandoned in favor of beardless varieties during the first half of our century. Now that hand work has gone out of wheat farming bearded (whiskered) varieties are again coming into use because of nutritive and other assets.

wrangler/wrangle. From the Mexican *caverango*—hostler. Man on roundup or trail drive who took care of the *remuda,* typically the least experienced hand in the outfit.

yodeling. Yodeling crept into western and cowboy singing in the 1930's. It is not to be confused with calls uttered to drive cattle.

Bibliography

Sources for a study of this kind are understandably varied: the standard publications dealing with the folklore, music, and popular literature of the American West; newspapers and other periodical literature of the American West; esoteric local publications and ephemeral printings of sheet music and popular song folios; popular recorded music of the 78-rpm era; our own field recordings and those of a score of fellow researchers who have contributed their significant cowboy and western items; ballet books, and sundry other manuscript resources.

Nearly all except the hard-core published items that are accessible in good research libraries have been assembled and entered in the ten volumes of the Fife Mormon Collection (FMC) and the thirty-two volumes of the Fife American Collection (FAC). Tapes (or acetate recordings on the earlier items) are preserved on all songs gathered from oral sources.

Large private collections, entered into the Fife Collection as integral volumes, are identified by appropriate independent abbreviations, and entered in this bibliography in alphabetical order. They are as follows:

GORDON: two volumes extracted from the Robert W. Gordon Collection at the Library of Congress.

HENDREN: five volumes from the private collection of Stella M. Hendren of Kooskia, Idaho.

JL: three volumes extracted from the manuscript collections of John A. Lomax in the archives of the Texas Historical Society, Austin.

PC-F: one volume from the private collection of Edwin Ford Piper at the State University of Iowa.

PNFQ: three volumes from the manuscript collection of the Pacific Northwest Farm Quad, Spokane, Washington.

Abbreviations used to refer to commonly cited sources appear in the bibliography in alphabetical order.

ABBOTT, E. C., and HELENA H. SMITH. *We Pointed Them North.* New York, 1939.

ABRAHAMS, ROGER. Private collection.

———— "The Cowboy in the British West Indies," PTFLS XXXII (1964), pp. 168–75.

ADAMS, RAMON F. *Western Words.* Norman, Oklahoma, 1946.

Adventure Magazine. See ROBERT W. GORDON, and ROBERT FROTHINGHAM.

"Allan's" Hillbilly and Western Folio. Melbourne, Australia, n.d.

ALLEN, FRANCIS. *Lone Star Ballads.* Galveston, 1878.

ALLEN, JULES VERNE. *Cowboy Lore.* San Antonio, 1933.

AMES, RUSSELL. *The Story of American Folk Song.* New York, 1955.

ANGELL, RUTH SPEER. "Background of Some Texas Cowboy Songs," M.A. thesis, Columbia University, 1937.

Arkansas Woodchoppers: Cowboy Songs with Yodel and Arrangements. Chicago, 1931.

Army Song Book. Washington, D.C., 1941.

ARNOLD, OREN, and J. P. HALE. *Hot Irons.* New York, 1940.

AUTRY, GENE. *Rhymes of the Range.* Evanston, Illinois, 1933.

BABER, D. F. *The Longest Rope: The Truth about the Johnson County Cattle War.* Caldwell, Idaho, 1940.

BARKER = *Barker's Biographical Dictionary of Musicians.* 5th ed., New York, 1958.

BARNES, WILL C. "The Cowboy and His Songs," *Saturday Evening Post,* June 27, 1925, pp. 14, 15, 122, 125, 128.

———— *Tales from the X-Bar Horse Camp.* Chicago, 1920.

BARRETT, LEONORA. "The Texas Cowboy in Literature," M.A. thesis, University of Texas, 1930.

BARRY, PHILLIPS. "Some Aspects of Folk-Song," JAFL, XXV (1912), pp. 277–80.

BEADLE, J. H. *The Undeveloped West.* Philadelphia, 1873.

BECK, EARL CLIFTON. *Lore of the Lumber Camps.* University of Michigan Press, 1948.

BELDEN = HENRY MARVIN BELDEN. *Ballads and Songs Collected by the Missouri Folk-Lore Society.* University of Missouri Studies, XV, 1. Columbia, Missouri, 1940.

BELDEN, *Song-Ballads* = HENRY MARVIN BELDEN. *Partial List of Song-Ballads and Other Popular Poetry Known in Missouri.* Columbia, Missouri, 1910.

Big Round-Up of Cowboy Songs. New York, 1934.

Big Slim, The Lone Cowboy Favorite Songs (folio). n.p., n.d. (after 1935).

BINNS = *Billy Binns' Ranch, Range and Home Songs* (folio). New York, c. 1936.

Blue Grass Roy, The Hamlins Korn Kracker, Book No. 4 (folio). Chicago, c. 1936.

BOATRIGHT, MODY C. *Backwoods to Border.* PTFLS, XVIII (1943).

BONI, MARGARET B. *Fireside Book of Favorite American Songs.* New York, 1952.

BOSWORTH, ALLAN R. *Sancho of the Long Long Horns.* Garden City, N.Y., 1947.

BOTKIN, BEN A. *American = A Treasury of American Folklore.* New York, 1944.

———— *Sampler* = "A Sampler of Western Folklore and Songs," *A Book of the American West,* Jay Monaghan, ed. New York, 1963, pp. 501–60.

———— *Western* = *A Treasury of Western Folklore.* New York, 1951.

———— and A. F. HARLOW. *A Treasury of Railroad Folklore.* New York, 1953.

BOTSFORD, FLORENCE H. *Folk Songs of Many Peoples.* New York, 1922.

BRADFORD, L. C. "Among the Cow-Boys," *Lippincotts Magazine* (June, 1881), pp. 565–71.

BRADLEY, W. A. "Song Ballets and Devil Ditties," *Harper's Monthly Magazine* (May, 1915), pp. 900–14.

BRANCH, E. DOUGLAS. *The Cowboy and His Interpreters.* New York, 1926.

BRATT, JOHN. *Trails of Yesterday.* Chicago, 1921.

BREIHAN, CARL W. *Great Gunfighters of the West.* San Antonio, Texas, 1962.

BRIEGEL, GEORGE F. *All Star = All Star Collection of Cowboy Ballads* (folio). New York.

———— *Rodeo* = *Collection of Rodeo Songs and Cow-Hand Ballads* (folio), New York, c. 1937.

———— *Souvenir* = *Souvenir Collection of America's Greatest Cowboy Songs for Piano and Voice* (folio). New York, c. 1938.

BROWN = *Frank C. Brown Collection of North Carolina Folklore.* Durham, N.C., 1952 ff. 7 vols.

BROWN, *Bass* = WILL C. BROWN. *Sam Bass and Company.* New York, 1960.

BROWNE, RAY. Private collection.

Buck Jones Rangers-Cowboys (folio). New York, 1932.

Bulletin of Folk Song Society of Northeast. Reprinted by American Folklore Society, Philadelphia, 1960.

BURT, OLIVE W. *American Murder Ballads and Other Stories.* New York, 1958.

CALDWELL, MABEL. "Gleanings from the By-ways of Oklahoma," *Chronicles of Oklahoma*. Oklahoma Historical Society, March, 1926, p. 46.

CALLISON, JOHN J. *Bill Jones of Paradise Valley, Oklahoma*. Kingfisher, Oklahoma, 1914.

CARLSON, A. D. "Cowboy Ballads at our Own Firesides," *Better Homes and Gardens*, X, 23 (November, 1931), pp. 61–62.

CARMER, CARL. *Songs of the Rivers of America*. New York, 1942.

The Cattleman. Fort Worth, Texas. (Periodical)

CHAMBERS, HENRY T. *Young Man's Country*. Bristow, Oklahoma, n.d.

CHENEY, THOMAS E. "Folk Ballad Characteristics in a Present Day Collection of Songs," M.A. thesis, University of Idaho, 1936.

CHITTENDEN, WILLIAM LAWRENCE. *Ranch Verses*. New York, 1893.

CLARK = CHARLES BADGER CLARK. *Sun and Saddle Leather*. Boston, 1912.

CLARK, *Cowboy* = KENNETH S. CLARK, *The Cowboy Sings*. New York, 1932.

CLARK, *Happy Cowboy* = KENNETH S. CLARK. *The Happy Cowboy*. New York, 1934.

CLARK, N. M. Co-author with Thorp of *Pardner of the Wind*, Thorp's autobiography.

CLIFFORD, JOHN. "Range Ballads," *Kansas Historical Quarterly*, XXV (Winter, 1955), pp. 588–97.

CLIFTON, BILL. *150 Songs: Old-Time Folk and Gospel* (folio).

COLDIRON, DAISY L. *Songs of Oklahoma*. Dallas, 1935.

COLEMAN, SATIO N., and ADOLPH BREGMAN. *Songs of American Folks*. New York, 1942.

Colorado Folksong Bulletin. ed. BEN G. LUMPKIN. Boulder, 1962–

COMBS, JOSIAH H. *Folk-Songs du Midi des États-Unis*. Paris, 1925.

———— and HUBERT G. SHEARIN. *A Syllabus of Kentucky Folk Songs*. Lexington, 1911.

COOLIDGE, DANE. "Cowboy Songs," *Sunset Magazine*, XXIX (November, 1912), pp. 503–10.

———— *Texas Cowboys*, New York, 1937.

COON, L. Field recordings in Library of Congress.

COURSEY, O. W. *Literature of South Dakota*. Mitchell, South Dakota, 1925.

Cowboy Songs (folio). Chicago, c. 1937.

Cowboy Tom's Round-Up Book (folio). New York, 1933.

Cox, *Historical* = JAMES COX. *Historical and Biographical Record of the Cattle Industry and the Cattlemen of Texas*. St. Louis, 1895.

Cox = JOHN HARRINGTON COX. *Folk Songs of the South*. Cambridge, Massachusetts, 1925.

Cox, *West Virginia* = JOHN HARRINGTON COX. *Folk Songs Mainly from*

West Virginia. American Folk-Song Publications No. 5, National Service Bureau Pub. 81-S, 1939.

CRADDOCK, JOHN R. "Songs the Cowboys Sing," PTFLS, XXVI (1934), pp. 184–92.

CRAWFORD, CAPTAIN JACK. *The Poet Scout: Verses and Songs.* San Francisco, 1879.

CRAWFORD, LEWIS F. *Rekindling Campfires.* Bismark, North Dakota, 1926.

CROMWELL, IDA M. "Songs I Sang on an Iowa Farm," WFQ, XVII, 4 (October, 1958), pp. 229–47.

DAVIS, *Songs* = ARTHUR KYLE DAVIS, JR. *Folk-Songs of Virginia.* Durham, North Carolina, 1949.

DAVIS, *Tip-Top* = JOE DAVIS. *Tip-Top Songs of the Roaming Ranger.* New York, 1935.

Delaney's Song Book (folio). New York, c. 1892.

DICK EVERETT. "The Long Drive," *Kansas Historical Collections,* XVII (1926–1928), pp. 27–97.

DOBIE, J. FRANK. Notes in his personal copy of Lomax, *Cowboy Songs,* copied by Fifes into their collection.

———— "Ballads and Songs of the Frontier Folk," PTFLS, VI (1927), pp. 121–83.

———— "A Buffalo Hunter and His Song," PTFLS, XVIII (1943), pp. 1–6.

———— *The Longhorns.* Boston, 1941.

———— "More Ballads and Songs of the Frontier Folk," PTFLS, VII (1928), pp. 155–80.

———— "Mustang Gray: Fact, Tradition and Song," PTFLS, X (1932), 109–26.

———— *Tales of Old-Time Texas.* Boston, 1955.

———— *Tone the Bell Easy,* PTFLS, X (1932).

DORSON, RICHARD M. Private collection in Indiana University Folklore Archives.

DOUBLEDAY, RUSSELL. *Cattle Ranch to College.* New York, 1899.

DUDGEON: *Frank Dudgeon's Old Time Song Book,* No. 1 (folio). c. 1932.

DUNCAN, BOB. Private collection given to Oklahoma City Library.

ECKSTROM, FANNIE H., and MARY W. SMYTH. *Minstrelsy of Maine: Folk-Songs and Ballads of the Woods and the Coast.* Boston and New York, 1927.

EDDY, MARY O. *Ballads and Songs from Ohio.* New York, 1939.

ELLARD, HARRY. *Ranch Tales of the Rockies.* Canon City, Colorado, 1899.

EMRICH, DUNCAN. *It's an Old Wild West Custom.* New York, 1949.

FAC = Fife American Collection. Private collection consisting of manuscripts, transcriptions of oral interviews, esoteric published items, made since 1956. Currently thirty-two volumes and still growing.

FELTON, HAROLD W. *Cowboy Jamboree: Western Songs and Lore.* New York, 1951.

FINGER, CHARLES JOSEPH. *Frontier Ballads.* New York, 1927.

Flag of Freedom. Puebla, Mexico, 1847. Newspaper of U.S. Army in Mexico.

FLANDERS, HELEN H. *The New Green Mountain Songster.* New Haven, 1939.

FLETCHER, TEX. *"The Lonely Cowboy" Song Book.* New York, 1940.

FMC = Fife Mormon Collection. Private collection consisting of manuscripts, transcriptions of oral interviews, esoteric published items, made between 1939 and 1956.

FMR = Fife Mormon Recordings. Acetate recordings made between 1939 and 1950, most of which are deposited in the Library of Congress.

FOWKE, EDITH. Private collection.

———— *American* = "American Cowboy and Western Pioneer Songs in Canada," WFQ, XXI (1962), pp. 247–56.

———— and RICHARD JOHNSTON. *Folk Songs of Canada.* Waterloo, Ontario, 1954.

FOX, OSCAR J. *Three Cowboy Desperado Songs.* Carl Fischer.

FRENCH, WILLIAM. *Some Recollections of a Western Ranchman.* London, 1927.

FREY, HUGO. *American Cowboy Songs.* New York, 1936.

FRIEDMAN, ALBERT B., ed. *The Viking Book of Folk Ballads of the English-Speaking World.* New York, 1956.

FROTHINGHAM, ROBERT. Edited "Old Songs That Men Have Sung," *Adventure Magazine,* for a short time prior to July, 1923.

FULD, JAMES J. *American Popular Music, 1875–1950.* Philadelphia, 1955.

GAINES, N. W. "Some Characteristics of Cowboy Songs," PTFLS, VII (1928), pp. 145–54.

GARD = WAYNE GARD. *The Chisholm Trail.* Norman, Oklahoma, 1954.

———— *Buffalo* = *The Great Buffalo Hunt.* New York, 1959.

———— *Law* = "The Law of the American West," *The Book of the American West,* ed. Jay Monaghan. New York, 1963, pp. 261–322.

GARDNER, EMELYN E., and G. J. CHICKERING. *Ballads and Songs of Southern Michigan.* Ann Arbor, 1939.

GARRETSON, MARTIN S. *The American Bison.* New York, 1938.

GAVIANI, FRANK. *Hill Billy, Cowboy and Standard Songs.* New York, 1935.

GERMAN, GEORGE B. *Cowboy Campfire Ballads.* Yankton, South Dakota, 1929.

GILLETT, JAMES B. *Six Years with the Texas Rangers.* Austin, 1921.

GILLIS, EVERETT A. "Literary Origins of Some Western Ballads," WFQ, XIII (1954), pp. 101–6.

GOLDSTEIN, KENNETH S. Private collection.

———— "The Texas Rangers in Aberdeenshire." PTFLS, XXXII (1964), pp. 188–98.

———— *The Unfortunate Rake*. Folkways Records FS 3805. 1960.

GOODWYN, FRANK. *The Black Bull*. New York, 1958.

GORDON, ROBERT W., founder of the Archive of American Folksong, Library of Congress. Manuscript collection in Library of Congress, consisting of items gathered through his column in *Adventure Magazine* (12 vols.). Cowboy and western materials from it entered in Fife collection under "Gordon no. —" (his numbering).

———— Edited "Old Songs That Men Have Sung," *Adventure Magazine*, July, 1923–November, 1927.

GRAY, OKLAHOMA = *Otto Gray and His Oklahoma Cowboys*. Stillwater, Oklahoma, 1930.

GRAY = ROLAND PALMER GRAY. *Songs and Ballads of the Maine Lumberjacks with Other Songs from Maine*. Cambridge, Massachusetts, 1924.

GREENWAY, JOHN. *American Folksongs of Protest*. Philadelphia, 1953.

GRINNELL, GEORGE BIRD. *Jack, the Young Cowboy*. New York, 1913.

HALEY, J. EVETTS. "Cowboy Songs Again," PTFLS, VI (1927), pp. 198–204.

HALL, SHARLOT M. "Songs of the Old Cattle Trails," *Out West* (March, 1908), pp. 216–21.

HALPERT, HERBERT. Private collection, some items of which are in the Library of Congress and some in the Western Kentucky Folklore Archives (WKFA).

HAND, WAYLAND D. *Butte* = "Songs of the Butte Miners." WFQ IX (1950) pp. 1–48.

———— *Strassen* = "Wo sind die Strassen von Laredo"? Die Entwicklungsgeschichte einer amerikanischen Cowboy Ballade. *Festschrift für Will-Erich Peuckert zum 60. Geburtstag dargebracht von Freunden und Schülern*. Berlin, 1955, pp. 144–61.

HENDREN, STELLA M. Private collection of manuscripts and newspapers, sources largely unknown. Cowboy and western materials entered in the Fife collection under "Hendren no. —."

HENRY, MELLINGER. *Folk-Songs of the Southern Highlands*. New York, 1938.

HIGH, FRED. *Old Old Folk Songs*. Berryville, Arkansas, n.d.

HINKLE, JAMES FIELDING. *Early Days of a Cowboy on the Pecos*. Roswell, New Mexico, 1937.

Hobo News: The Hoboes' Own Newspaper. Quarterly. New York City. (Issue consulted consisted of 28 unnumbered pages, comprising song texts and some tunes.) n.d.

HOFFMAN, FRANK. Private collection.

HOWARD, JOSEPH KINSEY. *Montana Margins*. New Haven, 1946.

HUBBARD, LESTER A. *Ballads and Songs from Utah*. Salt Lake City, 1961.

HUDSON, ARTHUR PALMER. *Folksongs of Mississippi and Their Background.* Chapel Hill, 1936.

HULL, MYRA. "Cowboy Ballads," *Kansas State Historical Quarterly*, VIII (February, 1939), pp. 35–60.

HUNTER, J. M. *The Trail Drivers of Texas.* Nashville, 1925.

Idaho Farmer. Originally published by Cowles Publishing Co., as a biweekly; now by Pacific Northwest Farm Quad. Spokane, 1895–.

ISUHM = Idaho State University Historical Museum, Pocatello.

IU = Indiana University, Archives of Folk and Primitive Music.

IVES, BURL. *The Burl Ives Song Book.* New York, 1953.

JAFL = *Journal of American Folklore*, 1888–.

JAMES = W. S. JAMES. *Cow-boy Life in Texas; or, 27 Years a Maverick!* Chicago, 1893.

JAMES, *Smoky* = WILL JAMES. *Smoky, the Cowhorse.* New York, 1926.

JEFFERS-JOHNSON, STRATFORD. "Lore from Leitram." *New York Folklore Quarterly*, V, 4 (Winter 1949), pp. 276–86.

JL = JOHN A. LOMAX, dossiers at Texas Historical Society.

JONES, BERTRAND L. "Folk-Lore in Michigan," *Kalamazoo Normal Record*, IV (May, 1914), pp. 297–302.

JORDAN, PHILIP D., and LILLIAN KESSLER. *Songs of Yesterday.* New York, 1941.

Ken Maynard's Songs of the Trails (folio). Chicago, c. 1935.

Kentucky Girls = *Radio Book of Favorite Mountain Ballads and Cowboy Songs as Broadcast by Kentucky Girls and Arkansas Woodchopper* (folio). c. 1929.

KINCAID, BRADLEY. *Favorite Old-Time Songs and Mountain Ballads.* No. 1 (1928); No. 3 (1930); No. 7 (1936); No. 8 (1936).

KLICKMANN, F. H., and S. SHERWIN. *Songs of the Saddle.* New York, 1933.

KORSON, GEORGE. *Pennsylvania Songs and Legends.* Philadelphia, 1949.

LANDECK, BEATRICE. "Get on Board," *A Collection of Folk Songs.* New York, c. 1944.

LARKIN, MARGARET, and HELEN BLACK. *Singing Cowboy.* New York, 1931. (Reprinted 1963 by Oak Publications.)

LARSON, KENNETH. Private collection.

LAWS, G. MALCOLM. *Native American Balladry.* Philadelphia, 1950.

LC = Archive of Folk Song, Library of Congress.

LEACH, MACEDWARD. *The Ballad Book.* New York, 1955.

LEAKEY, JOHN. *The West That Was.* Dallas, 1959.

LEE, JACK H. *Cowboy Song Book.* Butte, Montana, 1934.

——— *Songs of the Range.* Chicago, 1937.

——— *West of Powder River.* New York, 1933.

LEE, JAMES W., and RALPH ROBERTS. Private collection.

LINDROTH, RICHARD K. *The Cowboy and His Uke.* New York, 1950.

LOESSER, ARTHUR. *Humor in American Song.* New York, 1942.

LOMAX, JOHN A. Numbered dossiers of materials accumulated by him, now at the Texas Historical Society. Materials often unidentified. Cowboy and western materials entered in Fife collection under "JL no.—." In addition, there are materials in the Library of Congress, both manuscripts and recordings, from the Lomax collections.

———— *Cowboy Songs and Other Frontier Ballads* (identified as follows by copyright date):
    1910: New York, Sturgis and Walton. 191 pages.
    1911: New York, Sturgis and Walton. 326 pages. (Reprinted, 1915.)
    1916: New York, Sturgis and Walton. 414 pages. (Reprintings in 1917, 1918, 1919, 1927, 1929, 1930, 1931, 1933, 1936, without change, except published by The Macmillan Company from 1918 on.)
    1938: Revised enlarged and reset. 11th printing in 1957.

———— *Ballad* = *Adventures of a Ballad Hunter.* New York, 1947.

———— *Cattle* = *Songs of the Cattle Trail and Cow Camp.* New York, 1928.

————, and ALAN LOMAX.

———— *American* = *American Ballads and Folk Songs.* New York, 1934.

———— *Best Loved* = *Best Loved American Folk Songs.* New York, 1947.

———— *Singing* = *Our Singing Country.* New York, 1941.

———— *U.S.A.* = *Folk Song U.S.A.* New York, 1947.

LOMAX, (LILLY). "Trail Songs of the Cowpuncher," *The Overland Monthly* (San Francisco) 59: 24–29 (1912).

The Lone Ranger's Song Book. New York, 1938.

LUTHER, FRANK. *Americans and Their Songs.* New York, 1942.

LYNN, J. J. *Reminiscences of Fifty Years in Texas.* New York, 1883.

MACKENZIE, W. ROY. *Ballads and Sea Songs from Nova Scotia.* Cambridge, Massachusetts, 1928.

Mammoth = *Robbins Mammoth Collection of American Songs.* ed. Hugo Frey. No. 11. New York, 1941.

McCONATHY, OSBOURNE, JOHN W. BEATTIE, and RUSSELL V. MORGAN. *Music Highways and Byways.* New York, 1936.

McINTOSH, DAVID S. *Songs of Southern Illinois.* Mimeographed, 1940.

MOORE = ETHEL and CHAUNCEY O. MOORE. *Ballads and Songs of the Southwest.* Norman, Oklahoma, 1964.

MOORE, *Oklahoma* = ETHEL P. MOORE. "An Experiment in Collecting and Classifying the Folk-songs Sung in Oklahoma," M.A. thesis, University of Oklahoma, 1926.

MORRIS, ALTON C. *Folksongs of Florida.* Gainesville, 1950.

Nebraska Folklore: Cowboy Songs. WPA Writer's Project. Mimeographed. Nos. 1 and 11, 1937.

NEELY, CHARLES, and J. W. SPARGO. *Tales and Songs of Southern Illinois.* Menasha, Wisconsin, 1938.

O'BRYANT, JOAN. Private collection.

Oklahoma City Library. Collection of folk materials, including manuscripts and recordings.

OLNEY, MARGUERITE: Curator, Flanders Ballad Collection, Middlebury College, Middlebury, Vermont. Letter to A. E. Fife dated January 12, 1959.

O'MALLEY = JOHN WHITE. *D. J. O'Malley (Cowboy Poet).* Eauclaire, Wisconsin, 1934.

OWENS, WILLIAM A. *Texas Folk Songs.* Austin, 1950.

PACK = *Old Time Ballads and Cowboy Songs* compiled by LOYE PACK the Cowboy Singer (Cowboy Loye). N.p., n.d. (c. 1934).

PACK, *Song Book* = *Loye D. Pack Song Book* (folio, c. 1930's).

PARKER, JOHN MONROE. *An Aged Wanderer: A Life Sketch of J. M. Parker.* Cisco, Texas, c. 1915.

PATTERSON, PAT, and LOIS DEXTER. *Songs of the Round Up Rangers.* New York, 1933.

PC-F = EDWIN FORD PIPER private collection, now at Iowa State University. Cowboy and western materials entered in Fife collection under "PC-F No. —."

Pie Plant Pete and Bashful Harmonica Joe's Favorite Old Time Songs. Book No. 1. Chicago, c. 1937.

PIPER: see PC-F.

PNFQ = Song and poetry files of Pacific Northwest Farm Quad, Spokane, Washington. Publishers of four western farmers' magazines. The collection consists of contributions made by readers of a regular column which started in these newspapers in the 1920's and still continues.

POLLAN, LOY. "Provenience of Certain Cowboy Ballads," M.A. thesis, University of Oklahoma, 1938.

POUND, LOUISE. *American* = *American Ballads and Songs.* New York, 1922.

———— *Nebraska* = "Traditional Ballads in Nebraska," JAFL, XXVI (1913), pp. 351–66.

———— *Origins* = "American Folksong, Origins, Texts and Modes of Diffusion," SFQ, XVII (June, 1953), pp. 114–21.

———— *Pedigree* = "The Pedigree of a 'Western' Song," *Modern Language Notes,* XXIX, 1 (January, 1914), pp. 30–31.

———— *Syllabus* = *Folk-Songs of Nebraska and the Central West.* Nebraska Academy of Sciences Publications, IX, 3 (1915).

———— *Western* = "Some Texts of Western Songs," SFQ, III (1939), pp. 25–31.

PRICE, CON. *Trails I Rode.* Pasadena, California, 1947.

PTFLS = *Publications of the Texas Folklore Society,* 1916–.

RANDOLPH, VANCE. Field recordings in the Library of Congress.
—— Ozark Folksongs. Columbia, Missouri, 1946–1950. 4 vols.
REINBACH, EDNA. Music and Musicians in Kansas. Topeka, 1930.
REPUBLIC = Cowboy Songs sung by Longhorn Luke and His Cowboys for Republic Portland Cement Co. San Antonio, c. 1930.
RHINEHART, COWBOY SLIM. The Old Cowhand from the Rio Grand. (A Border Station folio.)
RICKABY, FRANZ. Ballads and Songs of the Shanty-Boy. Cambridge, Massachusetts, 1926.
RIDINGS, SAM P. The Chisholm Trail: A History of the World's Greatest Cattle Trail. Guthrie, Oklahoma, 1936.
RIOS, JOHN F. "Dogie Doggerels and Lugubrious Lyrics," Arizona Highways, XXXI (1955), pp. 4–6.
The Roaming Cowboy. (Cowboy Sam). Book No. 2. (A Border Station folio.)
ROBB, J. D. Private collection.
ROBERTSON, SYDNEY. Field recordings at the Library of Congress.
ROBINSON, CARSON J. Carson J. Robinson's World's Greatest Collection of Mountain Ballads and Old Time Songs. Chicago, 1930.
ROGERS, Cowboy = Roy Rogers Favorite Cowboy Songs (folio). New York, c. 1943.
Rogers' Favorite = Jesse Rogers' Favorite Songs (folio). New York, c. 1938.
Roundup Rangers = Songs of the Roundup Rangers (folio). 1932.
RUSH, OSCAR. The Open Range. Caldwell, Idaho, 1936.
SACKETT, S. J. Private collection.
SACKS, B. "Sylvester Mowry: Artilleryman, Libertine, Entrepreneur," The American West, I, 3 (Summer, 1964), pp. 14ff.
SANDBURG, CARL. The American Songbag. New York, 1927.
SANDOZ, MARI. The Buffalo Hunters. New York, 1954.
SCARBOROUGH, DOROTHY. A Song Catcher in Southern Mountains. New York, 1937.
SEEGER, CHARLES. Field recordings in the Library of Congress.
—— American Songs. Washington, U.S. Resettlement Administration No. 7.
SFQ = Southern Folklore Quarterly. 1937–.
SHAY, FRANK. My Pious Friends and Drunken Companions. New York, 1927.
SHERWIN, STERLING, and F. H. KLICKMANN. Songs of the Round-Up. New York, 1934.
SHERWIN, STERLING, and HARRY A. POWELL. Bad Man Songs of the Wild and Woolly West. Cleveland, 1933.
SHOEMAKER, H. W. Mountain Minstrelsy of Pennsylvania. Philadelphia, 1931.

———— *North Pennsylvania Minstrelsy.* 2nd ed. Altoona, Pennsylvania, 1923.

Sing 'em Cowboy Sing 'em: Songs of the Trail and Range. New York, 1934.

Sing Out (Periodical). New York: Peoples Artists, May, 1950–.

SIRES, INA. *Songs of the Open Range.* Boston, 1928.

SIRINGO, CHARLES A. *Riata and Spurs.* Boston and New York, 1927.

———— *A Song Companion of a Lone Star Cowboy.* Santa Fe, New Mexico, 1919.

SIZEMORE, ASHER. *Family: Asher Sizemore and Little Jimmie's Family Circle Songs.* c. 1937.

———— *Hearth: Asher Sizemore and Little Jimmie's Hearth and Home Songs.* c. 1934.

———— *Home: Asher Sizemore and Little Jimmie's Songs of Home and Heaven.* Laurel, Indiana, c. 1939.

———— *Old Fashioned: Old Fashioned Hymns and Mountain Ballads as Sung by Asher Sizemore and Little Jimmie.* 1933.

SMITH, E. D. "The Passing of the Cattle Trail." *Kansas Historical Collections,* X (1907–1908).

Song Hits. Dunellen, N.J., 1934. A monthly, with some exceptions.

SORRELS, ROSALIE. Private collection.

SOWELL, A. J. *Rangers and Pioneers of Texas.* 1884.

STANLEY, CLARK. *The Life and Adventures of the American Cowboy.* Providence, Rhode Island, n.d.

STEKERT, ELLEN. Private collection.

STOUT, EARL J. *Folklore from Iowa.* New York, 1936.

SULLIVAN, W. J. L. *Twelve Years in the Saddle for Law and Order on the Frontier of Texas.* Austin, 1909.

Surprise Lake Camp Book of Songs. Clipping file at New York Public Library.

SUTLEY, ZACK T. *The Last Frontier.* New York, 1930.

"Tex" The Texas Cowboy's Collection of Western Cowboy and Mountain Ballads As sung by Olus "Tex" Justus on NBC and Texas Quality Networks, etc. n.p., n.d.

Texas Centennial Song Book. Dallas, I (1936); II (1939).

THOMPSON, HAROLD W., and EDITH E. CUTTING. *A Pioneer Songster.* New York, 1958.

THORP, J. HOWARD ("JACK"). *Songs of the Cowboys.* Estancia, New Mexico, 1908.

———— *Songs of the Cowboys.* Boston, 1921.

———— "Banjo in the Cow Camps," *Atlantic Monthly,* CLXVI (1940), pp. 195–203.

———— *Tales of the Chuck Wagon.* Santa Fe, New Mexico, 1926.

———— and NEIL M. CLARK. *Pardner of the Wind.* Caldwell, Idaho, 1945.

TODD, CHARLES, and ROBERT SONKIN. Recordings made in California, now
in the Library of Congress.
Treasure Chest of Cowboy Songs. New York, 1935.
UAFA = University of Arizona Folklore Archives, Tucson.
U-Ill. Campus = *The Hell-Bound Train,* sung by Glenn Ohrlin. University
of Illinois, Campus Folksong Club Records, CFC 301. n.d.
Utah Cowboy's Album of Songs. (A Border Station, probably XERA.)
UTFA = University of Texas Folklore Archives, Austin.
WALLERICH, WILLIAM. *Air Force Airs.* New York, 1957.
WEADICK, GUY. "Kid White, N Bar N Cowhand," *Canadian Cattleman*
(February, 1952).
WEBB, WALTER PRESCOTT. "The Legend of Sam Bass," PTFLS III (1924),
pp. 226–30.
———— *The Texas Rangers: A Century of Frontier Defense.* Boston, 1935.
WEHMAN BROTHERS. *Good Old-Time Songs.* New York, 1910–1916. 4 vols.
WESTERMEIER, CLIFFORD PETER. *Trailing the Cowboy, His Life and Lore as
Told by Frontier Journalists.* Caldwell, Idaho, 1955.
WFQ = *Western Folklore Quarterly* (formerly *California Folklore Quar-
terly*). 1942–.
WHITE, *Lonesome* = *Cowboy Songs as Sung by John White "The Lone-
some Cowboy" in Death Valley Days.* Pacific Coast Borax Co., 1934.
WHITE, *Arizona* = STEWART EDWARD WHITE. *Arizona Nights.* New York,
1907.
WHITE, *Rawhide* = STEWART EDWARD WHITE. "The Rawhide," *McClure's
Magazine,* XXIV (December, 1904), pp. 175–76.
WHITE, JOHN, and GEORGE SHACKLEY. *The Lonesome Cowboy Songs of the
Plains and Hills.* New York, 1930.
WILGUS, D. K. Private collection.
———— *Anglo-American Folksong Scholarship Since 1898.* New Brunswick,
New Jersey, 1959.
———— "The Josiah H. Combs Collection of Songs and Rhymes," *Kentucky
Folklore Record,* VI, 4.
WILL, G. F. "Songs of Western Cowboys," JAFL, XXII (1909), pp. 256–61.
Williams Favorite = *Marc Williams Collection of Favorite Cowboy Songs.*
New York, c. 1937.
WISTER, OWEN. *Lin McLean.* New York, 1898.
WKFA = Western Kentucky Folklore Archives, University of California at
Los Angeles.
WPA = Material gathered by the WPA Writers' Project through 1930's and
early 1940's on file in Archive of Folk Music, Library of Congress.
WRIGHT, ROBERT M. *Dodge City, Cowboy Capital.* Wichita, Kansas, 1913.

Index of Titles

Index of First Lines

When I'm dead and a-goin' to my grave/One pleasant funeral let me have, 172

When my earthly trail is ended/And my final bacon's curled, 70

Where the Pecos river winds and turns in its journey to the sea, 245

While you are (you're) all so frisky, 24, 62, 63

Windy Bill was a Texas boy (man)/Said (and) he could rope you bet, 39, 41

Wrap me up in my old stable jacket/And say a poor buffer lies low, 171

You could see the tired cowboy as he is coming through the rain, 92

Comprehensive Index

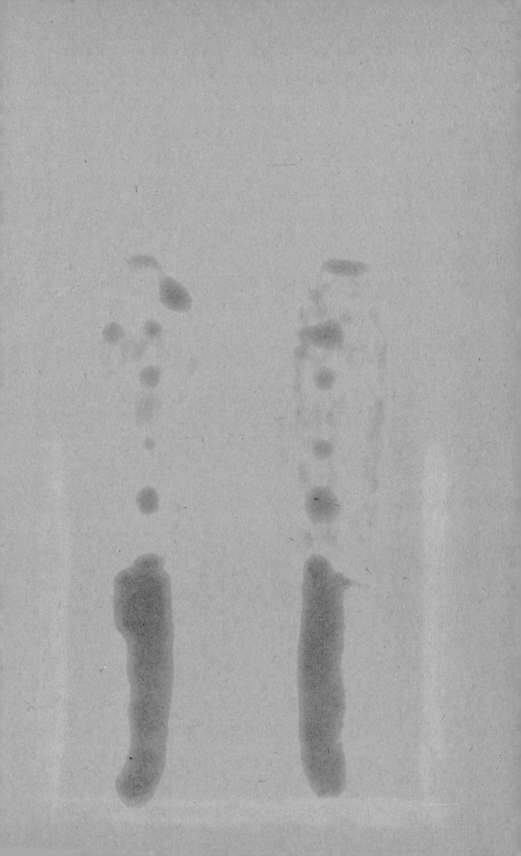

52769

ML
3551
T43

THORP, NATHAN
    SONGS OF THE COWBOYS.

DATE DUE

GAYLORD   PRINTED IN U.S.A.